Sam Brooks
David H. Carlson
Editors

Library/Vendor Relationships

Library/Vendor Relationships has been co-published simultaneously as *Journal of Library Administration*, Volume 44, Numbers 3/4 2006.

Pre-publication REVIEWS, COMMENTARIES, EVALUATIONS . . .

"Don't let this minimal title fool you; *Library/Vendor Relationships* is a TIMELY publication concerning the multifaceted partnerships that libraries and vendors engage in today. Brooks and Carlson set an affirming tone with their thoughtful introductions, outlining the mutual benefits of forming such working alliances. For libraries collaborating with database developers and vendors, this book OFFERS A METHOD FOR EXTENDING RESOURCES and a means for contributing to product development. In the same way, vendors benefit from customer feedback concerning their product or services through promoting open communications in advisory boards, focus sessions, users groups, and list serves.

The editors have comprised a balanced list of authors who contribute relationship examples that should appeal to all types of information providers. For example, the article suggesting guidelines for managing and preventing abusive database downloading should be required reading for every electronic resource librarian. Librarians wishing to be inspired by collaboration in progress should read the articles focusing on NISO standards, ANKOS consortia, book vendors' customer service, and OCLC's international collaborative council. . . . ENCOURAGES COOPERATION FOR THE BENEFITS OF MUTUAL DEVELOPMENT THAT LIBRARIES AND VENDORS WILL SURELY GAIN."

Michele Crump, MA, MA, MLIS
Chair, Acquisitions and Licensing Department
George A. Smathers Libraries
University of Florida

Library/Vendor Relationships

Library/Vendor Relationships has been co-published simultaneously as *Journal of Library Administration*, Volume 44, Numbers 3/4 2006.

Monographs from the *Journal of Library Administration*™

For additional information on these and other Haworth Press titles, including descriptions, tables of contents, reviews, and prices, use the QuickSearch catalog at http://www.HaworthPress.com.

1. *Planning for Library Services: A Guide to Utilizing Planning Methods for Library Management,* edited by Charles R. McClure, PhD (Vol. 2, No. 3/4, 1982). *"Should be read by anyone who is involved in planning processes of libraries–certainly by every administrator of a library or system." (American Reference Books Annual)*

2. *Finance Planning for Libraries,* edited by Murray S. Martin (Vol. 3, No. 3/4, 1983). *Stresses the need for libraries to weed out expenditures which do not contribute to their basic role–the collection and organization of information–when planning where and when to spend money.*

3. *Marketing and the Library,* edited by Gary T. Ford (Vol. 4, No. 4, 1984). *Discover the latest methods for more effective information dissemination and learn to develop successful programs for specific target areas.*

4. *Excellence in Library Management,* edited by Charlotte Georgi, MLS, and Robert Bellanti, MLS, MBA (Vol. 6, No. 3, 1985). *"Most beneficial for library administrators . . . for anyone interested in either library/information science or management." (Special Libraries)*

5. *Archives and Library Administration: Divergent Traditions and Common Concerns,* edited by Lawrence J. McCrank, PhD, MLS (Vol. 7, No. 2/3, 1986). *"A forward-looking view of archives and libraries. . . . Recommend[ed] to students, teachers, and practitioners alike of archival and library science. It is readable, thought-provoking, and provides a summary of the major areas of divergence and convergence." (Association of Canadian Map Libraries and Archives)*

6. *Legal Issues for Library and Information Managers,* edited by William Z. Nasri, JD, PhD (Vol. 7, No. 4, 1986). *"Useful to any librarian looking for protection or wondering where responsibilities end and liabilities begin. Recommended." (Academic Library Book Review)*

7. *Pricing and Costs of Monographs and Serials: National and International Issues,* edited by Sul H. Lee (Supp. #l, 1987). *"Eminently readable. There is a good balance of chapters on serials and monographs and the perspective of suppliers, publishers, and library practitioners are presented. A book well worth reading." (Australasian College Libraries)*

8. *Management Issues in the Networking Environment,* edited by Edward R. Johnson, PhD (Vol. 8, No. 3/4, 1987). *"Particularly useful for librarians/information specialists contemplating establishing a local network." (Australian Library Review)*

9. *Library Management and Technical Services: The Changing Role of Technical Services in Library Organizations,* edited by Jennifer Cargill, MSLS, MSEd (Vol. 9, No. 1, 1988). *"As a practical and instructive guide to issues such as automation, personnel matters, education, management techniques and liaison with other services, senior library managers with a sincere interest in evaluating the role of their technical services should find this a timely publication." (Library Association Record)*

10. *Computing, Electronic Publishing, and Information Technology: Their Impact on Academic Libraries,* edited by Robin N. Downes (Vol. 9, No. 4, 1988). *"For a relatively short and easily digestible discussion of these issues, this book can be recommended, not only to those in academic libraries, but also to those in similar types of library or information unit, and to academics and educators in the field." (Journal of Documentation)*

11. *Acquisitions, Budgets, and Material Costs: Issues and Approaches,* edited by Sul H. Lee (Supp. #2, 1988). *"The advice of these library practitioners is sensible and their insights illuminating for librarians in academic libraries." (American Reference Books Annual)*

12. *The Impact of Rising Costs of Serials and Monographs on Library Services and Programs,* edited by Sul H. Lee (Vol. 10, No. 1, 1989). *". . . Sul Lee hit a winner here." (Serials Review)*

13. *Creativity, Innovation, and Entrepreneurship in Libraries*, edited by Donald E. Riggs, EdD, MLS (Vol. 10, No. 2/3, 1989). *"The volume is well worth reading as a whole. . . . There is very little repetition, and it should stimulate thought." (Australian Library Review)*

14. *Human Resources Management in Libraries*, edited by Gisela M. Webb, MLS, MPA (Vol. 10, No. 4, 1989). *"Thought provoking and enjoyable reading. . . . Provides valuable insights for the effective information manager." (Special Libraries)*

15. *Managing Public Libraries in the 21st Century*, edited by Pat Woodrum, MLS (Vol. 11, No. 1/2, 1989). *"A broad-based collection of topics that explores the management problems and possibilities public libraries will be facing in the 21st century." (Robert Swisher, PhD, Director, School of Library and Information Studies, University of Oklahoma)*

16. *Library Education and Employer Expectations*, edited by E. Dale Cluff, PhD, MLS (Vol. 11, No. 3/4, 1990). *"Useful to library-school students and faculty interested in employment problems and employer perspectives. Librarians concerned with recruitment practices will also be interested." (Information Technology and Libraries)*

17. *Training Issues and Strategies in Libraries*, edited by Paul M. Gherman, MALS, and Frances O. Painter, MLS, MBA (Vol. 12, No. 2, 1990). *"There are . . . useful chapters, all by different authors, each with a preliminary summary of the content–a device that saves much time in deciding whether to read the whole chapter or merely skim through it. Many of the chapters are essentially practical without too much emphasis on theory. This book is a good investment." (Library Association Record)*

18. *Library Material Costs and Access to Information*, edited by Sul H. Lee (Vol. 12, No. 3, 1990). *"A cohesive treatment of the issue. Although the book's contributors possess a research library perspective, the data and the ideas presented are of interest and benefit to the entire profession, especially academic librarians." (Library Resources and Technical Services)*

19. *Library Development: A Future Imperative*, edited by Dwight F. Burlingame, PhD (Vol. 12, No. 4, 1990). *"This volume provides an excellent overview of fundraising with special application to libraries. . . . A useful book that is highly recommended for all libraries." (Library Journal)*

20. *Personnel Administration in an Automated Environment*, edited by Philip E. Leinbach, MLS (Vol. 13, No. 1/2, 1990). *"An interesting and worthwhile volume, recommended to university library administrators and to others interested in thought-provoking discussion of the personnel implications of automation." (Canadian Library Journal)*

21. *Strategic Planning in Higher Education: Implementing New Roles for the Academic Library*, edited by James F. Williams, II, MLS (Vol. 13, No. 3/4, 1991). *"A welcome addition to the sparse literature on strategic planning in university libraries. Academic librarians considering strategic planning for their libraries will learn a great deal from this work." (Canadian Library Journal)*

22. *Creative Planning for Library Administration: Leadership for the Future*, edited by Kent Hendrickson, MALS (Vol. 14, No. 2, 1991). *"Provides some essential information on the planning process, and the mix of opinions and methodologies, as well as examples relevant to every library manager, resulting in a very readable foray into a topic too long avoided by many of us." (Canadian Library Journal)*

23. *Budgets for Acquisitions: Strategies for Serials, Monographs, and Electronic Formats*, edited by Sul H. Lee (Vol. 14, No. 3, 1991). *"Much more than a series of handy tips for the careful shopper. This [book] is a most useful one–well-informed, thought-provoking, and authoritative." (Australian Library Review)*

24. *Managing Technical Services in the 90's*, edited by Drew Racine (Vol. 15, No. 1/2, 1991). *"Presents an eclectic overview of the challenges currently facing all library technical services efforts. . . . Recommended to library administrators and interested practitioners." (Library Journal)*

25. *Library Management in the Information Technology Environment: Issues, Policies, and Practice for Administrators*, edited by Brice G. Hobrock, PhD, MLS (Vol. 15, No. 3/4, 1992).

"A road map to identify some of the alternative routes to the electronic library." (Stephen Rollins, Associate Dean for Library Services, General Library, University of New Mexico)

26. **The Management of Library and Information Studies Education,** edited by Herman L. Totten, PhD, MLS (Vol. 16, No. 1/2, 1992). *"Offers something of interest to everyone connected with LIS education–the undergraduate contemplating a master's degree, the doctoral student struggling with courses and career choices, the new faculty member aghast at conflicting responsibilities, the experienced but stressed LIS professor, and directors of LIS Schools." (Education Libraries)*

27. **Vendor Evaluation and Acquisition Budgets,** edited by Sul H. Lee (Vol. 16, No. 3, 1992). *"The title doesn't do justice to the true scope of this excellent collection of papers delivered at the sixth annual conference on library acquisitions sponsored by the University of Oklahoma Libraries." (Kent K. Hendrickson, BS, MALS, Dean of Libraries, University of Nebraska-Lincoln) Find insightful discussions on the impact of rising costs on library budgets and management in this groundbreaking book.*

28. **Developing Library Staff for the 21st Century,** edited by Maureen Sullivan (Vol. 17, No. 1, 1992). *"I found myself enthralled with this highly readable publication. It is one of those rare compilations that manages to successfully integrate current general management operational thinking in the context of academic library management." (Bimonthly Review of Law Books)*

29. **Collection Assessment and Acquisitions Budgets,** edited by Sul H. Lee (Vol. 17, No. 2, 1993). *Contains timely information about the assessment of academic library collections and the relationship of collection assessment to acquisition budgets.*

30. **Leadership in Academic Libraries: Proceedings of the W. Porter Kellam Conference, The University of Georgia, May 7, 1991,** edited by William Gray Potter (Vol. 17, No. 4, 1993). *"Will be of interest to those concerned with the history of American academic libraries." (Australian Library Review)*

31. **Integrating Total Quality Management in a Library Setting,** edited by Susan Jurow, MLS, and Susan B. Barnard, MLS (Vol. 18, No. 1/2, 1993). *"Especially valuable are the librarian experiences that directly relate to real concerns about TQM. Recommended for all professional reading collections." (Library Journal)*

32. **Catalysts for Change: Managing Libraries in the 1990s,** edited by Gisela M. von Dran, DPA, MLS, and Jennifer Cargill, MSLS, MSEd (Vol. 18, No. 3/4, 1993). *"A useful collection of articles which focuses on the need for librarians to employ enlightened management practices in order to adapt to and thrive in the rapidly changing information environment." (Australian Library Review)*

33. **The Role and Future of Special Collections in Research Libraries: British and American Perspectives,** edited by Sul H. Lee (Vol. 19, No. 1, 1993). *"A provocative but informative read for library users, academic administrators, and private sponsors." (International Journal of Information and Library Research)*

34. **Declining Acquisitions Budgets: Allocation, Collection Development and Impact Communication,** edited by Sul H. Lee (Vol. 19, No. 2, 1993). *"Expert and provocative. . . . Presents many ways of looking at library budget deterioration and responses to it . . . There is much food for thought here." (Library Resources & Technical Services)*

35. **Libraries as User-Centered Organizations: Imperatives for Organizational Change,** edited by Meredith A. Butler (Vol. 19, No. 3/4, 1993). *"Presents a very timely and well-organized discussion of major trends and influences causing organizational changes." (Science Books & Films)*

36. **Access, Ownership, and Resource Sharing,** edited by Sul H. Lee (Vol. 20, No. 1, 1994). *The contributing authors present a useful and informative look at the current status of information provision and some of the challenges the subject presents.*

37. **The Dynamic Library Organizations in a Changing Environment,** edited by Joan Giesecke, MLS, DPA (Vol. 20, No. 2, 1994). *"Provides a significant look at potential changes in the library world and presents its readers with possible ways to address the negative results of such*

changes. . . . Covers the key issues facing today's libraries . . . Two thumbs up!" (Marketing Library Resources)

38. **The Future of Information Services,** edited by Virginia Steel, MA, and C. Brigid Welch, MLS (Vol. 20, No. 3/4, 1995). *"The leadership discussions will be useful for library managers as will the discussions of how library structures and services might work in the next century." (Australian Special Libraries)*

39. **The Future of Resource Sharing,** edited by Shirley K. Baker and Mary E. Jackson, MLS (Vol. 21, No. 1/2, 1995). *"Recommended for library and information science schools because of its balanced presentation of the ILL/document delivery issues." (Library Acquisitions: Practice and Theory)*

40. **Libraries and Student Assistants: Critical Links,** edited by William K. Black, MLS (Vol. 21, No. 3/4, 1995). *"A handy reference work on many important aspects of managing student assistants. . . . Solid, useful information on basic management issues in this work and several chapters are useful for experienced managers." (The Journal of Academic Librarianship)*

41. **Managing Change in Academic Libraries,** edited by Joseph J. Branin (Vol. 22, No. 2/3, 1996). *"Touches on several aspects of academic library management, emphasizing the changes that are occurring at the present time. . . . Recommended this title for individuals or libraries interested in management aspects of academic libraries." (RQ American Library Association)*

42. **Access, Resource Sharing and Collection Development,** edited by Sul H. Lee (Vol. 22, No. 4, 1996). *Features continuing investigation and discussion of important library issues, specifically the role of libraries in acquiring, storing, and disseminating information in different formats.*

43. **Interlibrary Loan/Document Delivery and Customer Satisfaction: Strategies for Redesigning Services,** edited by Pat L. Weaver-Meyers, Wilbur A. Stolt, and Yem S. Fong (Vol. 23, No. 1/2, 1997). *"No interlibrary loan department supervisor at any mid-sized to large college or university library can afford not to read this book." (Gregg Sapp, MLS, MEd, Head of Access Services, University of Miami, Richter Library, Coral Gables, Florida)*

44. **Emerging Patterns of Collection Development in Expanding Resource Sharing, Electronic Information, and Network Environment,** edited by Sul H. Lee (Vol. 24, No. 1/2, 1997). *"The issues it deals with are common to us all. We all need to make our funds go further and our resources work harder, and there are ideas here which we can all develop." (The Library Association Record)*

45. **The Academic Library Director: Reflections on a Position in Transition,** edited by Frank D'Andraia, MLS (Vol. 24, No. 3, 1997). *"A useful collection to have whether you are seeking a position as director or conducting a search for one." (College & Research Libraries News)*

46. **Economics of Digital Information: Collection, Storage, and Delivery,** edited by Sul H. Lee (Vol. 24, No. 4, 1997). *Highlights key concepts and issues vital to a library's successful venture into the digital environment and helps you understand why the transition from the printed page to the digital packet has been problematic for both creators of proprietary materials and users of those materials.*

47. **Management of Library and Archival Security: From the Outside Looking In,** edited by Robert K. O'Neill, PhD (Vol. 25, No. 1, 1998). *"Provides useful advice and on-target insights for professionals caring for valuable documents and artifacts." (Menzi L. Behrnd-Klodt, JD, Attorney/Archivist, Klodt and Associates, Madison, WI)*

48. **OCLC 1967-1997: Thirty Years of Furthering Access to the World's Information,** edited by K. Wayne Smith (Vol. 25, No. 2/3/4, 1998). *"A rich–and poignantly personal, at times–historical account of what is surely one of this century's most important developments in librarianship." (Deanna B. Marcum, PhD, President, Council on Library and Information Resources, Washington, DC)*

49. **The Economics of Information in the Networked Environment,** edited by Meredith A. Butler, MLS, and Bruce R. Kingma, PhD (Vol. 26, No. 1/2, 1998). *"A book that should be read both by information professionals and by administrators, faculty and others who share a collective concern to provide the most information to the greatest number at the lowest cost in the*

networked environment." (Thomas J. Galvin, PhD, Professor of Information Science and Policy, University at Albany, State University of New York)

50. **Information Technology Planning,** edited by Lori A. Goetsch (Vol. 26, No. 3/4, 1999). *Offers innovative approaches and strategies useful in your library and provides some food for thought about information technology as we approach the millennium.*

51. **Managing Multicultural Diversity in the Library: Principles and Issues for Administrators,** edited by Mark Winston (Vol. 27, No. 1/2, 1999). *Defines diversity, clarifies why it is important to address issues of diversity, and identifies goals related to diversity and how to go about achieving those goals.*

52. **Scholarship, Research Libraries, and Global Publishing,** by Jutta Reed-Scott (Vol. 27, No. 3/4, 1999). *This book documents a research project in conjunction with the Association of Research Libraries (ARL) that explores the issue of foreign acquisition and how it affects collection in international studies, area studies, collection development, and practices of international research libraries.*

53. **Collection Development in a Digital Environment,** edited by Sul H. Lee (Vol. 28, No. 1, 1999). *Explores ethical and technological dilemmas of collection development and gives several suggestions on how a library can successfully deal with these challenges and provide patrons with the information they need.*

54. **Collection Management: Preparing Today's Bibliographers for Tomorrow's Libraries,** edited by Karen Rupp-Serrano, MLS, MPA (Vol. 28, No. 2, 1999). *For both beginners and professional,* Collection Development *addresses your vexing questions that librarians continually face to assist you in creating a cost-effective and resourceful library.*

55. **The Age Demographics of Academic Librarians: A Profession Apart,** edited by Stanley J. Wilder (Vol. 28, No. 3, 1999). *The average age of librarians has been increasing dramatically since 1990. This unique book will provide insights on how this demographic issue can impact a library and what can be done to make the effects positive.*

56. **Collection Development in the Electronic Environment: Shifting Priorities,** edited by Sul H. Lee (Vol. 28, No. 4, 1999). *Through case studies and firsthand experiences, this volume discusses meeting the needs of scholars at universities, budgeting issues, user education, staffing in the electronic age, collaborating libraries and resources, and how vendors meet the needs of different customers.*

57. **Library Training for Staff and Customers,** edited by Sara Ramser Beck, MLS, MBA (Vol. 29, No. 1, 1999). *This comprehensive book is designed to assist library professionals involved in presenting or planning training for library staff members and customers. You will explore ideas for effective general reference training, training on automated systems, training in specialized subjects such as African American history and biography, and training for areas such as patents and trademarks, and business subjects.* Library Training for Staff and Customers *answers numerous training questions and is an excellent guide for planning staff development.*

58. **Integration in the Library Organization,** edited by Christine E. Thompson, PhD (Vol. 29, No. 2, 1999). *Provides librarians with the necessary tools to help libraries balance and integrate public and technical services and to improve the capability of libraries to offer patrons quality services and large amounts of information.*

59. **Management for Research Libraries Cooperation,** edited by Sul H. Lee (Vol. 29, No. 3/4, 2000). *Delivers sound advice, models, and strategies for increasing sharing between institutions to maximize the amount of printed and electronic research material you can make available in your library while keeping costs under control.*

60. **Academic Research on the Internet: Options for Scholars & Libraries,** edited by Helen Laurence, MLS, EdD, and William Miller, PhD, MLS (Vol. 30, No. 1/2/3/4, 2000). *"Emphasizes quality over quantity. . . . Presents the reader with the best research-oriented Web sites in the field. A state-of-the-art review of academic use of the Internet as well as a guide to the best Internet sites and services. . . . A useful addition for any academic library." (David A. Tyckoson, MLS, Head of Reference, California State University, Fresno)*

61. **Research Collections and Digital Information,** edited by Sul H. Lee (Vol. 31, No. 2, 2000). *Offers new strategies for collecting, organizing, and accessing library materials in the digital age.*

62. **Off-Campus Library Services,** edited by Ann Marie Casey (Vol. 31, No. 3/4, 2001 and Vol. 32, No. 1/2, 2001). *This informative volume examines various aspects of off-campus, or distance learning. It explores training issues for library staff, Web site development, changing roles for librarians, the uses of conferencing software, library support for Web-based courses, library agreements and how to successfully negotiate them, and much more!*

63. **Leadership in the Library and Information Science Professions: Theory and Practice,** edited by Mark D. Winston, MLS, PhD (Vol. 32, No. 3/4, 2001). *Offers fresh ideas for developing and using leadership skills, including recruiting potential leaders, staff training and development, issues of gender and ethnic diversity, and budget strategies for success.*

64. **Diversity Now: People, Collections, and Services in Academic Libraries,** edited by Teresa Y. Neely, PhD, and Kuang-Hwei (Janet) Lee-Smeltzer, MS, MSLIS (Vol. 33, No. 1/2/3/4, 2001). *Examines multicultural trends in academic libraries' staff and users, types of collections, and services offered.*

65. **Libraries and Electronic Resources: New Partnerships, New Practices, New Perspectives,** edited by Pamela L. Higgins (Vol. 35, No. 1/2, 2001). *An essential guide to the Internet's impact on electronic resources management—past, present, and future.*

66. **Impact of Digital Technology on Library Collections and Resource Sharing,** edited by Sul H. Lee (Vol. 35, No. 3, 2001). *Shows how digital resources have changed the traditional academic library.*

67. **Evaluating the Twenty-First Century Library: The Association of Research Libraries New Measures Initiative, 1997-2001,** edited by Donald L. DeWitt, PhD (Vol. 35, No. 4, 2001). *This collection of articles (thirteen of which previously appeared in ARL's bimonthly newsletter/report on research issues and actions) examines the Association of Research Libraries' "new measures" initiative.*

68. **Information Literacy Programs: Successes and Challenges,** edited by Patricia Durisin, MLIS (Vol. 36, No. 1/2, 2002). *Examines Web-based collaboration, teamwork with academic and administrative colleagues, evidence-based librarianship, and active learning strategies in library instruction programs.*

69. **Electronic Resources and Collection Development,** edited by Sul H. Lee (Vol. 36, No. 3, 2002). *Shows how electronic resources have impacted traditional collection development policies and practices.*

70. **Distance Learning Library Services: The Tenth Off-Campus Library Services Conference,** edited by Patrick B. Mahoney (Vol. 37, No. 1/2/3/4, 2002). *Explores the pitfalls of providing information services to distance students and suggests ways to avoid them.*

71. **The Strategic Stewardship of Cultural Resources: To Preserve and Protect,** edited by Andrea T. Merrill, BA (Vol. 38, No. 1/2/3/4, 2003). *Leading library, museum, and archival professionals share their expertise on a wide variety of preservation and security issues.*

72. **The Twenty-First Century Art Librarian,** edited by Terrie L. Wilson, MLS (Vol. 39, No. 1, 2003). *"A must-read addition to every art, architecture, museum, and visual resources library bookshelf." (Betty Jo Irvine, PhD, Fine Arts Librarian, Indiana University)*

73. **Digital Images and Art Libraries in the Twenty-First Century,** edited by Susan Wyngaard, MLS (Vol. 39, No. 2/3, 2003). *Provides an in-depth look at the technology that art librarians must understand in order to work effectively in today's digital environment.*

74. **Improved Access to Information: Portals, Content Selection, and Digital Information,** edited by Sul H. Lee (Vol. 39, No. 4, 2003). *Examines how improved electronic resources can allow libraries to provide an increasing amount of digital information to an ever-expanding patron base.*

75. **The Changing Landscape for Electronic Resources: Content, Access, Delivery, and Legal Issues,** edited by Yem S. Fong, MLS, and Suzanne M. Ward, MA (Vol. 40, No. 1/2, 2004).

Focuses on various aspects of electronic resources for libraries, including statewide resource-sharing initiatives, licensing issues, open source software, standards, and scholarly publishing.

76. **Libraries Act on Their LibQUAL+™ Findings: From Data to Action,** edited by Fred M. Heath, EdD, Martha Kyrillidou, MEd, MLS, and Consuella A. Askew, MLS (Vol. 40, No. 3/4, 2004). *Focuses on the value of LibQUAL+™ data to help librarians provide better services for users.*

77. **The Eleventh Off-Campus Library Services Conference,** edited by Patrick B. Mahoney, MBA, MLS (Vol. 41, No. 1/2/3/4, 2004). *Examines–and offers solutions to–the problems faced by librarians servicing faculty and students who do not have access to a traditional library.*

78. **Collection Management and Strategic Access to Digital Resources: The New Challenges for Research Libraries,** edited by Sul H. Lee (Vol. 42, No. 2, 2005). *Examines how libraries can make the best use of digital materials, maintain a balance between print and electronic resources, and respond to electronic information.*

79. **Licensing in Libraries: Practical and Ethical Aspects,** edited by Karen Rupp-Serrano, MLS, MPA (Vol. 42, No. 3/4, 2005). *Presents state-of-the-art information on licensing issues, including contract management, end-user education, copyright, e-books, consortial licensing software, legalities, and much more.*

80. **Portals and Libraries,** edited by Sarah C. Michalak, MLS (Vol. 43, No. 1/2, 2005). *An examination of the organization of Web-based and other electronic information resources with a review of different types of portals, attached services, and how to make the best use of them.*

81. **Evolving Internet Reference Resources,** edited by William Miller, PhD, MLS, and Rita M. Pellen, MLS (Vol. 43, No. 3/4, 2005 and Vol. 44, No. 1/2, 2006). *This book surveys the availability of online information, both free and subscription-based, in a wide variety of subject areas, including law, psychology, health and medicine, engineering, Latin American studies, and more.*

82. **Library/Vendor Relationships,** edited by Sam Brooks and David H. Carlson, MLS, MCS (Vol. 44, No. 3/4, 2006). Library/Vendor Relationships *examines the increasing cooperation in which libraries find they must participate in, and vice versa, with the vendors that provide system infrastructure and software. Expert contributors provide insights from all sides of this unique collaboration, offering cogent perspectives on the give and take process that every librarian, publisher, and database provider/producer can use.*

Library/Vendor Relationships

Sam Brooks
David H. Carlson
Editors

Library/Vendor Relationships has been co-published simultaneously as *Journal of Library Administration*, Volume 44, Numbers 3/4 2006.

The Haworth Information Press®
An Imprint of The Haworth Press, Inc.

New York • London • Victoria (AU)
www.HaworthPress.com

Published by

The Haworth Information Press®, 10 Alice Street, Binghamton, NY 13904-1580 USA

The Haworth Information Press® is an imprint of The Haworth Press, Inc., 10 Alice Street, Binghamton, NY 13904-1580 USA.

Library/Vendor Relationships has been co-published simultaneously as *Journal of Library Administration*™, Volume 44, Numbers 3/4 2006.

The development, preparation, and publication of this work has been undertaken with great care. However, the publisher, employees, editors, and agents of The Haworth Press and all imprints of The Haworth Press, Inc., including The Haworth Medical Press® and Pharmaceutical Products Press®, are not responsible for any errors contained herein or for consequences that may ensue from use of materials or information contained in this work. With regard to case studies, identities and circumstances of individuals discussed herein have been changed to protect confidentiality. Any resemblance to actual persons, living or dead, is entirely coincidental.

The Haworth Press is committed to the dissemination of ideas and information according to the highest standards of intellectual freedom and the free exchange of ideas. Statements made and opinions expressed in this publication do not necessarily reflect the views of the Publisher, Directors, management, or staff of The Haworth Press, Inc., or an endorsement by them.

Cover design by Jennifer M. Gaska.

Library of Congress Cataloging-in-Publication Data

Library/vendor relationships / Sam Brooks, David H. Carlson, editors.
     p. cm.
     "Co-published simultaneously as Journal of library administration, volume 44, numbers 3/4 2006."
     Includes bibliographical references and index.
     ISBN-13: 978-0-7890-3351-2 (alk. paper)
     ISBN-10: 0-7890-3351-8 (alk. paper)
     ISBN-13: 978-0-7890-3352-9 (pbk. : alk. paper)
     ISBN-10: 0-7890-3352-6 (pbk. : alk. paper)
     1. Libraries and electronic publishing. 2. Acquisition of electronic information resources. 3. Communication in library science. 4. Negotiation in business. 5. Online information services industry–Customer services. 6. Online databases–Marketing. I. Brooks, Sam, 1967- II. Carlson, David H., 1954- III. Journal of library administration.
Z716.6.L5435 2006
025.17'4–dc22
                              2006002789

Indexing, Abstracting & Website/Internet Coverage

This section provides you with a list of major indexing & abstracting services and other tools for bibliographic access. That is to say, each service began covering this periodical during the year noted in the right column. Most Websites which are listed below have indicated that they will either post, disseminate, compile, archive, cite or alert their own Website users with research-based content from this work. (This list is as current as the copyright date of this publication.)

(continued)

(continued)

(continued)

(continued)

Special Bibliographic Notes related to special journal issues
(separates) and indexing/abstracting:

- indexing/abstracting services in this list will also cover material in any "separate" that is co-published simultaneously with Haworth's special thematic journal issue or DocuSerial. Indexing/abstracting usually covers material at the article/chapter level.
- monographic co-editions are intended for either non-subscribers or libraries which intend to purchase a second copy for their circulating collections.
- monographic co-editions are reported to all jobbers/wholesalers/approval plans. The source journal is listed as the "series" to assist the prevention of duplicate purchasing in the same manner utilized for books-in-series.
- to facilitate user/access services all indexing/abstracting services are encouraged to utilize the co-indexing entry note indicated at the bottom of the first page of each article/chapter/contribution.
- this is intended to assist a library user of any reference tool (whether print, electronic, online, or CD-ROM) to locate the monographic version if the library has purchased this version but not a subscription to the source journal.
- individual articles/chapters in any Haworth publication are also available through the Haworth Document Delivery Service (HDDS).

Library/Vendor Relationships

CONTENTS

ABOUT THE EDITORS

Sam Brooks is the Senior Vice President of Sales & Marketing for EBSCO Information Services, the world's largest intermediary between libraries and publishers of journals and magazines. During the last fifteen years, Mr. Brooks has dedicated himself to working with libraries in every corner of the globe. He has visited institutions in more than eighty countries, and has worked extensively with ministries of education, ministries of science & technology, and ministries of culture in developing nations. In addition to authoring papers in peer-reviewed library science journals, he has been published in the library publications of more than a dozen countries, and has participated in panel discussions or appeared as the keynote speaker at many library conferences, including: ACRL Chapter Meetings, IFLA, The Charleston Conference, ALCTS Networked Resources and Metadata Committee Meeting, International Congress of Information, LITA Technology and Access Committee Meeting, NLA Tri-Round Table (Technical Services, Information & Technology), and many others. Mr. Brooks is active in the development of database resources for EBSCO, and acts as a primary liaison between EBSCO's customers, various library advisory boards and EBSCO's development teams.

David H. Carlson, MLS, MCS is Dean of Library Affairs at Southern Illinois University Carbondale. Morris Library at SIU Carbondale is a member of the Association of Research Libraries and the Greater Western Library Alliance, among other organizations. In January, 2006, the Library will begin a $42 million renovation and expansion of the main library structure, which was built in the early '50s. This initiative represents the largest single capital project in the history of the University. Mr. Carlson has a Master's in Library Science (University of Michigan) as well as a second Master's degree in Computer Science (University of Evansville). Reflecting this background, he began his career with positions in library systems and the implementation of integrated library systems in academic/research libraries. More recently, he has held positions with administrative responsibilities as Executive Director at the Triangle Research Libraries Network in North Carolina, Director of Libraries at Bridgewater State College in Massachusetts and his current position as Dean at SIUC in Illinois. Mr. Carlson has published a number of articles in library publications including *Library Journal, College and Research Libraries,* and *Information Technology and Libraries,* among others. Related to the topic of this issue, Mr. Carlson was an early advocate and founding member of the Academic Advisory Board for EBSCO Information Services.

Introduction:
The Importance of Open Communication
Between Libraries and Vendors

Sam Brooks

Among the 40-plus synonym entries in *Roget's New Millennium*™ Thesaurus, First Edition, for the term "relationship," interestingly, the term "dependence" appears.[1] When pondering the idea of relationships in terms of dependence, and more specifically, the relationships forged between libraries and vendors, a certain clarity is evident that may not exist in all relationships. After all, there may be no library/vendor relationship if there was no dependence in the first place. And further dissecting the terminology leads to the definition of dependence, which, in part, is "reliance" and "trust"–basic building-blocks in any fruitful relationship.[2]

The nature of relations between libraries and vendors is essentially different from typical customer/vendor relations. Much of this is to do with the fact that the staff of the library is most often not the end-user. Instead, the library staff is providing a service to their customers (patrons/students/faculty), which can be improved if the working relationship between the library staff and the vendor can also be enhanced. In a nutshell, libraries can provide better service to their end-users if vendors can better equip the libraries to do so. In order for vendors to accomplish this task, they often rely heavily upon libraries for the insight and direction to improve products and services. Thus, dependence is evident in this circular pattern, and forging strong relationships is key to

[Haworth co-indexing entry note]: "Introduction: The Importance of Open Communication Between Libraries and Vendors." Brooks, Sam. Co-published simultaneously in *Journal of Library Administration* (The Haworth Information Press, an imprint of The Haworth Press, Inc.) Vol. 44, No. 3/4, 2006, pp. 1-4; and: *Library/Vendor Relationships* (ed: Sam Brooks, and David H. Carlson) The Haworth Information Press, an imprint of The Haworth Press, Inc., 2006, pp. 1-4. Single or multiple copies of this article are available for a fee from The Haworth Document Delivery Service [1-800-HAWORTH, 9:00 a.m. - 5:00 p.m. (EST). E-mail address: docdelivery@haworthpress.com].

Available online at http://www.haworthpress.com/web/JLA
doi:10.1300/J111v44n03_01

1

the continued development of products and services for use by librarians and patrons.

In essence, open lines of communication and the basic sharing of information is at the core of library/vendor relations. Much of this stems from the willingness (by libraries) to freely share valuable improvement suggestions with vendors. Often this feedback is direct interpretations of suggestions or complaints voiced by their patrons. Thus, candid communication may result in specific enhancements to vendor products and services, and subsequently the ability for libraries to better meet the needs of the end-user. Much of the time, feedback comes from libraries to vendors through sales and service representatives, or through options on a vendor's customer support web site.

However, along with the power to help themselves through being vocal, libraries also have the ability to do damage to a vendor. As a community, academic librarians are often available to each other for assistance, and the very nature of the profession is to share and make available information. As such, an interesting and rather unique medium for librarians to share information and experiences with each other is that of the e-mail listserv. The basic idea with most library-specific listservs is to serve as a discussion platform for librarians, and provide a quick and easy way for librarians to gather insight from colleagues around the world (and sometimes vendors). For example, a popular listserv for academic librarians is LIBLICENSE-L (http://www.library. yale.edu/~llicense/index.shtml). According to a D-Lib magazine feature, "The LIBLICENSE Project was established to inform and educate members of the information supply chain, particularly (but not exclusively) librarians, about how effectively to contract for electronic information resources."[3] The value of these listservs is undeniable, and the larger listservs reach a great many librarians. Thus, just as positive comments may be beneficial to vendors, negative comments or reactions to a given vendor product in this open forum may prove damaging and difficult for a vendor to overcome.

Though the basic channels of communication from libraries to vendors largely have been established, improving upon this infrastructure is a constant undertaking. Some vendors continue to find ways to tap into the vast knowledge of library customers, and go to great lengths to learn more about issues facing libraries.

Perhaps the most important element in the library/vendor relationship is an understanding of needs. In other words, for vendors to provide the most valuable resources to libraries, vendors must have a thorough comprehension of the issues that face libraries, and the specific concerns, interests, etc., of the users whom these libraries serve. Of course, and as mentioned, direct communication with customers is paramount, but further still, vendors having librarians on staff, in essence, bring an every-day understanding of library issues closer to the source of the resources. EBSCO, for example, employs a large number of (MLS) librarians, many with years of experience in academic and other library settings. These individuals act in a wide variety of roles within the company including as on-site trainers, product managers, sales and service representatives, database developers, and other important positions. These librarians bring with them the critical experience that comes only from "hands-on" work in a library. It is this intimate knowledge and concern for the initiatives and challenges of libraries that further allows vendors to elevate their level of awareness, and in turn, create more suitable, beneficial resources.

Another powerful method of direct communication between vendors and libraries is through formal advisory groups. Advisory boards are used as forums for communication, feedback, and action, where the library advisory board provides guidance, direction, and insight on matters including policy and philosophy.[4] Some vendors have established a variety of advisory boards and seek their advice extensively. EBSCO, for example, maintains a number of advisory boards in place for differing, specific purposes. These range from broadly focused boards such as general advisory for a certain library-type (e.g., academic, public, business, etc.) as well as boards designed to assist in very specific aspects (e.g., database-specific, subject-specific, thesaurus creation, software, etc.). Advisory board members tend to be privy to information that is not yet available to the general public. As a result, it is common for vendors to have board members sign confidentiality clauses as a prerequisite to participation. Advisory boards may assist in virtually all phases of a vendor's business from product idea stages, product development and enhancements, to new initiatives and overall company direction. These advisory boards are often the initial sounding boards for company ideas, and tend to work closely with vendors through a combination of group meetings (in person), e-mail, and telephone exchange.

On a larger scale in terms of the number of libraries involved, but perhaps less encompassing in terms of the level of detail associated, are 'e-mail councils,' another form of library/vendor communication where vendors seek advice from customers. These e-mail councils tend to be sizeable groups of librarians segmented by library type, who are willing to provide insight strictly through e-mail. This feedback may come in the form of completed surveys, or simply e-mail responses to queries. E-mail councils are an effective way to quickly 'poll' customers to gain a strong sense of the overall feelings of a particular library group, rather than more in-depth insight into more involved topics that may be better suited for smaller or more focused advisory boards. E-mail councils provide a bi-directional sense of cooperation between vendors and customers, where opinions can be expressed and gathered expediently. Not every customer can be a member of an advisory board; thus, these e-mail councils provide an opportunity for many more libraries to voice their opinions and suggestions on specific topics in more of a formal forum than other more common/typical channels for providing unsolicited feedback.

Perhaps the most important element of communication is the actual personal involvement or participation it generates from all people affiliated with the library world. It is equally important for vendors and libraries to stay involved in furthering our professional development, and subsequently the value of the services that we provide. As professionals and interested parties, we stand to learn a great deal from our colleagues and counterparts. Vendors can learn from libraries and libraries can learn from vendors. This goes further than the back and forth communication between libraries and vendors as described previously. Being active in library/vendor communities means sharing experiences, passing along ideas, shedding light for others in areas where we may have expertise. As such, let this serve as my urging to anyone working in the library field to enlighten us with your perspective. Deliver conference papers. Contribute to library science journals (such as the *Journal of Library Administration*), write letters to editors of library industry publications, participate in panel discussions, etc. Whether it is finding ways to do our jobs more effectively, or learning what not to do, our participation is welcomed, respected, and needed. As such, we appreciate the contributions from both the librarians and vendors who have made this volume possible.

NOTES

1. Roget's New Millennium™ Thesaurus, First Edition (v 1.0.5). Available: http://www.thesaurus.com [November 2004].

2. The American Heritage® Dictionary of the English Language, Fourth Edition. Available: http://www.dictionary.com [November 2004].

3. Ann Okerson, "The LIBLICENSE Project and How it Grows," *D-Lib Magazine* 5 (September 1999), Available: http://www.dlib.org/dlib/september99/okerson/09okerson.html.

4. Anthea Stratigos, "Managing Up: Stakeholder Relationship Imperatives," *Online* 27 (March/April 2003), 69.

Introduction:
Forging Lasting Symbiotic Relationships Between Libraries and Vendors

David H. Carlson

The idea and genesis for this volume devoted to the topic of library and vendor relationships, began some twelve years ago. My professional background, education, and experience have focused on the application and development of computer systems in libraries. This expertise has impressed upon me the essential need for a positive and successful relationship between libraries and vendors. I fear that despite our mutual needs there are fundamental misunderstandings between libraries and vendors. In some cases, these misunderstandings lead to mistrust, broken relationships, and failed initiatives. These failings hurt both libraries and vendors.

Historically, the relationship between libraries and vendors is tightly linked to technological developments and applications. It starts with the technology that made today's modern libraries possible: the printing press. Authors worked with publishers to print, publicize, and distribute their works; libraries established arrangements and worked with publishers to acquire published materials. In the latter half of the twentieth century, with the development of office and information technologies, libraries began a new relationship with vendors of databases and integrated library systems. The application of information technologies has

[Haworth co-indexing entry note]: "Introduction: Forging Lasting Symbiotic Relationships Between Libraries and Vendors." Carlson, David H. Co-published simultaneously in *Journal of Library Administration* (The Haworth Information Press, an imprint of The Haworth Press, Inc.) Vol. 44, No. 3/4, 2006, pp. 5-10; and: *Library/Vendor Relationships* (ed: Sam Brooks, and David H. Carlson) The Haworth Information Press, an imprint of The Haworth Press, Inc., 2006, pp. 5-10. Single or multiple copies of this article are available for a fee from The Haworth Document Delivery Service [1-800-HAWORTH, 9:00 a.m. - 5:00 p.m. (EST). E-mail address: docdelivery@haworthpress.com].

Available online at http://www.haworthpress.com/web/JLA
doi:10.1300/J111v44n03_02

resulted in the development of some of the most important tools by which libraries interact with their patrons. Today, vendors provide the majority of the tools and databases that libraries depend on for mission-critical services.

The application of integrated systems in libraries follows a pattern of maturation that is closely tied to vendors. This timeline has three distinct stages:

1. *Research Stage.* In this earliest stage, the application of computers in libraries was exploratory and preliminary. The use and development of these new technologies in libraries were so different that the earliest applications are properly described as research applications–identifying the questions that need to be resolved for further development and success.

At this initial stage, libraries and librarians are the critical players; vendors have minimal roles. Libraries themselves are both customer and developer: building, applying, evaluating, and using their locally-developed systems for further development and application.

2. *Maturation.* In the second stage of application, maturation, there is further development of technologies which is informed by the lessons learned from early development. Libraries begin to implement and rely on systems that play mission-centric functions in circulation, cataloging, and public access. The vendor community takes notice, but the environment is a mixed one. There are for-profit vendors offering solutions but there is also robust competition from early systems developed by libraries that proved successful in early development. The integrated library management system, NOTIS, may be the best example of this. For a time, this system, developed by the libraries at Northwestern University, was the system of choice for academic/research libraries. At its height, the Northwestern-based NOTIS competed successfully with the for-profit vendor community and was an independent vendor to libraries across the nation and the world.

3. *Enterprise and Mission Critical.* In this final stage, for-profit vendors dominate the marketplace and systems are no longer experimental or marginal: they perform mission-critical functions in libraries. Nothing is more symbolic and reflective of this change than libraries first freezing, then removing, their card catalogs and relying on their online catalogs. Systems that began as locally developed initiatives–some with significant levels of success–are replaced by for-profit vendor systems. Libraries find that they cannot match the economies of scale and development that a for-profit vendor can provide through the resources of a national customer base. Thus, a system such as NOTIS is sold by North-

western University and becomes a product from a for-profit vendor. The only locally-developed systems that survive are those which have an extended state-wide application base, such as the University of California. More typical is the locally-developed BIS from the libraries in the Triangle area of North Carolina (Duke University, University of North Carolina Chapel Hill, and North Carolina State University). BIS is replaced in the late '90s by the for-profit DRA. Even these three strong research libraries, sharing a common research-based mission and close geographic proximity, find that they cannot compete with the functionality and development enabled by the economies of scale of the for-profit marketplace.

This three-stage sequence of development follows the application of integrated library systems beginning in the '60s and ending in the '90s. As this sequence matured in the '90s, this period saw a much different development of vendor involvement through the application of another automated solution: the availability of networked online full-text to libraries. Two primary approaches developed. First, some publishers offered platform-based solutions to libraries that offer exclusive access to the publisher's collection of journals. This approach worked fairly well for libraries with large stables of titles and critical journals, but not for the smaller publisher with limited offerings.

The second solution is what has been called the "aggregators." The two leading examples of this approach are EBSCO Information Services and ProQuest. These vendors gather together full-text from thousands of different journals and put them together in various packages under a shared interface and offer the solution to libraries with connectivity through the Internet and a standard web browser. For libraries, the aggregator offers an attractive solution with titles from various fields and at attractive prices compared to the print equivalent. For publishers, the aggregators bring a ready-made solution to offer a presence and solution in the electronic marketplace and a revenue stream in addition to the traditional print.

Unlike the development of integrated library systems, libraries did not play a central development role in these networked full-text solutions. Library involvement is limited to their voice as customer. This role is not insignificant but it is much different from a role as early developer and implementer.

There are many diverse elements and implications of these trends. The focus of this collection is the nature of the relationship between libraries and for-profit vendors. While the development of integrated library management systems and provision of networked full-text followed very different development patterns, they share one important outcome: in both cases, vendors are now providing services and solutions that are fundamental and mission-critical to libraries. In addition, libraries have given up their active role in the development and application of these systems to the for-profit vendor community except for a few regional and state-based approaches.

One of the most controversial aspects of this shift relate to the provision of electronic full-text. Librarians have concerns that the package of journals offered by publishers, whether in aggregator databases or as a smaller packages of publisher-specific titles, represent an abandonment of fundamental collection development responsibilities that *define* the nature and scope of the local library and its mission. It is not within the scope of this article to explore this important issue but the debate illustrates that with the advent of electronic systems in libraries through management information systems and the transmission of electronic full-text, third-party, for-profit vendors play an unprecedented role in libraries. Their decisions have significant impact on the ability of libraries to provide mission-critical services to their patrons.

My co-editor, Sam Brooks, begins his introduction by noting that the word "relationship" has elements of dependence; he is correct and the point is highly relevant. The dependence of modern libraries on vendors is unprecedented. It is the intent of this publication to explore the nature of this relationship and this dependency. By way of introduction to this work, I would like to address what I believe are some of the key elements of the relationship between vendors and libraries.

The relationship between libraries and vendors is not, by definition, negative. It is clear that libraries and vendors have fundamentally different roles and missions–libraries are non-profit and vendors exist to make money. While different, these missions do not have to be in conflict. They can be complementary. In his popular book on effective negotiation, *Getting to Yes*, author Roger Fisher makes this important point: "Agreement is often made possible precisely because interests differ [between parties]."[1] This is a critical point.

It is vital that libraries and vendors recognize our mutual dependency. This recognition means that we need to think carefully about our relationships and how to improve them. For vendors, the establishment of effective and meaningful user groups is an important step. There is a real temptation, however, for vendors to view and use these groups as little more than focus sessions of important customers or, even worse, marketing sessions. If these groups are to be effective it is essential that vendors give the libraries that participate meaningful roles in the strategic decisions and direction of the vendor. Vendors cannot turn over the management of their company to customer advisory groups, of course, but there is an important balance whereby the input and considerations of the advisory must have meaningful impact on company decisions and strategic direction. In the end, this will benefit both libraries and vendors.

Conversely, librarians must take their role in advisory groups seriously. The seriousness of this responsibility shows itself in several ways and the first is confidentiality. Libraries must respect the competitive nature of the marketplace and if they expect to have input into strategic directions, they must recognize the importance to the vendor of information that is private and confidential. This goes against our professional value of unrestricted information but it is inappropriate for libraries to share what they learn with colleagues when asked to keep information from vendors confidential.

In these advisory groups, it is also incumbent upon librarians to beware of being used as platforms for vendor endorsements of products or policies. There is nothing wrong with an individual librarian agreeing to a public endorsement of a vendor's product if that endorsement is honest and based on professional assessments. It may also be appropriate for an advisory group, on occasion, to review and provide an endorsement (if it can) of a controversial position or approach by a vendor in the marketplace if that endorsement is honestly given and based on professional interests. Indeed, there is not only nothing wrong with this approach, it is a reasonable expectation by vendors for librarians and it is one way that librarians can be a contributory partner. Nonetheless, the primary role of advisory groups should be in the confidential assistance to the vendor in assessment and feedback regarding its strategic plans and directions, not as opportunities for glossy endorsements of a product. The separation of these roles is important to maintain the integrity of the advisory group.

Finally, we need meaningful partnerships between libraries and vendors. One of the areas in which this can be done is through software development. Successful partnerships are very difficult to establish. Too often, librarians on the front lines of the application view these relationships as burdensome and providing no opportunity other than the troubling necessity of finding and dealing with errors in unstable software; library administrators may view these partnerships as opportunities for some publicity, national recognition, and/or software discounts from the vendor. Vendors, on the other hand, often do not take seriously the opportunity and ability of library technical staff to develop a product and they view the development effort by libraries as little more than a beta test. If libraries and vendors work together in real and meaningful development partnerships, where each is a trusted partner and each makes meaningful contributions to the relationship, there can be substantive improvement in these applications to the advantage of both.

For development partnerships to work there must be clear and formal expectations of what the vendor and the library will contribute to the effort and the contribution of each must be meaningful and important. Vendors need to be willing to trust librarians with access to some of their most important assets–their code–and librarians must be willing to honor this trust and they must be willing to provide staff with substantial commitments of time, effort, and talents.

CONCLUSION

It is interesting to note that the increase in the relationship between libraries and vendors is intimately connected to the deployment of technology. What began with the enabling technology of the printing press, has led to shared databases for cataloging, integrated library management systems, and full-text online databases. Libraries need vendors who provide mission-critical roles and services. The need is mutual as vendors need libraries to be successful and make a profit. Libraries and vendors do not compete–they complement. Through the implementation and use of meaningful advisory boards, successful development partnerships, and a mutual respect for the skills, talents, and perspective that each brings, the relationship between vendors and libraries can be improved and enhanced–to the benefit of both.

NOTE

1. Fisher, Roger, *Getting to Yes: Negotiating Agreement Without Giving In* (New York: Penguin Books, 1991), p. 43.

Managing the Unmanageable: Systematic Downloading of Electronic Resources by Library Users

Gayle Baker
Carol Tenopir

SUMMARY. During the past several years, vendors of electronic resources have been monitoring their systems for occurrences of the downloading of large volumes of material by individuals who access these systems through libraries. These incidents violate license agreements between libraries and vendors. The perpetrators may be legitimate authorized users of a library, or they may be unauthorized users who have found a temporary hole in network security and attain access through open proxy servers or other means. Some use technical tools, like robots, to facilitate quicker systematic downloading. These acts may result in cessation of access to the resource for a limited time until the library investigates the situation and reports its findings to the ven-

Gayle Baker is Professor and Electronic Services Coordinator, University of Tennessee Libraries (E-mail: gsbaker@utk.edu).

Carol Tenopir is Professor, School of Information Sciences, and Interim Director, Center for Information Studies, University of Tennessee (E-mail: ctenopir@utk.edu).

[Haworth co-indexing entry note]: "Managing the Unmanageable: Systematic Downloading of Electronic Resources by Library Users." Baker, Gayle, and Carol Tenopir. Co-published simultaneously in *Journal of Library Administration* (The Haworth Information Press, an imprint of The Haworth Press, Inc.) Vol. 44, No. 3/4, 2006, pp. 11-24; and: *Library/Vendor Relationships* (ed: Sam Brooks, and David H. Carlson) The Haworth Information Press, an imprint of The Haworth Press, Inc., 2006, pp. 11-24. Single or multiple copies of this article are available for a fee from The Haworth Document Delivery Service [1-800-HAWORTH, 9:00 a.m. - 5:00 p.m. (EST). E-mail address: docdelivery@haworthpress.com].

Available online at http://www.haworthpress.com/web/JLA
doi:10.1300/J111v44n03_03

dor. Librarians have options for investigating these incidents, working with vendors, and preventing such incidents from happening. *[Article copies available for a fee from The Haworth Document Delivery Service: 1-800-HAWORTH. E-mail address: <docdelivery@haworthpress.com> Website: <http://www.HaworthPress.com> © 2006 by The Haworth Press, Inc. All rights reserved.]*

KEYWORDS. License agreement violation, fair use, excessive downloading, systematic downloading, open proxy server, IP authentication, robots

INTRODUCTION

Receiving the first e-mail from a vendor about one or more incidents of excessive and/or systematic downloading of electronic resources can be alarming. This notification of a violation of the license agreement between the library and the vendor usually requests the library to investigate the incident and report the findings. Access to the associated electronic resource may be suspended for a time to one or more IP addresses related to the incident. With the first incident, a librarian may not know where to begin the investigation. The purpose of this article is to provide some guidelines to manage and prevent such incidents in the future.

THE ENVIRONMENT

With the costs of downloading large quantities of information decreasing due to improved network speeds from 300 baud to 10,000 baud in the 1980s, producers and vendors of databases became concerned with copyright and downloading. They developed downloading license agreements to deal with the length of time the files were stored, and the use and reuse of the data (Talab 1985).

The Internet today provides easy, high-speed access to vast amounts of information, much of which is free and easily downloaded. Unfortunately, this environment negatively affects the use of copyrighted and licensed electronic resources. Music and video piracy are common on many campus networks with file sharing software. Pressure from recording companies on college campuses has somewhat curbed the practice (Read 2004); however, many students do not recognize these practices as a problem and feel that any information on the Internet is there for the taking. Some students recognize that it is illegal to download music and videos, but do so anyway (Ishizuka 2004).

Academic libraries no longer pay connect time to access electronic resources. Instead, they usually pay a single amount for the right to access large collections of information, including full-text materials. Many libraries no longer have to mediate the access by having librarians serve as gatekeepers performing the search for and retrieval of information. Most searching is done by end users, many of whom see no difference between the information for which academic libraries spend large portions of their budgets and the information that they can freely access on the Internet.

LICENSE AGREEMENTS

Defining "authorized users" is a common component of license agreements for electronic resources. In higher education, "authorized users" usually are current students, faculty, and staff of the institution, while public institutions usually include "walk-ins" in this category, too. Authorized users are expected to follow Fair Use Provisions of U.S. Copyright Law when retrieving electronic materials. One of the factors to be considered in determining "fair use" is "the amount and substantiality of the portion used in relation to the copyrighted work as a whole" (Copyright Act of 1976). Many license agreements go beyond this and explicitly prohibit downloading in a systematic way.

Article 6 of Terms and Conditions for American Chemical Society (ACS) publications *ACS Web Editions* and *ACS Journal Archives* state that articles "are not to be systematically downloaded" and "may not be downloaded in aggregate quantities or centrally stored for later retrieval." The license also indicates that ACS may prevent the use of automated tools used for obtaining information from their online publications (American Chemical Society 2004). One of the common automated tools is a robot, a program which allows users to write code to automatically search for and retrieve information from web-based resources at speeds several times faster than a human being. A special form of a robot, called a "spider," has been used for years by search engines to seek out new web resources.

The license agreement for the Scitation online journals from the American Institute of Physics (AIP) is more specific about what is deemed excessive. It prohibits "systematic or programmatic downloading (e.g., the use of automated 'robots' or otherwise downloading or attempting to download in a short time period large amounts of subscribed-to or unsubscribed-to Scitation material such as all abstracts and/or full-text articles from entire journal issues or extensive search results . . .)" (American Institute of Physics 2004).

JSTOR "Terms and Conditions of Use" specifically state that one "may not download from the JSTOR archive an entire issue of a journal, significant portions of the entire run of a journal, a significant number of sequential articles, or multiple copies of articles" (JSTOR 2002).

License agreements usually contain some provision requiring the library to have appropriate security measures and make authorized users aware of appropriate use terms for the licensed product. While knowing that libraries cannot account for the actions of every user, vendors construct their license agreements to hold libraries responsible for investigating misuse of the product and initiating corrective action, if necessary (Rossingnol 2002).

UNAUTHORIZED USERS AND SYSTEMATIC DOWNLOADING

In 2002, JSTOR noticed that hundreds of complete issues of electronic journals in their archive had been downloaded in a systematic way. They learned that the downloading was being done via an open proxy server at an institution that had a JSTOR subscription (JSTOR 2002). Proxy servers authenticate users with data from institutional directories and facilitate remote, off-campus access for legitimate users to resources restricted to the campus IP address. The proxy server retrieves information requested and makes it available to the remote user. An open proxy server does no authentication, providing an open door to illegitimate users. Administrators of web servers on campus networks may be unaware that their servers are configured with open proxy capabilities. Unscrupulous persons search for these security holes and use them to access electronic resources available to the IP address of the server (Cain 2003).

Users can manually download material from a database of journal articles in a systematic way but this process is made much easier by robots. This systematic downloading of information poses a threat to vendors of electronic resources on two fronts–intellectual property and the integrity of the vendors' servers used to make electronic resources available to authorized users.

Marc Brodsky of the American Institute of Physics compared the use of robots to "cover-to-cover use of copying machines" (Bradley 2002). Robot programs facilitate the creation of rival or derivative electronic resources that may be sold for financial gain or used in lieu of a legitimate subscription.

A major threat of robots is their impact on vendor servers. Robot-generated requests for information can overwhelm a server with the sheer numbers of requests for information. This results in degraded response time, blocks legitimate users from access, and can eventually lead to a system crash (Butkevich and Orr 2004; Chesler and Treby 2004).

Vendors have developed automated tools to identify patterns of excessive and systematic downloading before they adversely affect their systems. They are reluctant to discuss specifics about limits that trigger an event of misuse, like the maximum number of articles downloaded during a session, because hackers would use this information to bypass their controls. Some vendor programs automatically shut off the offending IP address or IP range. Usually vendor personnel contact the library with information about the problem and ask that the library investigate and report their findings (Butkevich and Orr 2004; Chesler and Treby 2004).

INCIDENTS OF MISUSE

The number and type of incidents will vary from institution to institution. In 2004, the University of Tennessee (UT) Libraries dealt with excessive/systematic downloading incidents from three different vendors:

1. *Several journals through the Library's proxy server*–The vendor notified the Library that articles from several volumes of different journals had been downloaded on a specific date from an IP address that turned out to be the Library's proxy server. Access had been automatically turned off to that IP address. This was a serious problem because that proxy server facilitated remote access to electronic resources to authorized users. A review of the log file from the Library's proxy server revealed that the downloading actually occurred from an IP address that was later identified as being from another country. Access was restored and then cut off

automatically several times by the vendors monitoring programs during the process of gathering the information. Library staff eventually learned that the NetID and password of a graduate student was being used by someone through the foreign IP address. The NetID and password are used to authenticate users with the LDAP (Lightweight Directory Access Protocol) directory server for a variety of campus services. The department was contacted and we e-mailed the student. He stated that his NetID and password were stolen by a post-doctoral fellow who had recently left the country. He agreed to change his password and the misuse stopped immediately. Our findings were reported to the vendor without any identifying information about the student.

2. *Single journal from on-campus user*–The Library received notification of excessive/systematic downloading, including the IP address, date, journal title, and the number of articles that were downloaded. Once the library identified the location of the workstation using the IP address, we contacted the department and learned that it was associated with a workstation in a professor's office. The professor was contacted by e-mail about the incident. He called the library and explained that he was not aware that he was doing anything wrong by downloading over 300 articles in an hour. He had done this to create a database for his research interests. He apologized and said that it would not happen again.

3. *Articles from unspecified journals through an open proxy server*– The Library was notified that a vendor had identified an open proxy server at a specific IP address and that vendor had disabled printing and downloading from that address. The vendor asked to receive confirmation that the open proxy was disabled or security measures were added. No specific information was given as to which journals were downloaded or the amount downloaded. The Library learned that the IP address was for a server in a campus office. The server had been set up for the semester as a class project. The office manager was unconcerned about being unable to download from the vendor involved and did not wish to make any changes to the server. The Library enlisted the help of the campus network security office to help the office manager understand the security problem and to assist him in adding password access to their temporary proxy server. The downloading was obviously done by an unauthorized user who did not have a valid NetID and password to access the electronic resource through the library's proxy server.

What motivates an authorized user to use robots to download large amounts of material? Some desire to have their own archives of full-text materials available at their convenience. A librarian revealed in discussion on the CHMINF-L listserv that an international graduate student downloaded a large amount of material from a database to share with colleagues upon returning home (Bradley 2002). Others like the speed of access and not having to deal with network delays. They also like the portability and ability to access the data when they will not have network connections. Others have needs for large collections of text for research purposes, such as data or text mining (Lamoreaux 2004). Vendors, like the American Institute of Physics (Butkevich and Orr 2004) and the American Chemical Society (Chesler and Treby 2004), prefer to work with these researchers on a case-by-case basis in order to ensure that their servers are not compromised and that the use is legitimate research.

PREVENTION AND PREPARATION

Several concerns should be considered by libraries to be prepared to respond to vendors about misuse incidents and to prevent future incidents.

Policies and agreements on how information from electronic resources may be used are important to refer to when notifying a user of an infraction because they serve as a deterrent if they are made known to users. To make effective policies and use of policies:

- Review library policies for use of electronic information (Kaufman and Lowell 2002) and, if there are none, write policies for the library. Display the policies prominently to users on web pages associated with all types of electronic resources. Vendors suggest that, if possible, the policy be displayed at least once to everyone when they first log in to use the library's electronic resources (Chesler and Treby 2004). (This may not be possible if users are not required to log in to access electronic resources.)
- Scan existing print versions of license agreements for current electronic resources and provide links to them.
- Link to vendor web pages that explain their policies on abuse and misuse of electronic resources.
- Work to have the library's policy for use of electronic information included or referred to in the campus policy information use

policy. If there is no campus policy, then encourage and work with appropriate persons on campus to see that one is written. EDUCAUSE has a useful web resource on campus information policies (EDUCAUSE).

Identify persons who may be of assistance in the investigation:

- Retain a list of contacts in the campus network department (name, phone, e-mail, URL). Know who to contact for information on the location(s) of all workstations and servers with the IP address(es) to more easily identify the source of the problem.
- Identify appropriate contacts in the library systems office. Their expertise may be needed to interact with the campus network personnel, to interpret log data of sessions of excessive/systematic downloading and especially to obtain information from the library's proxy server. Their skills may also be needed to tighten security on public workstations in the library.

Take preventative action:

- Forty percent of the misuse of ACS materials is from unauthorized users, usually through an open proxy server (Chesler and Treby 2004). To minimize the risk of this security loophole, ask campus network security to scan for open proxy servers on a regular basis (Adinolfini 2003).
- Standard 5 of *Information Literacy Competency Standards for Higher Education* covers the understanding of ethical and legal issues involving information and its associated technology (American Library Association 2000). Work with the library's orientation program for new faculty and graduate students, as well as with instruction programs for individual departments. Consider programs for research personnel and visiting scholars who might not be otherwise informed of use guidelines for electronic information. Emphasize that noncompliance may result in loss of access to an electronic resource, not only for persons involved in misusing them, but also for the rest of the campus.
- Educate subject librarians about policies for use of electronic resources and provide them with appropriate materials to educate their clientele. Focus on librarians for departments in the sciences and technology where violations are most likely to occur. Suggest that the subject librarian speak at departmental faculty meetings

about the policies. When an incident of misuse occurs, consult with the subject librarian associated with the department involved, throughout the investigation.

- Be sure that vendors are updated with consistent appropriate contacts for problems, usually the technical or billing contact. For each incident at UT in 2004, the initial e-mail was sent to a different person in the library because personnel and responsibilities had changed since those initial contracts were signed.
- Do not publish passwords to electronic resources anywhere, except through a web page requiring user authorization. Advise patrons to not share these passwords and their personal passwords for accessing the library's proxy server (NebraskAccess 2005).

RESPONDING TO THE INCIDENT

Investigating these incidents involves a tension between the privacy rights of users and the protection of a library's investment in electronic resources. If the investigation is done in a discreet and professional manner, the user's privacy can be appropriately maintained and the library can report its findings to the vendor in order to restore access. Libraries should be cautious in taking on review of use data and corrective actions that are outside their authority (Liblicense 2004). Suggested steps in the process are as follows:

- Identify the location and department responsible for the site where the misuse occurred. This can usually be done by contacting campus network personnel and providing them with the IP address specified by the vendor. It may be necessary to obtain assistance from the department where the misuse occurred to identify the perpetrator of the misuse. Explain the situation, including the loss of access. The American Chemical Society has a sample e-mail, on their website, to notify a department of an incident of abuse that may be helpful (American Chemical Society 2004).
- Once the perpetrator has been identified, notify him/her in writing that the abuse has been identified. Refer to appropriate policies on use of electronic resources and explain the consequences of misuse. When they respond, determine the reason for their actions.
- Communicate with the vendor on the findings and resolution of the problem. This can be done without revealing the identity of any involved users and usually results in restoration of the service. In our

experience, vendors have not asked for information deemed private by the library. They have only asked for investigation into the problem and a cessation of the activities associated with misuse, all of which are usually required by the license agreements.

Complications may arise in identifying the perpetrator. The incident may occur on a public workstation, a workstation in a multi-user environment, or the library's proxy server. If there is no way to identify the perpetrator, then consider adding an extra layer of security, such as a log in on the public workstation. If the workstation is outside of the library and used by several persons, then confer with officials in the associated department about identifying the person responsible for the misuse incident. If the IP address is for the library's proxy server, consult with the administrator of the server to obtain information from the proxy log to identify who was doing the excessive downloading. This is important because access to the resource in question via the proxy server may continue to be cut off automatically until the misuse stops, and this affects all remote users.

Campus network personnel may need to be consulted to identify the location of open proxy servers on campus. They can also assist system administrators in uninstalling them.

Some research, like data or text mining and content analysis, requires the manipulation of large text datasets. Libraries should work with researchers and vendors to negotiate the acquisition of significant portions of an electronic resource for educational and/or research purposes.

License agreements usually prohibit excessive downloading and require the library's assistance in investigating such incidents. This can be done without revealing any identifying information about the perpetrator to the vendor. It is another facet in managing an electronic collection.

AFTER RESOLUTION

After reporting findings about the incident to the vendor, take time to review policies, procedures, and user education.

Identify any information use policy loopholes that may have arisen and update current library policies as needed. If the incident was caused by an open proxy server, check with network security officials on when the most recent scan for open proxies was performed. If over six months ago, request that the scan be done more often, at least once a semester.

Work with the subject librarian to follow-up with the department where the infraction occurred. If the person involved in the misuse was not aware of wrongdoing, then it might be appropriate for the subject librarian to communicate with the faculty and students about the incident and the appropriate use of electronic resources.

CONSEQUENCES AND THE FUTURE

"The power to abuse digital resources is enormous and the consequences fall not on the individual, but the university community, both in access and financial consequences" (Lamoreaux 2004). Libraries are spending a greater percentage of their budgets on electronic resources (Young and Kyrillidou 2004). Loss of access not only means lost financial resources for the library, it could even affect researchers' information needs in the institution during crucial grant writing.

The time spent investigating these incidents can be expensive and take personnel away from other duties. At the University of Tennessee, the resolution of the incident involving the library's proxy server and a stolen NetID and password for the local LDAP server took over two weeks to resolve. Extra programming was needed to temporarily add the NetID to the proxy server log data and time needed to review the log data. Care was taken to turn off the option to record the NetID on the proxy server log once personnel determined the identity of the person whose NetID information was stolen.

Vendors vary in how they monitor excessive downloading. In the incident above, while examining the University of Tennessee proxy server log file, we learned that a very large number of articles from another publisher's site were downloaded in a systematic order by the same off-campus perpetrator through the proxy server. This was stopped when the stolen password was changed. This vendor did not contact us about any misuse. Excessive downloading can only be monitored on a comprehensive basis at the vendor's server.

Use statistics generated by vendors includes these incidents and usage is now a factor in some new pricing models (Kaser 2004). Libraries hit with misuse by unauthorized users may be subject to price increases that do not reflect real use patterns if their subscription is based upon this pricing model. Vendors should consider removing misuse data from these statistics or providing specific information about the number of misuse sessions and associated downloaded articles.

Some libraries, like the Yale University Library, scan their license agreements and make them available to users, along with a summary of some of the license terms. To make license agreements easier for users to understand, Adam Chesler and Jill Treby of the American Chemical Society (2004) suggest that vendors try to make the language of license agreements less technical. This can be done by having an easily identifiable section on what users can and cannot do with database records and electronic full-text, with explanations of terms like "excessive downloading."

Look into new methods of authorization and authentication. The JSTOR experience brought to light the problem when access is controlled by IP addresses and open proxy servers help unauthorized users look like they are coming from a valid IP address. JSTOR is working with new access control methods, like Shibboleth, which are independent of IP addresses. Shibboleth is a project of Internet2 and is designed to make it easier for member institutions to collaborate. For databases, it can authenticate remote users using campus authentication servers without having to use a proxy server. It can also be used to provide selected access to resources based upon attributes associated with each individual (JSTOR 2003). Although it may not be popular, this may begin a trend by making everyone on campus log in to access databases. One could then identify first time users, display use guidelines, and, possibly, ask for agreement with the guidelines before allowing the user access to the electronic resource.

Libraries may not be able to prevent misuse of electronic resources, but they can minimize the occurrence. If an incident occurs, investigate it as required by the license agreement, report the findings to the vendor and learn from the experience. Dealing with these incidents is part of the stewardship of an electronic collection.

WORKS CITED

American Chemical Society. 2004. "Tools to Curb Abuse." http://pubs.acs.org/liblink/abuse.html.

American Institute of Physics. 2004. "Permitted and Prohibited Uses of Scitation's Online Journals." http://scitation.aip.org/jhtml/scitation/pp_uses.jsp.

American Library Association, Association of College and Research Libraries. 2000. Information Literacy Competency Standards for Higher Education. http://www.ala.org/ala/acrl/acrlstandards/standards.pdf.

Adinolfi, Daniel. 2003. Open Web Proxies on the Cornell University Network. http://www.cit.cornell.edu/computer/security/openweb/.

Bradley, David. "Sshhh, I'm Downloading." *The Alchemist*, June 12, 2002, http://www.chemweb.com/alchemy/articles/1023287427971.html.

Butkevich, Tom and Orr, Christine. Telephone interview by Gayle Baker. Knoxville, Tenn. December 7, 2004.

Cain, Mark. 2003. "Cybertheft, Network Security, and the Library Without Walls." *Journal of Academic Librarianship* 29 (4): 245-248.

Chesler, Adam and Treby, Jill. Telephone interview by Gayle Baker. Knoxville, Tenn. December 9, 2004.

Copyright Act of 1976. United States Code, Title 17, Section 107.

EDUCAUSE. "Information Policies." http://www.educause.edu/content.asp?page_id=645&PARENT_ID=109&bhcp=1.

Ishizuka, Kathy. 2004. "Kids: Stealing Digital Data OK." *School Library Journal* 50 (8): 18.

JSTOR. 2002. "Open Proxy Servers: Gateways to Unauthorized Use of Licensed Resources." *JSTORNEWS* 6 (3), http://www.jstor.org/news/2002.12/open-proxy.html.

JSTOR. 2002. "Terms and Conditions of Use." http://www.jstor.org/about/terms.html.

JSTOR. 2003. "Shibboleth: A Potential Alternative to IP-based Authentication." *JSTORNEWS* 7, (3), http://www.jstor.org/news/2003.10/shibboleth.html.

Kaser, Dick. 2004. "A Thousand Points of Price." *Information Today* 21 (8): 29.

Kaufman, Paula and Lowell, Gerald R. 2002. "Checklist for Drafting Electronic Information Policies." http://www.arl.org/newsltr/196/checklist.html.

Read, Brock. 2004. "College and record executives tell congress of steps to curtail music piracy." *Chronicle of Higher Education* 511 (2): A37.

Lamoureaux, Seldon Durgom. Telephone interview by Gayle Baker. Knoxville, Tenn. December 2, 2004.

LibLicense: Licensing Digital Information. 1996. "License Performance Obligations." http://www.library.yale.edu/~llicense/perflcls.shtml.

NebraksAccess. 2005. "Licensing Terms and Subscriber Obligations." http://www.nlc.state.ne.us/nebraskaccess/toolbox/statedbterms.html.

Rossignol, Lucien R. 2000. "Realistic Licensing or Licensing Realities: Practical Advice on License Agreements." *The Serials Librarian* 38 (3/4): 357-361.

Talab, Rosemary S. 1985. "Copyright and Database Downloading." *Library Journal* 10 (18): 144-147.

Yale University Library. 2004. "Permitted Uses of Online Resources." http://www.library.yale.edu/journals/licensing.html.

Young, Mark and Kyrillidou, Martha. 2004. *ARL Supplementary Statistics, 2002-2003*. Washington, DC: Association of Research Libraries. http://www.arl.org/stats/pubpdf/sup03.pdf.

RESOURCES

Selected library policies and guides about use of electronic resources:

- Harvard. "Copyright and Licensing Restrictions." http://lib.harvard.edu/e-resources/copyright.html.

- Kansas State. "Responsible Use of CATnet's Electronic Resources." http:// catnet.ksu.edu/help/eresource_appropriate_use.html.
- Texas A&M University. "Intellectual Property, Fair Use, and Academic Integrity." http://ednetold.tamu.edu/vgn/portal/tamulib/content/renderer/footer/0,2876,1724_ 1001640,00.html.
- University of North Carolina, Chapel Hill. "User rights and restrictions." http:// eresources.lib.unc.edu/eid/restrictions.php.
- University of Tennessee. "Electronic Resource Use Guidelines." http://www. lib.utk.edu/~elecserv/dbuse.htm.
- University of York. "Copyright Guidance Notes." http://www.york.ac.uk/services/ library/guides/copyright.htm.

Library/Vendor Relations:
The APA Experience

Linda Beebe

SUMMARY. When an information provider works with multiple vendors, the library/vendor/producer relations can be complex, as the American Psychological Association (APA) has discovered. APA's philosophy of "we want to be where our customers want to find us" appears to serve both customers and the association well, but putting this philosophy into practice requires careful attention. The benefits and complications related to delivering a provider's products on multiple platforms are reviewed, using the APA experiences as a model. APA seeks librarian counsel and subsequently puts the advice into practice. *[Article copies available for a fee from The Haworth Document Delivery Service: 1-800-HAWORTH. E-mail address: <docdelivery@haworthpress.com> Website: <http://www.HaworthPress.com> © 2006 by The Haworth Press, Inc. All rights reserved.]*

KEYWORDS. Electronic products, psychological information, vendor relations, databases, journals, books, PsycINFO, librarian feedback, advisory boards, database licensing

Linda Beebe is Senior Director of PsycINFO for the American Psychological Association (E-mail: LBeebe@apa.org). In her role at APA, she directs the development and production of APA's electronic databases. Previously, she was President of Parachute Publishing Services, which provided consulting services to a wide range of publishers. For many years, she was the Associate Executive Director for Communications for the National Association of Social Workers, where she directed the scholarly press, public information, general interest publications, and marketing.

[Haworth co-indexing entry note]: "Library/Vendor Relations: The APA Experience." Beebe, Linda. Co-published simultaneously in *Journal of Library Administration* (The Haworth Information Press, an imprint of The Haworth Press, Inc.) Vol. 44, No. 3/4, 2006, pp. 25-42; and: *Library/Vendor Relationships* (ed: Sam Brooks, and David H. Carlson) The Haworth Information Press, an imprint of The Haworth Press, Inc., 2006, pp. 25-42. Single or multiple copies of this article are available for a fee from The Haworth Document Delivery Service [1-800-HAWORTH, 9:00 a.m. - 5:00 p.m. (EST). E-mail address: docdelivery@haworthpress.com].

Available online at http://www.haworthpress.com/web/JLA
© 2006 by The Haworth Press, Inc. All rights reserved.
doi:10.1300/J111v44n03_04

Maintaining a strong, thriving relationship among database providers, vendors, and libraries requires a delicate balance. The library is the mutual customer for the provider and vendor; consequently, the customer needs must be paramount with both provider and vendor working to avoid any conflict in policies and procedures. At the same time, both provider and vendor have business requirements that also must be met.

Third-party vendors are an important component in the delivery of psychological information to libraries. In early 2005, the American Psychological Association (APA) produced five electronic databases, and approximately 85 percent of the business is conducted in collaboration with third-party vendors.

ABOUT APA

Founded in 1892, the American Psychological Association is the largest national psychological society in the world with 150,000 members. Fifty-three APA divisions, most of which are related to specialty areas, demonstrate the breadth of psychology as a discipline. The association's dedication to advancing the science of psychology is reflected in its large and growing scholarly publications program. An elected Publications & Communications Board governs the program. Candidates for election must have strong editorial and publishing experience, and each slate is nominated with an eye toward achieving diversity in subject expertise, as well as gender and race.

APA has a long history of working with vendors. The first electronic delivery of psychological abstracts occurred in 1967, and by 1971 the bibliographic records were available on Dialog (VandenBos 1992). For a few years after PsycLIT was launched in CD-ROM format in 1986, it was available only on SilverPlatter. Subsequently, APA greatly expanded its alliances with third-party vendors. In 2005, PsycINFO was available on twelve platforms including APA's own PsycNET, whereas PsycARTICLES was offered on eight platforms. (See Table 1 for a list of third-party vendors and the APA products they distribute.) There is considerable variance in the number of vendors for two reasons: (1) PsycINFO has been available to vendors for a much longer time than the newer products; (2) some vendors do not distribute full-text products.

The association seems to be somewhat unusual in the array of vendors that offer APA products, particularly for full-text. Most primary publishers seem to offer their full-text content almost entirely from their own platforms. If they work with third-party vendors, they generally

TABLE 1. Vendors for PsycARTICLES and PsycINFO in April 2005

Vendor	PsycARTICLES	PsycINFO	PsycBOOKS	PsycEXTRA	PsycCRITIQUES
APA	X	X	X	X	X
CSA	X	X	X^1		X^1
DataStar		X^2			
Dialog		X^2			
DIMDI		X^2			
EBSCO	X	X	X	X	X
Hogrefe & Huber	X	X			
OCLC	X	X	X^1		
Ovid Technologies	X	X	X		
ProQuest	X	X			
ScienceDirect	X	X			
Thomson ISI		X			

[1]Contract signed, but not selling or delivering yet.
[2]Transactional services only, no site licenses.

place content in aggregated collections. A quick survey of web sites for major bibliographic databases in early 2005 found that only Inspec listed more vendors than PsycINFO. CAB Abstracts, for example, showed seven vendors plus CAB Direct from CABI Publishing. EconLit listed seven vendors, whereas, CINAHL listed four vendors in addition to Cinahl Information Systems, and BIOSIS also seemed to be available through four vendors. Despite the complications of working with so many companies, APA's philosophy of "we want to be where our customers want to find us" has served the association well from both mission and business perspectives.

APA Primary Journals

In 2005, APA published twenty-seven APA journals plus seventeen journals in its Educational Publishing Foundation (EPF). Several of the EPF journals were published under contract with other societies and APA divisions. (See Table 2 for a list of journals.) APA no longer publishes *Prevention & Treatment*, its only all-electronic journal; however, all previously published issues are included in the electronic PsycARTICLES database. From 1956 to 2004, APA also published *Contemporary Psychology: APA Review of Books*. In 2005, the journal was transformed

TABLE 2. APA and EPF Journals in 2005

APA Journals	EPF Journals
American Psychologist	American Journal of Orthopsychiatry
Behavioral Neuroscience	Consulting Psychology Journal: Practice & Research
Developmental Psychology	Cultural Diversity and Ethnic Minority Psychology
Emotion	Dreaming
Experimental and Clinical Psychopharmacology	Families, Systems, & Health
Health Psychology	Group Dynamics: Theory, Research, and Practice
Journal of Abnormal Psychology	History of Psychology
Journal of Applied Psychology	International Journal of Stress Management
Journal of Comparative Psychology	Journal of Occupational Health Psychology
Journal of Consulting and Clinical Psychology	Journal of Psychotherapy Integration
Journal of Counseling Psychology	Psychoanalytic Psychology
Journal of Educational Psychology	Psychological Services
Journal of Experimental Psychology: Animal Behavior Processes	Psychology of Addictive Behaviors
Journal of Experimental Psychology: Applied	Psychology of Men and Masculinity
Journal of Experimental Psychology: General	Psychotherapy: Theory, Research, Practice, Training
Journal of Experimental Psychology: Human Perception and Performance	Rehabilitation Psychology
Journal of Experimental Psychology: Learning, Memory, and Cognition	Review of General Psychology
Journal of Family Psychology	
Neuropsychology	
Professional Psychology: Research and Practice	
Psychological Assessment	
Psychological Bulletin	
Psychological Methods	
Psychological Review	
Psychology and Aging	
Psychology, Public Policy, and Law	

into the PsycCRITIQUES database with weekly electronic releases replacing the bimonthly print journal.

Rigorous peer review and careful attention to science characterize APA journals. Editors serve six-year terms, and the APA Publications & Communications Board conducts extensive outreach in a very formal process to fill each vacancy. The Board must also approve each official journal description, as well as editorials.

In addition to primary journals, APA publishes the *Clinician's Research Digest: Briefings in Behavior Science*, a newsletter designed to highlight current published research. The APA Journals department also produces the print index journals. *Psychological Abstracts*, first published in 1927, is still produced monthly in print from the PsycINFO database, although the print version does not include all of the records released weekly in the electronic form. Three specialty index journals also appear in print form: *PsycSCAN: Clinical, Neuropsychology Abstracts*, and *Psychoanalytic Abstracts*.

APA Books

With more than ten million copies sold, the most widely known APA book is the *Publication Manual of the American Psychological Association.* The *Publication Manual* serves as the style manual for a large proportion of journals in the social and behavioral sciences, as well as for research reports in graduate education. The fifth edition was published in 2001.

In the first half century of its existence, APA published almost no books. From the mid 1950s to the late 1980s, the association published books sporadically. APA now publishes sixty to seventy books each year in its professional book program, as well as multi-volume reference works, all designed to support the science and practice of psychology and related disciplines. The association also produces two trade book imprints: LifeTools publishes self-help books for adults on an occasional basis, and Magination Press publishes children's books on subjects such as divorce, adoption, ADHD, death and dying, and character development. Magination Press releases about twelve books a year. In addition, the APA Books Department produces several series of psychotherapy training videos; in early 2005 nearly 100 videos were available.

APA Electronic Databases

APA's lengthy experience with PsycINFO and its ownership of the secondary database were instrumental in the development of other databases. The fielded data and strong indexing support full-text databases. As much as possible, APA has attempted to use the same field labels and structure to make it easy for an experienced PsycINFO user to move to other databases with no steep learning curve.

PsycINFO

Commercially available since 1971, the bibliographic database has gone through several transformations, adding historical data, picking up abstracts for dissertations, and including additional fields. One of the most notable changes was the addition of cited references in 2002. The PsycINFO record now includes the citation lists from nearly all journal articles and book chapters added to the database. The references appear in an expanded record with links to PsycINFO records when they exist and to the actual full-text if APA can acquire a link. In addition, the user can search a cited references database to track the literature backward and forward.

Another landmark year for the database was 2004 as the database reached the two million record mark, and staff produced a significantly increased number of records. The 106,100 records produced in 2004 represented a 36 percent increase over 2003 production.

Since APA discontinued the CD product PsycLIT in 2000, most institutions subscribe to the full PsycINFO database; however, there are still some users of the PsycFirst database (bundled searches) offered through OCLC.

PsycARTICLES

In 2005, this full-text database includes forty-five primary journals published by APA, plus three journals from the Canadian Psychological Association, and five from Hogrefe & Huber. Because APA's mission is to disseminate information widely, the primary journals are not offered as single titles. PsycARTICLES was conceived as a database of journal articles, and the initial offering downplayed the individual titles. First offered to members in 1998, the database was not made widely available to institutions until 2001. There were two forays into institutional use earlier. In 1999, APA offered a package of PsycINFO, PsycARTICLES (then simply titled APA's Database of Full-Text Journal Articles), and print journals to very small institutions in a program called Small College Access. This program was available only through APA and was discontinued when vendors began offering PsycARTICLES.

Then starting in late 2000, APA beta tested the full-text database with Michigan State University, the University of Michigan, and the WALDO Consortium in New York. The idea was to work with university libraries that had been direct load customers for PsycINFO, so that we would not favor or slight any vendor. Between pop-up surveys for end users, discussions with the librarians, and focus groups with several audiences at the two schools in Michigan, we learned just how many details we had to change. Being able to search across titles easily was indeed a very positive experience for end users; however, browsing was difficult. Even more crucial was the fact that there was no way to put titles in the OPAC when we did not distinguish them. That change was made rapidly. The end users' requests for PDF, phrased loudly enough to be characterized as demands, led quickly to the addition of the PDF option.

By the end of 2001, both EBSCO*host* and Ovid were offering the database, although the clean-up we needed to do extended into 2002. About ten journals have been added to the database since 2001, and in early 2005 it included more than 42,000 articles back to 1985. APA has digitized almost all of its backfiles (with the earliest journal in 1894). After considering several options for business models, APA's decision was that we will provide the legacy content to any institution who maintains a site license at no additional charge. Content from 1984 back to 1894, when the first issue of the first APA journal was published, is being delivered to customers in June 2006.

PsycBOOKS

This full-text database offers books and book chapters from APA and other distinguished publishers. The Classics Collection from other publishers includes about 100 books dating back to the early 19th century. In addition to the 500 book titles in the initial release, the database includes the 1,500 entries from the Encyclopedia of Psychology, which APA co-published with Oxford University Press in 2000. In early 2005, PsycBOOKS included 619 complete volumes.

PsycBOOKS was built in similar fashion to PsycARTICLES, which is a database of full-text journal articles with title browsing capabilities and individual URLs for each title so they can be linked to the OPAC. Likewise, PsycBOOKS is a database of book chapters with browsing capabilities for title, author, and year of publication. APA is also delivering MARC records for each of the books. The database was launched for free trials in August 2004 and made available for sale in October.

PsycEXTRA

In the past few years, two conflicting messages reached us over and over. We received many requests from librarians and end users to cover content outside the scholarly literature, such as conference presentations, newsletters, and other professional materials. Yet we heard repeatedly, "Keep PsycINFO the clean database it is. Restrict it to scholarly content." We concluded that it was time to develop a gray literature database.

Discussions began in early 2003 and continued through the early summer. By the time the APA Council of Representatives approved the new product in August 2003, staff were ready to acquire and process the content. Because gray literature is often difficult to find and availability is often transitory, especially in online editions, we decided to include full-text in this bibliographic database whenever possible. (We found the fleeting nature of some gray literature particularly prevalent on federal web sites. Often something we looked at a few weeks earlier was gone when we returned.) It did not seem very useful to serve as a discovery tool to content that the user might not be able to obtain. Consequently, about 60 percent of the more than 56,000 records in the database in early 2005 included full-text for a total of more than 150,000 pages. The major exception is the magazine and newspaper bibliographic records APA licenses from EBSCO Publishing. Although it appeared useful to have these materials indexed with psychological terms, it seemed counter-productive to include the full-text that libraries already would be buying elsewhere. By including only the bibliographic data for these materials, APA could keep the price of the database much lower.

PsycEXTRA launched for free trials June 1, 2004 and was made available for sale October 1, 2004. The goal now is to increase the content significantly, particularly for technical reports and conference presentations.

PsycCRITIQUES

Planning for this database began with the recruitment of a new editor in 2003, as APA sought to cure the problems it faced with the print journal *Contemporary Psychology*. Chief among them was the fact that by the time a book was reviewed and the review published, the book was easily two years old, and often it was older. Further, the bimonthly print journal accommodated fewer than 300 reviews a year, and estimates of the number of books published annually in psychology exceeded 2,000. Yet the message we heard consistently from librarians was that a book review product was important, if it could be made current and more extensive than the print journal.

The new editor embraced the idea of an all-electronic product that would combine very new content released weekly with a database of reviews published back to 1995. Using the automated tools APA built, he recruited more than 1,100 potential reviewers who agreed to return reviews in a month. By year's end he had received 555 reviews of 2004 copyright books, and published nearly 300 in weekly releases offered as free trials. With the official start of PsycCRITIQUES: Contemporary Psychology–APA Review of Books as Volume 50, Issue 1 on January 5, the challenge was to publish all of the remaining 2004 reviews, while making room for reviews of 2005 books.

DELIVERY OF ELECTRONIC CONTENT THROUGH VENDORS

All five of APA's electronic databases are available through third-party vendors in 2005 (see Table 1). Because of the way it was developed, PsycEXTRA will be available only through APA PsycNET and EBSCO*host* for the next several years. Vendor contracts and delivery for PsycBOOKS and PsycCRITIQUES were still in flux in early 2005. Some vendors are delivering the databases; some have signed contracts and engaged in loading; some are still negotiating.

Benefits of Working with Vendors

The main reason to work with multiple vendors is customer satisfaction. Our experience has been that many libraries prefer to have their choice of a vendor. Their decisions on which vendor and how many vendors have a major influence on their workload in many areas, such as license negotiations, legal processing, technical services, and user instruction. Further, librarians are responding to their users' preferences. Often we find that an institution will choose to access an APA database on more than one vendor's platform because of conflicting requests from major constituencies. For example, the psychology program may prefer PsycINFO on EBSCO, while the medical school wants it on Ovid. There are many different combinations with the various vendors at many institutions. In these instances, the library pays just one data fee for each APA database.

We try to offer librarians a choice of as many vendors as feasible for each database. Working with multiple vendors places APA products where our customers want to find them, and it allows us to take advantage of the relative strengths each vendor has in a given market. Working with many vendors also fosters healthy competition among vendors. For the customer, this competition helps ensure that customer needs are better served; for APA it encourages vendors to be more responsive to APA needs in selling our databases.

There are other benefits for APA. To start, we gain far more exposure with existing and potential customers when we're listed in the catalogs and on the web sites of many vendors. In addition, third-party vendors can spread their costs across hundreds of databases, whereas APA has only five databases. Therefore, the vendors can afford larger sales forces, regional offices, larger customer service departments, bigger IT units, and much stronger technology infrastructures. To serve all of our thousands of customers directly through APA would require a very substantial investment, one that few associations could afford.

Complications in Working with Vendors

In all relationships there is the potential for complications. When the relationship is a three-way one, as it is with an information provider, the third-party vendor, and the customer, the potential for complications and misunderstandings increases. Working with multiple vendors further complicates issues. In addition, while we save on many areas because of our relationship with vendors, there is a significant cost for supporting the delivery of our products on other platforms.

Licensing and Reporting Issues

In the mid-1980s, APA began requiring customer licenses. The association wanted to highlight the fact that APA is connected to the customer and concerned about them, regardless of the platform they are using. Staff expected that licensing would bring APA closer to the customer and that it would make it easier for the organization to hear issues and respond to them appropriately. Over the years, as we have added vendors and launched new products, we have steadily increased the number of APA staff who process licenses.

In our relationships with all vendors, we have consistently asserted that customers for APA products are mutual customers and that APA has the right to communicate directly with those customers. Therefore, we require that customers sign license agreements directly with APA, in addition to any agreement they may have with the vendor. We set our data fees, which we supply to vendors, and all multi-institution price quotations for data fees must come from APA.

APA has worked with vendors to try to simplify the process and keep the licensing and reporting from being any barrier to service. The APA director of sales, Peter Gaviorno, and his staff spend considerable time meeting with vendor representatives to hear issues, communicate APA concerns, and negotiate reporting processes that are mutually agreeable *and* that meet our auditors' requirements. Even with ongoing communication, considerable trust is required because often we know customers have subscribed only when the vendors tell us. APA staff work with vendors and their distributors to jointly serve customers better.

Matching Product with Interface

When APA launches a new product, we provide the vendors with technical specifications that describe the product in considerable detail. The specifications include definitions for each field and describe how APA would like to see the features implemented. We also revise specifications for each annual new edition of PsycINFO and now for the newer products (APA released the first PsycARTICLES revised edition in October 2004). Our contracts with vendors mandate that APA must approve the vendor rendition of our products on their platform before they are officially launched.

In planning new features or a new product, the information provider who is the sole purveyor need consider only the needs of buyers and users and the limitations of their own platform. The information provider who works with multiple vendors must consider all their interfaces as well. Consequently, APA staff review all major potential changes with all of their vendor counterparts. Nonetheless, problems still arise. For example, when APA considered moving to XML for PsycINFO, all vendors agreed it would be better than the delivery in U.S. MARC and said they would be ready to accept it with the 2003 edition, which we released in June 2003. Unfortunately, technology changes do not always move as rapidly as planned, and we continued to deliver U.S. MARC to several vendors for many months.

For many years, APA had one staff person assigned to technical liaison with vendors. In 2003, PsycINFO was reorganized to include a Product Development office under Alvin Walker that works with APA programmers on product development and the enhancement of our production systems and with vendors on the delivery of our products. Initially, two staff worked on reviewing product releases and vendor delivery of our products. We expanded the office in 2005 and will add more staff in 2006. PsycINFO and PsycCRITIQUES release weekly, new issues of journals in PsycARTICLES go out at least weekly, PsycEXTRA is on a biweekly schedule, and PsycBOOKS goes out monthly. Ideally, we should be reviewing vendor presentations of APA products constantly. With our current staffing, we often hear about problems with a product on a vendor platform when we see the problem discussed on a library listserv.

No matter how well we and our vendor partners try to coordinate, there are undoubtedly several versions of a product in the market at one time. For example, some vendors load the annual new editions of PsycINFO very quickly; others do not. Issues of new journals are posted immediately on some platforms and less rapidly on others. Sometimes a single article does not get picked up until someone is made aware of the fact that it is missing. And sometimes a change in data means a journal is sorted out of order so it appears that an issue is not available when it actually is. All of these are frustrating to users and librarians, and we are working with vendors to minimize the differences.

Communication Issues

For librarians, perhaps the biggest communication issue is knowing when changes take place in the product and when they appear in the interface they are using. APA is developing a Librarian Resource Center on the APA web pages, and the plan is to post information about when changes take place on all platforms. Building the table for journal issues posted on eight platforms is an interesting task, but once it is in database form, maintaining it should be less difficult.

For APA, one of the biggest frustrations is that, when something goes wrong with one of our products on a vendor platform, the problem is always seen as an APA product problem. In December 2004, for example, data was corrupted on one vendor's platform; consequently, bizarre information was displayed in the source field. The news went out immediately that PsycINFO had this odd problem. APA first determined that the problem existed only with one vendor, then worked with that vendor to correct the problem; in the meantime we sent out the word about what the problem really was. We walk a fine line in working to provide our customers with accurate information without pointing fingers at any supplier.

APA takes care to provide a level playing field for all vendors. We post our data fees for all products on our web pages, and we use the same basis to provide price quotations to all vendors for a given institution. Vendor requests for quotations for a set of institutions may be configured differently with different vendors. However, APA works hard to ensure that all our vendors understand our pricing and can trust the fairness of our process. Some factors àre also out of our control. For example, APA does not control either the final prices that vendors offer to customers or the division of prices that consortia offer to their members. With so many parties involved, there is always the possibility for misunderstanding in the process of quoting and finalizing large consortium deals that involve multiple vendors. We often find that we must reiterate the fact that the consortia, not APA, determine which vendors they will use.

Librarians have written about the issues on their end of the process. In a technical services report of a 2002 conference presentation (Baker 2003), Davis noted the number of library staff who need to be included in discussions about a decision to purchase access. "Bibliographers or selectors, reference librarians, IT staff as well as serials or acquisitions personnel should participate in discussions." She went on to describe the departments at the publisher who are involved as "customer service, sales, technical support, and the legal group." When the publisher works with third-party vendors, there are two sets of many of those departments involved, and the potential for miscommunication increases. It is sometimes difficult to obtain sufficient information to provide good customer service. For example, APA's customer relations staff struggle to find the right name for the recipient of welcome packages.

Another major communication issue is keeping all key vendor staff informed about APA products. APA sales staff meets regularly with the sales forces for the major vendors. PsycINFO staff talks frequently with their vendor counterparts. The difficulty is assuring that all of the people–APA staff and staffs at all of the various vendors–understand the details about the products. That difficulty is further complicated by the fact that no database is a static product.

TRAINING AND SUPPORT

Like most bibliographic databases, PsycINFO once had an active training program; consequently, we remained close to our customers. Then, like other producers, we began to make the assumption that everyone knew how to use a computer and therefore training was no longer necessary. Recently, the most frequent request we get from librarians is for training. They tell us that training from the vendors is not adequate for our products. Those trainers know their interface and their own products, but the librarians find that they are showing the vendor trainers how PsycINFO or one of the other APA products work on their platform. Librarians ask us for web-based tutorials for all of the vendor systems, quick reference cards, good help screens, and on-site training.

APA has heard those concerns and is increasing our attention to training and support. In 2005, we will be producing new search guides for vendor platforms and updating our user manuals. A new Documentation and Training Specialist joined the Customer Relations staff in January 2005, and we expect to add other staff resources shortly. Because we cannot visit every campus or institution every year, our first priority will be to build web-based tutorials and institute web-cast training sessions.

Working with multiple vendors is a two-edged sword in many ways. By tracking the delivery of our products on multiple platforms, we learn a great deal about the potential for the products and how we might improve them. However, it is time-consuming and costly to track all the interfaces and to publish all of the collateral documents and training material needed to support their delivery.

RECENT TRENDS

Three trends stand out. First, like all information providers, we have seen a significant increase in consortium sales. Not only are there more consortium sales, the deals themselves are more complex. Often today, there is a mix of institution types: universities, community colleges, hospitals, high schools, and so on. Also, there are often multiple vendors involved.

Another trend is the migration of institutions from one vendor to another. Whereas an institution previously might have stayed with a vendor for several years, they now might go from one to another. With shrinking budgets, the overall street price is likely to have a much greater influence on the vendor decision. The impact for APA is much more paperwork. We are signing more licenses, not just because our sales are increasing, but because of the migration from one vendor to another.

The third trend has to do with the complexity of licenses. While we have been trying to simplify our licenses, we are discovering that more and more institutions are required to add provisions to our basic license

(Beebe n.d.). One example is the lengthy addendum that the Florida Center for Library Automation (FCLA) must add to every license they sign (Newberry 2004). The FCLA provisions are typical of those that library systems may add. (See Table 3 for some common concerns.) The California Digital Library (2005) posts its requirements on the Web. One of the complications of working with vendors is that many of the provisions required by universities or state laws refer to interface issues, such as ADA requirements or guaranteed availability. We cannot sign those provisions because we do not control the vendor interface. In these instances, the license may go back and forth two or three times before there is clarity on who can affirm what.

There is a fourth issue that I find interesting, but could not characterize as a trend. Five years ago, we had a significant number of direct load customers. That is, they did not use our interface or a vendor platform, preferring to load the data into their own delivery systems. Up until 2004, that number declined every year with no new direct loads being added. When we asked about it, librarians replied that they were finding it increasingly difficult to maintain delivery systems that could accommodate a large number of information providers, many of whom are making changes to their product every year. In 2004, we suddenly had two or three new direct load customers. I will be curious to see if they continue to load on their own and if more customers decide to build or buy their own loading and delivery systems. My suspicion is that customers installing their own delivery systems expect to save on service and delivery fees over time.

ONGOING FEEDBACK AND DEVELOPMENT

Although we survey end users and talk to them as much as we can, we rely heavily on feedback and advice from librarians for the development

TABLE 3. Example of License Issues

Sample Requirements for Inclusion	Sample Requirements for Deletion
A&Is updated weekly	Limitation of time to bring suit
Failsafe operations	Arbitration
Indemnification by Licensor	Indemnification by Licensee
Content linkable and linked	Reporting requirements for Licensee
Usage statistics in standard form	Escalation of costs
Governing law in the library's state	Punitive charges

and refinement of APA's electronic products. We gather that information in several ways.

We have hosted breakfast roundtables at meetings of the American Library Association (ALA) for several years. The discussions at those meetings are invaluable to us in planning changes and dealing with potential problems in delivery of our content. At the ALA meetings, we have been pleased to have an opportunity to meet with the Education, Behavior, and Social Sciences Committee (EBSS at www.lib.msu.edu/corby/ebss/) and the Psychology-Psychiatry Committee, which is a sub-committee of EBSS. The mutual exchange of information is very beneficial to us, and we appreciate librarians making time for us in their busy schedules, at their formal meetings, and our roundtables.

APA exhibits at several other library meetings to communicate face to face with our customers and our vendor partners. In addition to the two ALA meetings, APA will exhibit publications and databases at the following in 2006: Computers in Libraries, Association of College and Research Librarians, American Educational Research Association, Medical Library Association, Special Libraries Association, Canadian Library Association, Internet Librarian, and Online Information London.

In 2002, APA expanded the Electronic Resources Advisory Committee, a subcommittee of the Publications & Communications Board, to include a librarian. Having Marietta Plank from the University of Maryland on that committee has been very helpful. The experience with her was so positive that the chair of the search committee for the new editor of *Contemporary Psychology* invited another librarian, Leslie Bjorncrantz from Northwestern, to join the search committee. Again, the librarian input was extremely helpful, especially in shaping the search for someone who would be amenable to a totally new way of operating.

In 2004, APA constituted its own Library Advisory Council, which met for the first time in October. (See Table 4 for the first APA Library Advisory Council.) We sought out a mix of subject experts and experts in other areas of library administration and were pleased to receive acceptances from all we invited. One example of the value of meeting with this group was our careful planning for a business model for the PsycARTICLES backfiles. We were glad we had shared it with this group before we announced it to the world, because they made it clear that our original plan would not work. All of the senior staff in the APA Publications & Databases department are looking forward to further work with this group.

TABLE 4. APA Library Advisory Council 2005

Larry Alford	Vice Provost	Temple University Paley Library
Leslie Bjorncrantz	Curriculum Librarian & Bibliographer for Education, Linguistics, Management, and Psychology	Northwestern University
Betty Day	Director of E-Content Management and Delivery	University of Maryland
Margaret Landesman	Head, Collection Development	University of Utah
Michele Newberry	Assistant Director	Florida Center for Library Automation
Darlene Nichols	Psychology and Sociology Librarian	University of Michigan
Dorothy (Dottie) Persson	Head, Psychology Library	University of Iowa
Marietta Plank	Assistant to the Dean for Special Projects	University of Maryland
Diana Ramirez	Associate Professor, Social Sciences Reference Librarian	Texas A&M

We also had the opportunity to meet twice with EBSCO Publishing's Academic Advisory Board consisting of university libraries from many regions. On the first occasion, Julia Frank-McNeil, APA's director for books, and I went to talk about turning a law book series into a database. Following their wise counsel that it likely would not have a very sizable audience saved us considerable effort. I met again with the group in Orlando in June 2004 to get feedback on PsycEXTRA. That meeting was also useful, as have been all of our meetings with librarians.

We are eager to find more opportunities to solicit feedback and advice from librarians. We maintain a listserv; however, that seems to be primarily a means for us to communicate to librarians. We did receive superb advice from three librarians on the U.S. MARC records in reply to a request on the listserv. We particularly appreciated their efforts, because they invested considerable time in reviewing documents in an area in which we had no experience. Susan Hillson, our customer relations manager, has begun some e-panels, and we have received good advice on other specific areas. In my experience, librarians by nature reach out to be helpful. We learn a great deal about how libraries are operating by observing the interactions on the library listservs, and we are grateful for all the information we obtain, even when the message is not the one we hoped to hear.

CONCLUSION

The APA experience has been that our library customers like having choices of vendors for APA electronic products. In addition, the association benefits from the resources multiple vendors bring to selling access to our products. At the same time, working with multiple vendors requires considerable investment in communications and in providing support for selling and delivering content on all of those platforms. Product development is also complicated by the need to consider multiple platforms.

APA has been fortunate to receive good advice from librarians in several different ways. In the future, it is likely that we will create additional advisory councils. These might be informal, planned around a specific event or process, or they might be more formal, such as advisory councils for specific products. There may be opportunities as well to build more iterative processes with our vendors. What is clear is that we will continue to work with librarians and vendors to build on current good relations and improve the processes further.

WORKS CITED

Baker. B., editor. 2003. Technical Services Report. *Technical Services Quarterly* 20, p. 63.

Beebe. n.d. Licensing APA Products at APA. *The Serials Librarian. Proceedings of the North American Serials Interest Group (NASIG) 2004.*

California Digital Library. n.d. Vendors & Content Providers. Retrieved from http://www.cdlib.org/vendors. January 4, 2005.

Newberry, M. Letter to author. March 29, 2004.

VandenBos, G. 1992. The APA Knowledge Dissemination Program: An Overview of 100 Years. pp. 347-381. In *100 Years–The American Psychological Association: A Historical Perspective*, Evans, R.B., Sexton, V.S., & Cadwallader, T.C., Editors.

Managing Customer Relationships:
A Book Vendor Point-of-View

George Coe

SUMMARY. The most important thing for a book vendor in managing customer relationships is successfully managing the company's own resources. Book vendors must be able to hire and train staff who understand the changing needs of libraries and who are able to influence the company's strategic direction and daily operation so that these needs are met. In recent years, book vendors have had to go beyond bookselling, and provide technical services to help libraries to become more efficient. This has required new levels of expertise from book vendors, who today work more closely with their customers then ever before. *[Article copies available for a fee from The Haworth Document Delivery Service: 1-800-HAWORTH. E-mail address: <docdelivery@haworthpress.com> Website: <http://www.HaworthPress.com> © 2006 by The Haworth Press, Inc. All rights reserved.]*

KEYWORDS. Library vendors, book vendors, bookselling, technical services, library/vendor relations, outsourcing

George Coe is President, Institutional Division, Baker & Taylor, Inc., 2550 West Tyvola Road, Suite 300, Charlotte, NC 28217 (E-mail: coeg@btol.com).

The author would like to acknowledge the assistance of Baker & Taylor and YBP Library Services colleagues Bob Nardini, Gary Shirk, and Michael Utasi.

[Haworth co-indexing entry note]: "Managing Customer Relationships: A Book Vendor Point-of-View." Coe, George. Co-published simultaneously in *Journal of Library Administration* (The Haworth Information Press, an imprint of The Haworth Press, Inc.) Vol. 44, No. 3/4, 2006, pp. 43-55; and: *Library/Vendor Relationships* (ed: Sam Brooks, and David H. Carlson) The Haworth Information Press, an imprint of The Haworth Press, Inc., 2006, pp. 43-55. Single or multiple copies of this article are available for a fee from The Haworth Document Delivery Service [1-800-HAWORTH, 9:00 a.m. - 5:00 p.m. (EST). E-mail address: docdelivery@haworthpress.com].

doi:10.1300/J111v44n03_05

43

Successful companies find ways to ensure that every staff member in every department understands that the immediate task at hand, no matter how deeply embedded within an organization, is connected to customers. A customer orientation must become part of a company's innate structure, informing everything from process design, to marketing campaigns, to compensation systems.

UNDERSTANDING THE BOOK VENDOR

The biggest mistake for a book vendor, in customer relationships, would be to attempt to manage them.[1] The warehouse, the LAN, freight costs, the 401(k) program, the travel budget, the cardboard box stock, these and a thousand other things need to be managed. But managed toward the one real goal for a book vendor, strong and lasting customer relationships. If the vendor's shipping department, for example, operates under its own logic, heroic attempts to "manage" the customer relationship will in the end fail to disguise the fact that books are not being reliably delivered. If a business is managed poorly, no customer relationship wizardry will help. If managed well, customers will notice and the business will thrive. In short, managing customer relationships, for a book vendor, means managing yourself.

Does this make book vendors unique? Of course not. But within the larger library marketplace, bookselling has some characteristics that set it apart. Historically, library firm orders have been far more portable than business placed with serials or systems vendors, for example. A library can move firm orders from one book vendor to another, quickly, quietly, and with relatively little effort. Today, this flexibility is more limited than in the past, due to more complex library workflows, to the growth of contractual arrangements, and to the rise of approval plans. Even so, all book vendors know that if they do not stay close to a customer today, tomorrow that library might be another vendor's customer.

At the same time, book vendors have a unique opportunity in customer relationships. What other vendor has the chance to deliver to the library, over and over, a new assortment of objects that will please and even delight many members of the library staff? These are books, of course, which arrive in boxes bearing the vendor's name, address, and logo. Librarians will associate the books at least as closely with their vendor as with the publishers who actually made them. Like Bill Murray in *Groundhog Day*, book vendors wake up each morning and nothing has changed. But for them it is not a bad dream. Instead, book vendors have the chance to deliver customized shipments of books every week, every month, and every year. No other type of library vendor enjoys a foundation like this for building customer relationships.

Today, with the focus often elsewhere, it needs to be reinforced that the principal business of book vendors is selling books. Libraries still buy books in great number.[2] They depend upon their book vendors. Unlike most other suppliers, at the heart of the relationship between library and vendor is a physical object, a book, placed inside of another physical object, a box. More to the point, according to a library's size, hundreds, thousands, even tens of thousands of books will arrive at the library each year. They must arrive quickly, they must arrive regularly, they must arrive undamaged, they must be the correct ones–no easy thing in itself–and they must arrive so that a library can process them efficiently. With everything else a book vendor must do today–provide technical services, maintain complex online databases, offer sophisticated customer support–it is easy to slight the difficulty of delivering the right books quickly and in good condition, week in and week out. Little else matters if this does not happen, since the foundation of a library-vendor relationship will have fractured.

When all goes well and a book vendor delivers, however, customers notice and business will grow. Vendor capacity will need to grow with it. All successful book vendors build an operation that is nimble as well as substantial. The books–physical objects–must be identified, bought, received, described, moved, stored, moved again, gathered, often stamped and labeled and otherwise processed, invoiced, boxed, and shipped–week after week without interruption. It is easy for a vendor to say to a librarian that the company's focus is on customers. However, it is anything but easy to say the same thing on the floor of a warehouse, for example, where much of the work is a series of repetitive human tasks tied together by any number of complex, interlocking, and co-dependent automated systems.

Those systems were designed to answer a defined set of library needs. But as libraries evolve, their needs evolve too. Periodically, a book vendor has to make changes in operations and supporting systems, sometimes fundamental changes. Does maintaining focus on customer relationships mean that the vendor jumps to it whenever a library requests a new invoice configuration, an unusual shipping cycle, or a special way of packing or labeling books? Ideally, yes, since ideally a vendor will have built procedures and systems to accommodate the requests libraries are likely to make.

In the real world, though, there will be requests a vendor isn't able to handle routinely. Has the vendor built an organization that will enable new requests to reach the warehouse floor, for example, to gain a hearing in the first place? Then, does the vendor have staff with the awareness to properly balance the daily imperative of moving books–"books in, books out" is the classic shorthand for describing what book vendors do–with the longer-term imperative of recognizing, understanding, and responding to the changing needs of libraries? Is it solely up to sales and customer service to handle customers, or do customer relationships become everyone's job?[3]

If "yes" is the ideal answer to library requests, "no" is sometimes the only practical answer, since a vendor needs to be aware of the impact of exceptions on the overall performance of systems–on the ability to serve *all* customers, not just the one who has an exception. "We can't now, but please tell us more," will often be the best answer, and the necessary first step in responding to changing customer needs.

UNDERSTANDING THE CUSTOMER

Vendors aren't the only ones who run substantial operations. So do libraries. The complexity of behind-the-scenes library operations is always a surprise to outsiders, who might guess that maintaining an OPAC or mounting a database require considerable expertise, but who in general would have no idea what it takes in people, processes, systems, and equipment to put a book on the shelf, let alone tens of thousands of books. The largest libraries can hold their own for complexity with nearly any type of organization, and even small libraries need to replicate to scale most of the processes found in a university research library or in the downtown hub of a large public library system. Beyond the intricacies of their operations, every library creates a culture of its own within the larger library culture, one affected by local political and economic forces which, likewise, spin within the wider orbits of the library world.

If a book vendor does not understand libraries, library operations, and the contexts in which libraries exist, then the operation a vendor builds might turn out to be the wrong one. In order to understand libraries, a vendor first needs staff who are able to talk with librarians and listen to librarians–staff able to create systems and services that will make sense to librarians. Online customer support systems, for example, will often be the first choice of customers and are a necessary service today for book vendors. But even when a service like this reduces the degree of personal contact between library and vendor, the interface presented to customers must be built by people who understand libraries.

Book vendors need staff who can understand the jargon and technical language of librarianship; who read the same journals and newsletters and visit the same web sites as librarians; who know what kinds of humor librarians will find funny and what kinds they will not; who will have an idea of how library staff in Acquisitions and Collections and Cataloging and Public Services are liable to work with one another; who will know when to talk about books and when not to; and who above all will see local obstacles and opportunities as clearly as librarians see them. Selling books to libraries is a world apart from the stereotypes of salesmanship.[4]

Hiring librarians, in fact, makes sense for book vendors.[5] While librarians who decide to work for a vendor may hear from library colleagues that they have gone over to the "dark side," many have made successful careers this way and book vendors often count librarians among their most valuable employees.[6] When librarian talks to librarian, obviously some communication barriers come down. Can non-librarians do as well? In fact some can, as proven by the track records of many book vendor representatives who entered the field from another area of bookselling, from non-degreed library work, from an entirely unrelated career, or who simply worked their way up within a vendor's organization. For a book vendor, everything starts with selecting and nurturing staff who are capable enough and interested enough to understand libraries, and who are willing to commit to the ongoing effort this requires.

These staff members must also be able to express to their vendor colleagues in the office what it is that libraries need. When necessary, they must convince those who might need convincing that a change in the vendor's processes or services has to be made. For example, about ten years ago, as a cost-saving measure, many libraries began to prefer paperbacks over hardcover editions whenever possible.[7] For book vendors this was unwelcome news. Important parts of their operations needed to change in order to substitute a book lower in price, and so probably lower in profit, for a higher-priced one. While the case had to be made—first by libraries to vendor representatives, then by those representatives to their vendor colleagues—paperback preference became a standard vendor service option.

At about the same time, by contrast, CD-ROMs emerged on the marketplace. The format had a bright future, it seemed, as libraries began to collect and network these new devices. Book vendors had a choice. Should they retool in order to give CD-ROMs special focus? Some people thought so.[8] CD-ROMs did not disappear, of course, but before long were surpassed by then-unimagined breakthroughs and never became a mainstay for book vendors.

Like all organizations, library vendors continuously face choices. Today's stagnant library market for books is a fact presenting every book vendor with choices that can't be avoided.[9] Most of these choices amount to bets on a company's success in selling books against competitors, as well as bets on the future of the book itself. CD-ROMs aside, what about eBooks, talking books, out-of-print books, rare books, used books, children's books, foreign books, music scores, maps, music CDs, DVDs, videos, databases, even periodicals? Libraries buy all of these things and the vision of a super-vendor able to handle all materials, even three or four different types of materials, even one more than a vendor is doing at the moment, can be a tempting one. "Look at Amazon," an ambitious vendor might say. "Look at Wal-Mart."

Some book vendors have made the choice to include several or more different types of materials in their services to libraries. For a vendor able to channel multiple product types through a single sales and marketing operation, building and diversifying business in such streamlined fashion can be an attractive equation. Libraries can also benefit, since their vendor contacts and possibly their operations are correspondingly streamlined when one vendor fills multiple roles. The library's buying power will likely increase too. Product diversification is one way for book vendors to strengthen and broaden customer relationships.

In a stagnant book market there is another way to grow, selling books into *different* markets. Are academic library budgets being slashed? Then what about public libraries? Are the publics doing poorly? Then how about schools? Are economies growing in Asia? Then why aren't we there? Don't corporate libraries buy books? Why can't we figure out retail? What about everyone going to Amazon or Barnes & Noble? That's millions of books sold online every day. Why can't we get some of that? Most book vendors today have found that entering international markets is a necessary step to remain healthy and to grow. Why can't we sell anything, anywhere, to anyone?

That dream might become a nightmare for the staff at headquarters whose job will be to make things happen. Another nightmare might be in store for the library whose vendor has diverted resources away from the core business and is undergoing the ups and downs of new formats or new markets. No vendor–no business–wants to miss opportunities for growth. And no library will be well-served by a complacent book vendor. But the necessary first step toward sustainable growth for a book vendor is to understand everything about the core market, so that within that core and beyond, the best choices will be made and the right priorities set. Can your staff talk to librarians and do they understand libraries? For a book vendor, no question is more important than this.

WHAT LIBRARIES WANT

Until the 1990s–only late last century, although it can seem like a century ago–a book vendor's customer relationships were entirely about books. While books are still central, about ten or fifteen years ago book vendors began to learn that customers wanted something more. What libraries have wanted since then are vendors able to help them adapt to new economic and technological circumstances.

The new economics came first, during the 1980s. Businesses, governments, and institutions of every other type were forced to work more efficiently. Many libraries took a close look at backroom operations such as technical services departments.[10] Before long, book vendors who had to handle the books anyway were handling everything about a book, just short of placing it on a library shelf themselves. It was called outsourcing, a term which, difficult as it is to recall today, was once unfamiliar to librarians.[11] Cataloging records, ownership stamps, labels, barcodes, bookplates, security devices, whatever a given library had decided was necessary to put books into the hands of patrons passed first through the hands of the book vendor. None of this was entirely new, especially in the public and school library segments of the market, but the scale and scope of what was expected from book vendors were definitely new.[12]

Vendors learned that they could forget about maintaining customer relationships, let alone managing them, without technical services capabilities. Changing the operation to handle more paperbacks was nothing compared to gearing up for technical services. But vendors had little choice. Without technical services–in a reselling industry where it is difficult in the market for one vendor to differentiate its own core services from the services of others–the business would go elsewhere. "We made our choices based mainly upon technological support," was the matter-of-fact but representative conclusion of one librarian summarizing a firm order vendor review, "since all the vendors evaluated were comparable in discounts and services."[13] Within the span of just a few years, organizations with barely anyone on staff able to read a MARC record had taken in much of the routine technical services work for dozens and then hundreds of libraries.

The focus of these vendor-library relationships shifted from books to an esoteric area where only a handful of people at the library had much knowledge. Naturally, library politics changed. Selectors ceded to technical services departments some of their authority in vendor decisions. Vendor contacts within the library widened. Agendas for visits grew longer. Vendor representatives, to be able to talk to their library contacts and to their expert colleagues at the office, needed to understand the basics of technical services. It was even better if they developed real expertise.

Not long after the economics changed, the technology changed too. While library technology has never been static, the onset of the World Wide Web qualifies as an epochal change by any standard. For book vendors, so was the proliferation of ways to exchange electronic files with libraries. Tapes, diskettes, and modems were miraculous in their day; then as e-mail, FTP, and the Web sped past they seemed as antique as typewriters. In many libraries, the sizable backroom operations for sorting, searching, and keying that had always been needed to build book collections began to seem as ancient as the manual labor that built the pyramids.

Stories of successful technological innovations spread quickly, through conference presentations, journal articles, and personal networks. It seemed everyone was asking the same question: "How can *my* library take advantage of this?" Libraries and their book vendors learned how together. Libraries studied workflows associated with manual procedures developed over decades. Selecting, searching, funding, ordering, receiving, returning, paying, cataloging: some librarians were surprised to learn that buying books required all of these steps, each one a sub-system carried out under procedures perhaps known only to the staff members who performed them, staff who did not automatically agree that workflow changes were necessary or prudent. Sometimes change came by mandate, sometimes by consensus. Sometimes the *status quo* held.

Book vendors joined in when libraries invited them to participate. Usually vendors did so eagerly, because there was no better marketing angle than to be a partner in one of these success stories. At times libraries outpaced their vendor partners. For example, in the early days of online outsourced cataloging, the mid-1980s, most vendors were not equipped to supply the MARC tapes libraries wanted. When filling a void became clearly beneficial to both parties, libraries and vendors found occasion to work together closely. A good example, one that followed tapes in the evolution of vendor services, was the co-development of OCLC's PromptCat service, which has since streamlined cataloging for many libraries.[14]

Today technological innovation and economics have converged. Most book vendors are fluent in discussing how their own web interface can support a variety of library selection and ordering workflow models and can describe the different ways that cataloging records might accompany books. They have become adept at building interfaces to integrated library systems, modifying bibliographic records to suit individual library needs, delivering title records via FTP and EDIFACT (among other electronic options), and providing all the physical processing necessary to turn a generic book into a particular library's book. In short, while economics drove libraries to seek low-cost outsourced services, technology made it possible for vendors to respond.[15] Libraries asked for more service and lower costs. When they had the resources to answer, book vendors pleased customers and thereby increased sales.[16]

Once it was the norm for a library to maintain relationships with several book vendors. Then libraries learned that the cost of acquiring a book was an issue as important, or more so, than the cost of the book itself; and learned too that consolidation with a single vendor offered benefits beyond straight cost savings.[17] Book vendors, those that survived, learned the same lesson. If "save the time of the user" was an old precept in librarianship, then "save the time of the library" became a new one for book vendors.[18]

This created a challenging new business model.[19] Delivering what libraries needed required substantial investment. In an industry with modest margins, those investments were larger than many vendors could absorb on their own. With few realistic choices, smaller vendors began to seek alliances with larger ones. Beginning in the 1990s, some were ultimately absorbed in a still-unfinished series of consolidations.[20]

WHAT BOOK VENDORS WANT

It has become common for one vendor to supply nearly all of a library's books. Obviously, these vendors like having a substantial amount of business practically guaranteed for the year. But the benefits may not stop there. Some libraries choose to work with their vendor in a way that goes beyond the traditional customer-supplier relationship. When a library collaborates with a vendor to develop and test new services, in effect the two become partners in creating something of value to both. The library becomes something like a development laboratory.[21] Library and vendor may ask: "How could electronic invoicing for a particular integrated library system be delivered?" "Could the library load pre-order records from the vendor's system and accommodate all necessary local data fields?" "How must vendor or library change procedures to take advantage of EDIFACT ordering?" The best way to find out is to work together to research a question, develop a project plan, and then execute it.

Successful collaborative projects add to a vendor's stock-in-trade. The example of Library A can help to win business at Library B. Soon someone at Library C will be asking why *we* aren't doing things that way. For vendors who have developed substantial technical services expertise, this can be a wondrous cycle.[22] Not only does business grow but expertise grows too. As one and then another set of local problems are studied and solved, vendor and library staff learn from one another as their work progresses. If there are any moments in library bookselling that might be called exhilarating, one would be when vendor and library both witness gains and declare success in a collaborative project to engineer change.

Vendors are grateful when libraries dedicate talented staff, at considerable expense, to solve problems of mutual interest; and grateful again when it is acknowledged that the vendor is doing the same thing. However, vendors are not always so fortunate. If some library staff believe that a high discount should be the main factor in their vendor relationship, while others see a more encompassing role for the vendor, no amount of technical expertise on the vendor's part might be enough to solidify a position at that library. The greatest challenge in customer relationships for book vendors today is to convince as many librarians as possible that the price of a book is not an adequate measure of the value a vendor can bring to a library.[23]

Closer customer relationships bring a vendor closer as well to whatever factionalism might exist within a library. Stalled or half-started workflow redesign projects are common and can be a troublesome component of customer relationships for book vendors. When staff have not reached consensus on workflow change, or do not fully understand the capabilities of their own integrated library system, or perhaps have not spoken to OCLC about its capabilities, the book vendor might be asked for help. Does Acquisitions favor using PromptCat? Well, Cataloging may have a different idea. The Director has mandated a shelf-ready approval plan. Has anyone spoken to Collections? Questions like these can lead to disagreement. One group may see the vendor as an ally, but another may take the opposite view. Remaining neutral and objective is always the best course. Even so, library politics can put the vendor in a hard position, vulnerable to criticism, whether or not earned, but without standing to fashion a solution.

Internal library issues are not the only ones that might confront the book vendor. Today's complex service arrangements also require closer contact with third parties. While nurturing relationships with book publishers and other product vendors has always been important, today a book vendor must also work closely with less familiar organizations such as eBook aggregators, bibliographic utilities, and systems vendors. Can, for example, a particular system handle library funds in purchase order records? The answer will affect what the vendor is able to arrange for a library. Sometimes vendors find themselves in the role of library advocate when speaking to third parties, who of course have their own set of priorities and for whom a book vendor is not necessarily a customer. This can be a challenging role, but relationships with third parties have become crucial to book vendor/customer relationships.[24] While vendors must do all they can to advocate the library position, they must also remind libraries that vendors have to work within limits set by other parties involved in library book acquisitions, an activity that has proven highly resistant to standardization.[25]

The best approach for book vendors, with libraries and third parties alike, is to be truthful about a company's own capabilities; to avoid raising unrealistic expectations; to discuss competitors and third parties with respect; and to make sure that lines of communication are as open as they can be in all directions. In selling books or anything else to librarians, whose profession is infused with as much and probably more altruism than most others, it is wise and also smart to carry out business in an ethical way.[26] If their trust were diminished, libraries and book vendors would find their relationships diminished too.

SUCCESS IN CUSTOMER RELATIONSHIPS

For a book vendor, success in customer relationships depends on building an organization that can perform thousands upon thousands of small transactions nearly flawlessly, every day, for years. Success also means finding ways to see what lies ahead more clearly than others do.

There are no easy formulas and no redi-mix solutions. Success requires hiring the right people, teaching them the right skills, and asking them to understand the customer completely, from dock to director's office. For a book vendor, success in customer relationships is earned, not managed.

NOTES

1. Many librarians would say *they* are the ones who need to "manage effectively our relationships with these suppliers": Marilu Goodyear and Adrian W. Alexander, "Libraries as Customers: Achieving Continuous Improvement through Strategic Business Partnerships," *Library Acquisitions: Practice & Theory* 22, no. 1 (1998): 7.

2. In 2003, public libraries in the U.S. devoted over 41 percent of their acquisition expenditures to books, while for U.S. academic libraries the corresponding figure was just under 20 percent. Together, the two library types spent well over $650 million on books. *The Bowker Annual: Library and Book Trade Almanac*, 49th ed. (Medford, NJ: Information Today, 2004), 428-431.

3. "Communication between the two organizations takes place not just between two individuals, but between all relevant employees from each organization": Goodyear, "Libraries as Customers," 8.

4. Adam Bennington, "Everything I Know about Promoting the Library I Learned from Bad Sales Reps," *Information Outlook* 8, no. 3 (March 2004): 37-43.

5. Rick Anderson, *Buying and Contracting for Resources and Services: A How-to-Do-It Manual for Librarians* (New York: Neal-Schuman, 2004), 79.

6. Andrew K. Pace, *The Ultimate Digital Library: Where the New Information Players Meet* (Chicago: American Library Association, 2003), xi-xvi.

7. Randy Silverman and Robert Speiser, "Buying Publishers' Trade Paperbacks versus Hardbacks: A Preventive Conservation Strategy for Research Libraries," in *Advances in Librarianship*, Irene P. Godden, ed. (San Diego: Academic Press, 1992), 127-151; Glen Worley, "Squeezing the Most Out of the Approval Plan Budget: The University of Texas at Austin and Blackwell's Book Services Preferred Edition and Paper Preferred Option," *Against the Grain* 12, no. 3 (June 2000): 16-26; Dana Courtney, "The Cloth-Paper Conundrum: The Economics of Simultaneous Publication," *Journal of Scholarly Publishing* 33, no. 4 (July 2002): 202-229.

8. Michael Gorman, "The Academic Library in the Year 2001: Dream or Nightmare or Something in Between?" *Journal of Academic Librarianship* 17, no. 1 (1991): 5.

9. Brian Alley, "Vendor's Lament: The Shrinking Library Marketplace and the Shortage of Better Mouse Traps," *Technicalities* 14, no. 10 (October 1994): 1.

10. Sha Li Zhang, Dan Miller, and Don Williams, "Allocating the Technology Dividend in Technical Services through Using Vendor Services," *Library Collections, Acquisitions, & Technical Services* 26 (2002): 379-393.

11. Gary M. Shirk, "Contract Acquisitions: Change, Technology, and the New Library/Vendor Partnership," *Library Acquisitions: Practice & Theory* 17 (1993): 145-153; Gary M. Shirk, "Outsourced Library Technical Services: The Bookseller's Perspective," *Library Acquisitions: Practice & Theory* 18 (1994): 383-395.

12. Dana L. Alessi, "Raising the Bar: Book Vendors and the New Realities of Service," *Journal of Library Administration* 28, no. 2 (1999): 25-40.

13. Cynthia Hsieh, "Book Vendor Evaluation from a Small Academic Library's Perspective," *Against the Grain* 16, no. 4 (September 2004): 80-81.

14. Mary M. Rider and Marsha Hamilton, "PromptCat Issues for Acquisitions: Quality Review, Cost Analysis and Workflow Implications," *Library Acquisitions: Practice & Theory* 20, no. 1 (Spring 1996): 9-21.

15. Kathleen L. Wells, "Hard Times in Technical Services: How Do Academic Libraries Manage? A Survey," *Technical Services Quarterly* 21, no. 4 (2004): 17-30.

16. Janet L. Flowers and Scott Perry, "Vendor-Assisted E-Selection and Online Ordering: Optimal Conditions," *Library Collections, Acquisitions, & Technical Services* 26 (2002): 395-407.

17. Goodyear, "Libraries as Customers," 8; Luke Swindler and Terry B. Hill, "The Africana Collections at the Libraries of the University of North Carolina at Chapel Hill and Duke University," *Against the Grain* 16, no. 1 (February 2004): 26-30.

18. "Save the time of the user" is S.R. Ranganathan's Fourth Law of Library Science. M.A. Gopinath, "Ranganathan, Shiyali," in *Encyclopedia of Library and Information Science*, Allen Kent et al., eds., vol. 25 (New York: Marcel Dekker, 1978), 61.

19. Zhang, "Allocating the Technology Dividend," 391.

20. John R. Secor, "Why Some Vendors Will Endure and Others Will Not," *Against the Grain* 8, no. 1 (February 1996): 20-24; John R. Secor and Gary M. Shirk, "The Coming Restructuring of Library Book Vending," *Libri* 50 (2000): 104-108; Pace, *Ultimate Digital Library*, 12-14.

21. Pace, *Ultimate Digital Library*, 16-17.

22. Gary M. Shirk, "The Wondrous Web: Reflections on Library Acquisitions and Vendor Relationships," *Acquisitions Librarian* 5 (1991): 1-8.

23. Goodyear, "Libraries as Customers," 8.

24. L. Hunter Kevil, "Vendor Partnerships: CEOs, Systems, and the Future," *Library Acquisitions: Practice & Theory* 21 (Fall 1997): 244-247.

25. Katharine Treptow Farrell and Marc Truitt, "The Case for Acquisitions Standards in the Integrated Library System," *Library Collections, Acquisitions, & Technical Services* 27 (2003): 483-492.

26. Cynthia H. Goldstein, "Ethics in Technical Services," *LLA Bulletin* 58 (Summer 1995): 34-38; Anderson, *Buying and Contracting for Resources and* Services, 139-147.

Library/Vendor Relations:
An Academic Publisher's Perspective

Keith Courtney

SUMMARY. Communication with customers (libraries) is vital to the overall success of academic publishers. Ongoing interaction and involvement with the library community through conference participation, institution of focus groups and other such means allow publishers to better serve the evolving needs of libraries. With foresight and direction, the acquisition of smaller publishing entities by larger organizations can result in a mutually beneficial situation for all parties. Through partnerships with online full-text database aggregators, academic publishers can increase their overall range of exposure and gain more name recognition in areas of the world where, previously, access to that publisher's content was not easily attainable. The use of online pre-publication services allows academic publishers to make the latest articles available to researchers even before the article is made available in print. By assigning Digital Object Identifiers (DOIs) to every article made available through a pre-publication service, researchers are able to fully cite such articles and thus make full use of the information provided in their own studies. Comprehensive online support services provide libraries with a variety of essential subscription management services and

Keith Courtney is Sales Director, Taylor & Francis Ltd, 4 Park Square, Milton Park, Abingdon, Oxfordshire OX14 4RN, UK (E-mail: keith.courtney@tandf.co.uk).

[Haworth co-indexing entry note]: "Library/Vendor Relations: An Academic Publisher's Perspective." Courtney, Keith. Co-published simultaneously in *Journal of Library Administration* (The Haworth Information Press, an imprint of The Haworth Press, Inc.) Vol. 44, No. 3/4, 2006, pp. 57-68; and: *Library/Vendor Relationships* (ed: Sam Brooks, and David H. Carlson) The Haworth Information Press, an imprint of The Haworth Press, Inc., 2006, pp. 57-68. Single or multiple copies of this article are available for a fee from The Haworth Document Delivery Service [1-800-HAWORTH, 9:00 a.m. - 5:00 p.m. (EST). E-mail address: docdelivery@haworthpress.com].

help to increase the overall level of interaction between library and publisher. The Open Access (OA) issue is multi-dimensional in nature and has often been misconstrued by many in the publisher and library communities. As the Open Access concept is still being defined, academic publishers must pay close attention to its development and attempt to incorporate such access into their offerings so as to best serve the needs of their subscribers. *[Article copies available for a fee from The Haworth Document Delivery Service: 1-800-HAWORTH. E-mail address: <docdelivery@haworthpress.com> Website: <http://www.HaworthPress.com> © 2006 by The Haworth Press, Inc. All rights reserved.]*

KEYWORDS. Academic libraries, academic publishers, acquisitions, Digital Object Identifier, DOI, focus groups, full-text databases, Gordon and Breach, imprints, library/vendor relations, mergers, online support, pre-publication service, subscription agents, Taylor & Francis, open access, pricing models, journals

Successful relationships, in general, are built upon a foundation of mutually beneficial goals and aspirations. The strength of relationships between academic publishers and libraries is a direct reflection of the commitment of each party to the continuing development of academic research and the benefits it fosters. If academic publishers are to provide the appropriate high-quality products and services that their library customers require, an open line of communication must be maintained at all times between both parties. Such cooperative interaction is vital to the success of both academic publishers and the libraries that they serve.

For over two centuries, Taylor & Francis has sought to publish the highest-quality periodicals and monographs with the foremost aim of promoting the exchange of scholarly information amongst academics worldwide. In 1798, Richard Taylor founded the *Philosophical Magazine* with the intent of creating a new scientific journal that would be produced in close collaboration with the academic community. Joined by Dr. William Francis in 1852, they continued their practice of producing high-quality journals in cooperation with the members of the academic community for which the publications were intended to serve. The relationship forged by such a close alliance of publisher and scholars continues to this day.

When it comes to key characteristics of publishers and the consistent availability of journal content, academic and other research libraries prefer to work with those publishers that exude strong qualities of stability and longevity.[1] Such qualities help to provide libraries with a sense of ease and comfort in knowing that the publisher has a long-standing, reliable track history in terms of performance and viability.

Thus, in order to best serve the needs of libraries, an academic publisher must stay active and current in the library community. Attending key conferences and participating in organizations such as the United Kingdom Serials Group (UKSG) and the North American Serials Interest Group, Inc. (NASIG) are ways in which a publisher can develop and maintain a solid relationship with the library community. Such a strong relationship helps to provide publishers with the information and direction that they require in order to best serve the needs of their customers. By directly interacting with current customers (and potential customers), a publisher can understand the concerns and needs of their individual library customers, and reflect those concerns in the products and services that they provide. Much of the value derived from developing these relationships comes not only from many years of interaction, but the willingness on part of both parties to become involved, rather than remain passive and non-communicative.

Another way in which academic publishers can interact with the library community for mutual benefit is through the institution of formal focus groups (or sessions). In fact, focus sessions are being used more often as a research technique of publishers that are looking for qualitative feedback in various areas such as general editorial evaluations of existing products with regard to future directions, new product development (including review and analysis of prototypes when necessary), the development of new sales models, and other assessment issues.[2] Not to be confused with advisory boards, which are typically intended to function in an ongoing, long-term capacity, focus groups are formed on an as-needed basis, and are disbanded once they have fulfilled their intended purpose. In order to receive the greatest possible return from a focus group, academic publishers must create focus groups with care and with a very specific purpose in mind.

The principal objective of creating a focus group must be clearly delineated at the onset so as to provide the publisher with the necessary direction for the group's formation. Once the objective has been determined, the publisher needs to invite potential participants from the appropriate library communities. Though this process may be time-consuming, assembling the appropriate panel inevitably pays dividends toward the desired outcome. Library communities of interest to the publisher may be global in geography while simultaneously being very homogenous in terms of library type (e.g., a cross section of academic libraries from around the world). The opposite scenario may also be a viable option if a publisher wishes to limit the group's membership by geography and not by library type. However, the scenario that is most often actualized is when a publisher elects to obtain feedback from a specific library type in a limited geographic region (e.g., academic libraries in the UK) to ascertain highly refined and detailed information. Such details are ultimately determined by the specific agenda of the meeting. The key factor is that the publisher keeps their final objective in mind when organizing the focus group, conducting the meetings, and incorporating their findings toward the eventual conclusion.

Academic libraries should seek out publishers that have a long-standing practice of making frequent use of such focus groups in helping to shape the companies' products and services. In fact, publishers may wish to pursue a policy of always seeking the advice of libraries before introducing any new publishing initiatives. By strictly adhering to such a foundational policy, academic publishers can be successful at keeping pace with the needs and desires of their customers.

Over the last few years, Taylor & Francis has been working closely with a number of key library customers to develop a sales model, which allows access to a wider range of journals at affordable prices, with usage as a key factor in determining customer needs. The initial feedback is that one size may not fit all and therefore a need for more flexible, transparent models offering choice may be a preferred route over the next few years. Ultimately, the aim is to match content with faculty needs. This is one example of how feedback obtained from focus groups plays an important role in the development and implementation of new publishing initiatives.

As smaller publishing companies are slowly acquired by larger organizations and their publications absorbed into the catalogs of such larger companies, many in the library community worry about how this continuing trend will affect libraries and their patrons in the long run. An acquisition may be deemed successful if it results in mutually beneficial situations for the acquired publisher, the acquiring publisher, and the library community. Acquisitions should be made only after a careful consideration of the consequential effects on the library community at large. For instance, acquisitions by Taylor & Francis are subject to the overall aim of the company, which is to make each journal the best available in its respective area(s) of study. Therefore, by using the acquisition of other publishing entities to further enhance the value of all affected journals, the applicable research communities benefit, through the availability of higher-quality information, as does the acquiring publisher, through increased and lasting revenue.

Academic publishers, when planning to acquire another publishing entity, should do so with the customers' best interests in mind. Existing subscribers of the publishing entity that is to be acquired should not be inconvenienced as a part of the acquisition process. In fact, such an acquisition or merger should provide the customer with better service and an improved product overall. Taylor & Francis, in particular, has developed the necessary skills to successfully integrate acquisitions into the company's overall structure. The company is thus able to make the acquisition of another publishing entity as seamless as possible in order to best serve the needs of its readers/subscribers.

An excellent example of an acquisition that has proven to be of benefit to all parties is that of the Gordon and Breach Publishing Group in 2001. Although many of their journals were already considered to be of first-rate quality, Gordon and Breach suffered from a lack of consistency and regularity that made it especially difficult for libraries to manage and catalog their subscriptions to Gordon and Breach titles. The publisher had long operated under a system by which they would publish academic research papers as soon as they had received enough submissions to constitute a full issue. While this method may have provided libraries with some limited advantages, there were far more disadvantages in the long run. For example, if a particular Gordon and Breach journal received a large number of article submissions in a given year that resulted in additional issues being published, then subscribers to that title would be presented with a supplemental bill for the additional content provided during the year. This policy made it very difficult for individual libraries to budget for their Gordon and Breach subscriptions from year to year. Through this acquisition, Taylor & Francis set out to provide all existing and future subscribers with a more manageable and predictable subscription model for upcoming volumes.

The fusing of Gordon and Breach's high-quality content with Taylor & Francis's highly-efficient and stable infrastructure has resulted in an exceptional synergy. Gordon and Breach journals have received the direction and structure that they needed in order to better deliver their content to the marketplace. Much of this improvement was facilitated through the implementation of enhanced quality rules along with a strict adherence to budget, targets, and deadlines, all of which has resulted in the consistent and timely delivery of high-quality journals.

Another key benefit that has resulted from the acquisition of smaller publishing entities by Taylor & Francis is the enhanced support and distribution that a larger publisher can provide for the publications of such smaller organizations. Through such acquisitions, highly respected journals that originated with organizations such as Routledge, Carfax, Swets & Zeitlinger Publishers, Marcel Dekker, and Frank Cass & Co are able to benefit considerably from the additional editorial and financial support provided by the larger company. Furthermore, these journals benefit from a broader range of distribution made possible through a major publisher and its distribution partners, enabling them to reach a much wider audience of researchers. Also, many of the journals from smaller publishers will benefit from enhanced electronic (e-journal) access through such acquisitions. Through acquisitions of publishing entities, a greater number of libraries world-wide benefit from increased access to content that may previously have been more difficult to obtain. The Taylor & Francis Group now publishes more than 1,000 individual journals, previously published under a variety of imprints such as Routledge, Brunner-Routledge, Carfax Publishing, Frank Cass, Martin-Dunitz, Psychology Press, Routledge, Spon Press, Gordon and Breach, and Taylor & Francis. From 2005 all Scientific, Technical, and Medical titles are published under the single imprint of Taylor & Francis, and the Social Science and Humanities titles are published under the Routledge imprint. The aim was to provide heightened awareness in the academic, policy, and business communities for all journals and by providing a more integrated presence at the many conferences attended each year. With the aim of publishing the leading journal in each field of scientific research, the company continues to refine its catalog of publications so as to offer its customers the most comprehensive collection of titles available with an emphasis on quality scholarship.

In addition to acquisitions, partnerships with other companies provide benefits for the academic research community. By working with other companies that serve the library community, an academic journal publisher can increase the range and depth of their product distribution in a positive manner. Serials agents serve as the backbone of distribution for academic publishers as most college and university libraries rely almost exclusively on the use of serials agents for their periodical acquisitions. By partnering with such agents for the management of customers' subscriptions, academic publishers are able to allocate a greater quantity of time and resources towards the development of quality content for their publications.

Furthermore, through participation in aggregated full-text database initiatives, academic publishers can reach out to a large quantity of potential readers that normally would not have easy access to the publisher's content. EBSCO Publishing, for instance, is a key partner for Taylor & Francis in the area of aggregated full-text databases and enables access to content for researchers in parts of the world that were previously unexposed to said content. By making their content available through such databases, academic publishers can obtain a higher degree of exposure for their journals than would normally be possible through traditional subscription models. For example, a small library that has a very limited serial acquisition budget may never have been able to afford subscriptions to many of the titles provided by a particular publisher, yet the library is able to afford a subscription to an aggregated full-text database. If the database happens to include full-text coverage of that same publisher's journals, then the small library benefits from the additional content that they would not have been able to afford otherwise, and the publisher benefits from the increased exposure and name recognition that comes with such access.

While full-text databases offer obvious benefits to libraries, understanding the differences between individual journal subscriptions (print or electronic) and access to journals via aggregated full-text databases is of utmost importance for librarians in order to maintain continuous, valuable access to journals via databases. As much as participation in full-text databases allows for additional exposure and revenue streams for publishers, this is secondary to the core subscription business, which allows publishers to continue to thrive, expand, and improve journal offerings for libraries. If libraries were to view databases as a means for canceling journal subscriptions, this would be a blatant misuse of these resources, and consequently may have adverse effects on library collections. Indeed it is likely that publishers would withdraw their content from these databases. Certainly, the greatest value of a full-text database is the level of content it may bring to a library that was otherwise not available. "Databases should be viewed as a complement (not a replacement) to the core print and electronic journal collections in academic libraries."[3] In addition to providing this supplemental access to journals for ARLs and other universities in developed nations, aggregated full-text databases are often the primary means for accessing scholarly information in emerging nations as well. Taylor & Francis is proud to partner with EBSCO Publishing in providing content as part of academic databases reaching "information-starved countries."[4] Such initiatives benefit libraries in developing regions that might otherwise have little or no budget available for individual journal subscriptions. Some libraries receiving access to EBSCO*host* databases through projects such as eIFL Direct (http://www.eifl.net/) and INASP (http://

www.inasp.info/) literally increase their access to important journals from a small handful to several thousand titles, whilst the publisher benefits from the increased readership and usage.

Just as the selection of content that makes up a particular journal package is of utmost importance to a library, so is the currency of the research that is distributed through those journals. In an ideal world, libraries and their patrons would have access to the latest research as soon as the article is ready for publication. With the aim of turning this ideal into a reality, and in response to feedback provided by academic librarians, Taylor & Francis has fashioned a new service entitled *prEview*. This new initiative is an online-first publication service that allows subscribers to avoid the delays that are often associated with print (and even e-journal) publication and thereby gain swift access to the latest research findings. Nearly one hundred journals are currently covered by *prEview*, and many more are scheduled to be added in the near future.

The full-text articles available via this service are essentially advance copies of the same pieces that will be formally published under specific volume and issue numbers in the future. All such papers have been put through the peer-review process, revised and fully approved by the editors of their respective journals. In addition, these pre-publication versions have undergone all final copy-editing, typesetting, and proof approval (by the author). Once available via *prEview*, a document will not receive any additional revisions or edits. If a researcher only has access to the "working paper" version of a particular article, they may find that a number of the details could potentially change prior to final publication. While working papers can certainly provide valuable contributions to one's understanding of a topic, they are not as readily citable as the pre-publication documents available through a service such as *prEview*. Therefore, when a researcher accesses an article in this way, they are reading nothing less than the final, definitive version of the piece as it will appear in the formal publication.

As the articles made available through a pre-publication service have not yet received volume and issue designations, one may wonder how they can be of use to scholars interested in using the new information in their own research. Academic publishers can solve this problem by assigning each article a DOI (Digital Object Identifier), which effectively serves as a virtual watermark. "The International DOI Foundation defines DOI as an entire system for 'persistent identification and interoperable exchange of intellectual property (IP) on digital networks.' In other words, DOI is used to identify ownership and track the use of IP in cyberspace. DOI has been called 'the bar code for intellectual property.'"[5] The use of DOIs at this stage in the publication process allows researchers to fully cite and track the articles available to them without any concern as to how such documents may be located following formal publication. In fact, even upon formal publication, when an article is removed from a pre-publication service and relocated to the print and online versions of the journal with full bibliographic data (volume, issue, etc.), the article's unique DOI will remain intact so as to facilitate a constant means of reference to that article. This type of availability benefits researchers in that it provides them with rapid access to the latest research without sacrificing quality or accessibility. By having access to the final pre-publication versions of each paper, scholars may fully incorporate the information provided into their own research. The use of static DOIs further enhances the value of pre-publication articles as scholars can easily access and formally cite the latest research that otherwise may have been difficult for end readers to locate.

Quality of journal content is the basis for many ranking formulas and studies, and is generally the primary factor used by librarians in determining the value of these journals. However, an area of great importance that is often overlooked by publishers, but which may enhance the quality of working relationships between publishers and libraries, is that of service. Outstanding customer service is vital to the long-term relationships between libraries and publishers/vendors. In addition to providing libraries with the content that they require, a publisher should also be responsible for offering a diverse range of services to support libraries' use of such content. Services such as online administrative support for e-journal access, up-to-date notification of bibliographic changes (e.g., title name and ISSN), subscription management information, journal alerting services, special offers, usage statistics for e-journals, and general news and information regarding the company and its services are all important to a solid customer service program.

A publisher can best serve the needs of its customers by not only providing a comprehensive array of support services, but by also making the majority of such services (if not all of them) available from a single access point. Convenient access to all of these services helps to ensure that customers will utilize them to their full potential and therefore experience the best possible relationship with the publisher. As many facets of the information industry are now situated online, the ideal location for a single point of access is the publisher's web site. In this digital age, easy access to support services is increasingly necessary for librarians who are forced to manage a rapidly growing body of elec-

tronic information. To address this need, Taylor & Francis has made online customer service one of its foremost priorities.

With the development of the "LibSite,"[6] Taylor & Francis has as-
sured that librarians can easily access the information that they need to
effectively manage their subscriptions in a timely and convenient manner. In addition to offering quick and easy access to all of the aforemen-
tioned services, the LibSite provides additional features and benefits not
commonly available for large academic publishers. For example, not
only does this service offer subscribers access to complete usage data
for their e-journals, but such usage reports are now available in
COUNTER 1-compliant format. This is due in part to Taylor & Francis's role as a founding sponsor of COUNTER[7] and the company's ongoing commitment to providing the comprehensive usage statistics that
librarians require in a clear format.

As a support web site should truly meet the needs of customers, the
publisher should solicit feedback from customers regarding the site on a
continual basis. This is necessary as such feedback is vital to the development and enhancement of support and other publisher services. In order to gather as much information as possible, the publisher must
provide an easy method whereby customers can submit their comments
and suggestions. The chances of a customer providing constructive
feedback increase in direct proportion to the level of ease with which
they can make their submission. With a simple online form, valuable information can be garnered with minimal effort by the customer.

Open Access (OA) has become one of the major issues in the journals
business but there are some misconceptions about it. One can distinguish between: OA as a lobbying issue; OA as a business model, with
the increasing number of peer-reviewed titles being OA; and OA as au-
thor/institutional repositories of scholarly information which could
form the basis of a virtual global research archive.

The lobbying issue is driven by a number of enthusiastic proponents,
whose most cogent argument is that there should be universal free access to taxpayer-funded research. This has found resonance in governments and their agencies as the movement towards e-government and
e-democracy becomes a political and cultural spin-off of technological
advance. Some research funders (but not all) have taken this position
and have endorsed it.

The OA business model–or 'author-pays'–has been around a lot longer than recent incarnations such as BioMedCentral and Public Library
of Science, mainly via controlled circulation publications and page
charge/author fee-based journals. Sometime before headline announce-

ments such as Springer Open Choice and OUP's Nucleic Acids Research as a 'hybrid,' Taylor & Francis was experimenting with a 'hybrid' OA medical title, and postings to open archives.

This remains a unique strength of Taylor & Francis–being flexible and nimble enough to meet the needs of academic and learned society partners, while bringing business acumen to the process so that editors and societies are properly funded to undertake a number of OA publishing experiments, as our academic partners require, and we feel well placed to make them successful.

We firmly believe that funding, supporting, and organizing first-class peer review communities in all subject areas is a key, continuing role for the academic publisher–whatever the business or sales model. We also bring traditional editorial and marketing skills to the table, along with a host of new skills for the online age:

- organizing metadata and identifiers for version control, search, and retrieval
- highlighting, data feeds, alerting, etc.–an extension of traditional marketing techniques
- reader and researcher tools
- researcher community networks within subjects
- contextualization of content and publisher organizational values
- quality control, authentication, validation, and branding

The third aspect of OA–the repository–is tied in with authors' rights. Taylor & Francis already allows pre-prints–where the editor of a journal accepts that such 'prior publication' is not a barrier to submission. We are also developing a post-print policy which allows authors the right to post a final version in a repository, yet which enables the definitive, published version to have a clear identifier in the online environment.

As with all of our business practices, we are simply following the centuries-old policy of providing products and services that meet both the continuing and changing needs of the scholarly and scientific communities. In order to stay on top of those needs, it is vital that academic publishers strive to maintain a high level of communication and mutual interaction with the communities that they serve. Such a proactive approach helps to ensure that publishers enjoy lasting and highly successful relationships with their library customers.

NOTES

1. Sam Brooks and Thomas J. Dorst, "Issues Facing Academic Library Consortia and Perceptions of Members of the Illinois Digital Academic Library," portal: *Libraries & the Academy* 2, no. 1 (2002): 48.

2. Mary Elizabeth Clack and John Riddick, "The balance point: Focus on serials issues," *Serials Review* 16, no. 1 (Spring 1990): 91.

3. Sam Brooks and Thomas J. Dorst, "Issues Facing Academic Library Consortia and Perceptions of Members of the Illinois Digital Academic Library," portal: *Libraries & the Academy* 2, no. 1 (2002): 50.

4. Blazej Feret, Michael Kay, Anna Maria Balogh, Peter Szanto and Sam Brooks, "eIFL-Electronic Information for Libraries: A Global Initiative of the Soros Foundation Network," 67th IFLA Council and General Conference August 16-25, 2001. Available online at: http://www.ifla.org/IV/ifla67/papers/117-141e.pdf.

5. Shin Kennedy, "DOI," *Computers in Libraries* 24, no. 2 (February 2004): 19.

6. http://www.tandf.co.uk/libsite.

7. Taylor & Francis Press Release, "T&F Announce Availability of COUNTER Compliant Usage Statistics April 2004," (available at: http://www.tandf.co.uk/libsite/news.asp).

ANKOS and Its Dealings with Vendors

Phyllis L. Erdogan
Bulent Karasozen

SUMMARY. The Anatolian University Libraries Consortium (ANKOS) was formally created in 2001 following joint licensing projects by four libraries in 1999 and twelve in 2000. The consortium has grown to encompass eighty-nine libraries in 2005, and the number of its contracts has increased to twenty-five. Members include Turkish university libraries and research libraries attached to hospitals and government offices. A voluntary association, ANKOS is run by a Steering Committee composed of the directors of nine member libraries with the help of staff members from those libraries. The first agreements were for print+e-access for journals and for an aggregator database, and these were mostly informal subscription arrangements. An early activity was the development of a model Turkish National Site License. That license now forms the basis for negotiations with vendors, which culminate in formal license agreements. Beginning in 2004, ANKOS contracts are for electronic-only access and are often for multiple years. *[Article copies available for a fee from The Haworth Document Delivery Service: 1-800-HAWORTH. E-mail address: <docdelivery@haworthpress.com> Website: <http://www.HaworthPress.com> © 2006 by The Haworth Press, Inc. All rights reserved.]*

Phyllis L. Erdogan is Vice President, Bilkent University, 06800 Ankara, Turkey (E-mail: librdirector@bilkent.edu.tr). She was formerly a member of the ANKOS Steering Committee and Library Director, Bilkent University, 06800 Ankara, Turkey.

Bulent Karasozen is ANKOS Chairman and Library Director, Middle East Technical University, 06531 Ankara, Turkey (E-mail: bulent@metu.edu.tr).

[Haworth co-indexing entry note]: "ANKOS and Its Dealings with Vendors." Erdogan, Phyllis L., and Bulent Karasozen. Co-published simultaneously in *Journal of Library Administration* (The Haworth Information Press, an imprint of The Haworth Press, Inc.) Vol. 44, No. 3/4, 2006, pp. 69-83; and: *Library/Vendor Relationships* (ed: Sam Brooks, and David H. Carlson) The Haworth Information Press, an imprint of The Haworth Press, Inc., 2006, pp. 69-83. Single or multiple copies of this article are available for a fee from The Haworth Document Delivery Service [1-800-HAWORTH, 9:00 a.m. - 5:00 p.m. (EST). E-mail address: docdelivery@haworthpress.com].

Available online at http://www.haworthpress.com/web/JLA
© 2006 by The Haworth Press, Inc. All rights reserved.
doi:10.1300/J111v44n03_07

KEYWORDS. ANKOS, consortia, consortium, pricing models, cost distribution, database licensing, multi-year contracts, price negotiations, library/vendor relations, Turkey, international

INTRODUCTION

The Turkish academic library community entered a new era with the creation in May 2001 of the Anatolian University Libraries Consortium. Known by its Turkish acronym, ANKOS, the consortium's development has been documented in an article written by two members of its steering committee.[1] In that article is to be found a complete list of licensed databases since the first ANKOS contracts in 2002, including those signed for 2004. The present article will bring the reader up to date on ANKOS work for 2005.

BACKGROUND

In 1946, the year that the National Library was established, there were three Turkish universities; by 1981 their number had risen to nineteen. In that year, a revision of the Turkish law governing institutions of higher education brought all post-secondary education into the university system, provided for an increase in the number of state universities, and following a change in the Turkish Constitution, permitted private higher education on the condition that such institutions be non-profit and that their students be admitted according to the national policy of *numerus clausus* whereby all candidates to enter higher education are subject to a central entrance examination and placed in a specific university department according to the results. Since the passage of that law, twenty-four universities and two vocational schools at post-secondary level have been opened by private foundations. Another thirty-one universities and two institutes of technology have been opened by the State. These, together with the nineteen institutions dating from prior to 1981, two international universities located in Kyrgyzstan and Kazakhstan operated jointly by their own and Turkish authorities, three military academies, and five universities in the Turkish Republic of Northern Cyprus, are all potential members of ANKOS. Membership is also open, subject to case-by-case decisions, to special (research) libraries. Participation in at least one ANKOS agreement with a product supplier constitutes membership in ANKOS.

Of the fifty-nine institutions created following the 1981 law, the state universities were often located outside the large metropolitan areas and were without library collections or technological infrastructures. Not surprisingly, they found it difficult to attract teaching staff and students. Thus, when the National Academic Network and Information Center (ULAKBIM) was close to completing its mission of providing all universities with Internet connections, it was time for ANKOS in 2002 to undertake to arrange licenses to provide access to electronic resources for as many institutions as possible.

Given the extreme diversity of conditions of the universities, this has been a challenge. For example, ANKOS member institutions' budgets for collection expenditures (books, periodicals, other non-book items, and electronic resources) in 2004 varied between $100,000 and $3,000,000.[2] Enrollments vary from fewer than 100 to over 50,000.[3] English language knowledge of staff and students ranges from almost none (no English preparatory classes and no instruction in English) to institutions where the medium of instruction is English.[4] All these institutions need to use resources, but to what extent can they afford them, and how effectively can they be used and by how many users? These are problems for ANKOS as well as for the libraries in other southern European countries, which greatly affect negotiations with publishers and vendors. It was in recognition of this communality of problems less frequently encountered in some other countries, that consortia from Greece, Italy, Portugal, Spain, and Turkey banded together to form SELL, the Southern European Libraries Link,[5] to discuss mutual problems and approaches to vendors.

Added to the problems posed by the range of institutions is the dearth of knowledge of English among librarians and the lack of experience of librarians in negotiating contracts and prices. Certain firms with which ANKOS has contracts have Turkish agents, which facilitates communications with the members but does not always lead to easier contract negotiations since it means an extra layer to pass through.

GROWTH OF ANKOS

Since its establishment in 2002, ANKOS has grown rapidly both in terms of member libraries and total number of database subscriptions. In the first year, ANKOS members had a total of 235 database subscriptions through the consortium. This number increased to 402 in 2003 and 564 in 2004. It is expected that there will be a total of 729 subscriptions for 2005 when all details are finalized for the deals for twenty-five databases. Twelve of these are from commercial publishers, nine from society publishers, three are aggregator databases, and one is a database of electronic books. The average number of ANKOS contracts per member library increased from 5.4 in 2003 to 7.2 in 2004 and 8.6 in 2005. This data shows that despite insufficient financial resources, Turkish academic and research libraries are still trying to enrich their electronic collections and that saturation level has not yet been reached. This can be explained in part by the establishment of new universities (the Government has announced that fifteen more will be chartered in 2005). At the same time, probably both as a result of the ANKOS-aided increased access to research publications and funding from the European Union and other foreign sources, the number of research publications emanating from Turkey increased by an average of 25 percent annually between 2002 and 2004. For the first time the Turkish Scientific and Technical Research Council (TUBITAK) has also announced significant financial support for research, in the amount of US $400,000 for 2005.

Usage statistics for the ANKOS full-text databases have monitored rapid growth: from a total number of full-text downloads of 2,300,000 in 2002 to 6,020,000 in 2003, and to 8,470,000 in 2004. Only eleven of the ANKOS databases were COUNTER-compliant in 2004, and ACS, Emerald, and Taylor & Francis were first licensed by ANKOS in 2004 so it is not possible to compare usage statistics for those databases with earlier years. Among the COUNTER-compliant databases, Oxford University Press e-journal usage increased by 56 percent from 2003 to 2004, with 169,000 full-text downloads. Similar increases were observed for ScienceDirect (41 percent increase to 4,600,000 full-text downloads in 2004) and Blackwell Synergy (30 percent increase, to 383,000 downloads). The increase in usage of aggregator databases was low: ProQuest databases with 491,000 and EBSCOhost with 795,000 full-text downloads in 2004 showed increases of about 6 percent and 10 percent, respectively.

To foster awareness and use of the databases, ANKOS arranges several education seminars per year in different areas of the country. In 2004, user education was given for EBSCOhost, Elsevier Science Direct, IEEE/IEE Electronic Library (IEL), Kluwer Online Journals (now part of Springer), ProQuest, Web of Science, and Wiley InterScience.

To overcome the lack of sufficient English of both librarians and users, ANKOS has collaborated with vendors to translate database brochures into Turkish and distribute them to the member libraries. The first three such Turkish publications were for the American Chemical Society, Elsevier Science Direct, and Web of Science. Some of the vendors, for example ProQuest and the Institute of Physics, also make Turkish interfaces available on their web sites. In 2005, ANKOS will concentrate more on evaluating usage statistics and user education, especially during the annual meeting to which vendors come to introduce their products.

THE ANKOS MODUS OPERANDI

ANKOS is a voluntary association of academic libraries, together with a few research and special libraries, which operates through the efforts of the nine heads of libraries who form its Steering Committee. The Steering Committee members are in turn assisted by members of their staffs who serve as "ANKOS liaisons" for each product or vendor with whom negotiations are undertaken. A visit to the ANKOS English-language web site[6] will provide information about this structure and other details.

Proposals of products come to the Steering Committee from members and vendors. If the Steering Committee finds a product worthy of consideration by ANKOS, one of the Committee members is requested to appoint a liaison librarian to arrange for a trial, announce the trial to the ANKOS membership, receive usage statistics from the vendor at the end of the trial, and collect information about the members' desires to subscribe to the product. If there is sufficient interest, the liaison person then ensures that the vendor is aware of the ANKOS licensing principles and the Turkish National Site License (TRNSL).[7] The TRNSL is a model license which was developed by the ANKOS "Licensing Working Group" composed at that time of two library directors and an American legal librarian who was working in one of the ANKOS member libraries. The text of the TRNSL was drawn up following a review of many model consortial licenses, with the addition of requirements specific to the Turkish situation such as the necessity of individual invoices and vendor support for user education with Turkish-language materials. Both the principles and the TRNSL can be consulted on the ANKOS web site. Negotiation of the contract is conducted by the Licensing Working Group together with a member of the Steering Committee.

At the same time that the text of the contract is taking shape, pricing is negotiated. Until now, price negotiations have been carried out in some cases by the liaison librarian and sometimes by a member of the

Steering Committee. At a recent Steering Committee meeting, however, it was proposed that the role of the Licensing Working Group should gradually be expanded to include price negotiations, because it was recognized that this is also an area requiring an accumulation of experience and the development of expertise.

TRIALING OF DATABASES

Trials of subscribed and proposed databases play an important role in the ANKOS selection process and decisions about continuation of contracts, and they are a preferred practice by vendors and libraries. ANKOS is offered some twenty trials a year by publishers. At the end of each trial, the usage statistics are collected by the ANKOS liaison, who also collects the reactions of the trialing libraries. For 2005, as a result of the trials in 2004, ANKOS made new agreements with SIAM (ten members), JSTOR (ten new members so far in addition to previously subscribed libraries), and Serials Solutions (eleven members). Trials also led to the enlargement of existing consortial agreements: the number of OVID members rose from fifteen to twenty-seven; Taylor & Francis from seventeen to thirty-five; Blackwell Synergy from twenty-six to thirty-seven; and MathSciNet from fifteen to twenty-three. Trials with ALPSP (Association of Learned Professional Society Publishers), BMJ (British Medical Association Journals), CSA (Cambridge Scientific Abstracts), CAB Abstracts, Economist Intelligence Unit, GeoRef, ISI Emerging Markets, Safari, Sage, and the World Bank did not result in contracts, either due to prices that the members could not afford or low usage. In a few cases there were disagreements about the licensing terms. Although there were several attempts at systematic downloading and robot usage during the trials, ANKOS was able to stop such misuse before it endangered the consortium as a whole. (The infrequent examples of such illegal use by subscriber institutions' users have been promptly dealt with also to the satisfaction of the vendors.)

EXPERIENCES WITH VENDORS

ANKOS licenses in 2004 were with journal publishers (e.g., Cambridge University Press, Elsevier), aggregators such as EBSCO Publishing and ProQuest, indexing services (including MathSciNet and the ISI Web of Science), and e-book suppliers. Some of these products had originally been subscribed to jointly by the libraries which subsequently formed ANKOS, and at the beginning, the subscriptions continued without the benefit of a license for the consortium. As the years pass, and with the help of the model Turkish National Site License, these relationships are gradually being formalized, which we believe is to the benefit of both parties. During these years, our contacts with vendors have shown us that while ANKOS may not be a sophisticated negotiator, in this new library world neither are a number of the firms we deal with. All of us are groping for the best way to proceed, and mutual goodwill and an open line of communication are the most important factors in reaching results that are mutually satisfactory.

Multi-year contracts provide a means for consortia to guarantee a price cap over the period of the contract. With ANKOS affairs being handled by a group of volunteers who all have full-time library jobs, three-year contracts are looked upon also as a way to decrease the workload of the liaison librarians, the Licensing Working Group, and the Steering Committee. By staggering starting dates there will eventually be fewer contracts to negotiate per year. The contracts are designed to allow new members to join after the first year, with all member contracts ending together when the original contract term is ended. The Licensing Working Group is also careful to include in the agreements a clause whereby the supplier guarantees not to rescind the contracts of all ANKOS members for the breach of contract of any single library, with a view especially to protecting the consortium against non-payment by an individual member.

As mentioned previously, ANKOS is a voluntary association, and despite a great deal of consideration and consultation, no means has been found to establish a legal bond between the members. In practical terms this means that each member institution signs a license for each product. It also means that ANKOS cannot collect funds from the members in order to pay a single consortium invoice, which would undoubtedly bring financial advantages apart from the fact that some vendors have refused to consider a deal which required individual invoices for the members.

According to Turkish law, the state universities have to spend their budgets for services received within the year; they cannot pay license fees for the next year. Also, the budgets of the state universities are opened during the year in installments, and the first funds are made available in April. Sometimes library funds are withheld or diverted by the university administration to other uses. These are among the situations which ANKOS must arrange with the vendors, and the solution to this one is often to employ an intermediary willing to pay the vendor on time and collect from the libraries later, charging a commission. This solution is favored by many vendors who, it should be recognized, have been very patient with delayed payments. We hope that the payment issues will be resolved by the expected change in regulations which will allow universities to move to a multi-year budgeting system.

A modification in ANKOS contracts since 2004 has been the decision to license only electronic access to the sources. This leaves the print subscriptions to be sorted out by the individual members who wish to continue receiving them. This decision was taken in connection with ANKOS' desire to base fees not on each member's previous individual print holdings but on the overall consortial holdings and total fees paid previously by the members, with the total ANKOS fee to be divided up by ANKOS among the members. It was also a result of the difficulties encountered subsequent to the passing of a new tender law affecting state universities, which requires that the universities call for competing bids by several vendors for the supply of print subscriptions. Where there is only one possible supplier, the law requires that state universities present a document guaranteeing that the supplier has the exclusive right to market the product in Turkey and an Embassy document ("Apostille") certifying the guarantee.

PRICING NEGOTIATIONS AND FEE DISTRIBUTION

Cost division models are new for many consortia, and we want to mention three which have been presented at E-ICOLC meetings. The Swedish consortium BIBSAM and the Finnish consortium FinELib[8] have models similar to each other in that they are both based on FTEs and prior fees or, if usage statistics are available, they may be used to identify user groups and their populations. FinELib uses the same cost division model for all databases subscribed to by the consortium, whereas BIBSAM has several models, taking into account the size of the potential user group. Both groups acknowledge that fee distribution is an ongoing process that needs to be transparent so that member libraries feel that it is fair. In this connection they have both found it useful to limit the range of costs to members by setting maximum and minimum fees. As will be seen below, both models have similarities with models applied by ANKOS, although in ANKOS there has not been a conscious setting of upper and lower limits to prices. The BIBSAM and FinELib use of FTE is also different, in that students and teachers/researchers are weighted differently and according to field of study, whereas in the ANKOS case this was done only for the IEEE agreement.

Another cost division model, applied by the Consortium of Academic Libraries of Catalonia, was discussed at length by Lluis Anglada and Nuria Comellas in their 2002 article.[9] This model is based on "dimensions or characteristics" of the institutions and the cost of their print holdings. Anglada and Comellas emphasize the difference in teaching between universities in the USA, UK, and northern Europe and those in the southern European countries, where the traditional method of large classes and lecture notes is also the case for the majority of Turkish universities. They also criticize the definition of FTE as used in the English-speaking countries because education authorities in many European countries do not record their student data in terms of FTE. On this subject, however, Turkey is similar to the English-speaking countries, since there is a time limit for completion of studies and detailed statistics on researchers and students according to level and department are available from the Council of Higher Education.[10]

Pricing is an aspect of the ANKOS agreements which requires time, innovative thinking, and patience. Most, if not all, early ANKOS contracts for electronic access were based on print subscriptions held by the ANKOS members. In the first years this seemed an obvious and even fair approach. As pointed out earlier, however, many Turkish universities, especially the newest ones, have no or very few print subscriptions, and the pricing schemes of the publishers were allowing them access at a tiny fraction of the amounts paid by older members. Initially this situation was accepted by the larger or better funded libraries as a way to bring resources to the less fortunate institutions. As the years passed and the better-off libraries were supporting an ever increasing number of members at higher and higher percentages of the costs, the Steering Committee undertook to convince the vendors to agree to a total price for the consortium and leave the distribution to ANKOS. This has been accomplished with several three-year contracts, both with aggregators and journal publishers, although with expressions of concern from the libraries whose yearly subscription rates increased more than they had expected.

The first publisher with whom ANKOS signed an agreement which included an ANKOS-dictated fee structure was the Thomson Company for Web of Science (WOS). All ANKOS/WOS members subscribe to two indexes (in all but one case *Science Citation Index* and *Social Sciences Citation Index*) and may choose to subscribe also to the third. Member libraries were grouped by ANKOS into four "tiers" according to a formula which gave points to each library for the number of its full-time equivalent (FTE) four-year undergraduate students, postgraduate students, and teaching staff;[11] its collection budget; and the degree to which English is taught and/or used for instruction in the institution since all ANKOS contracts are, so far, for English-language materials.

The first three-year Thomson contract which used the ANKOS tiering system ended on December 31, 2004. For the new three-year contract certain changes were made by ANKOS in the membership of the pricing tiers, taking into account the amount of use made by the members of the database agreement (use per FTE). In these calculations, FTE, budget, and use/FTE were weighted equally and extent of English use was given a lesser weight. Another modification was the addition of a fifth tier, which allows disadvantaged institutions to join at a greatly reduced fee. Tier 1 members pay the highest amount with the new Tier 5 paying 22 percent of the amount paid by Tier 1. An auxiliary benefit to ANKOS members, although not reflected in the current license agreement, is a favorable price for back years, again based on the ANKOS tiers. The 2005-2007 agreement has been accepted by fifty-nine libraries.

Another publisher with whom ANKOS has a tier arrangement is IEEE. A first abortive attempt at forming an ANKOS/IEEE consortium for 2003 was followed by more successful negotiations for 2004, whereby twenty-two ANKOS members had access to the IEL. That agreement was for one year, and the ANKOS libraries that joined were grouped according to FTE figures for the respective university's departments of electrical and electronics engineering, computer engineering, physics, physics engineering, and biomedical engineering, as follows: the number of undergraduate students was multiplied by a factor ranging from 0.1 to 1 assigned to the institution according to the amount of English instruction there. (Institutions where teaching is entirely in English were assigned the factor 1.) To that number was added the total of postgraduate students and teaching staff multiplied by 3. The universities were then divided into three groups according to their total FTE as calculated, so that the institutions with FTE > 1,399 were assigned to Group 1, FTE = 800-1,399 to Group 2, and FTE < 800 to Group 3. Group 1 libraries paid the highest amount, Group 2 paid 25 percent less, and Group 3 paid 50 percent less for the IEL database. In addition, TUBITAK paid a special price for access by its various installations across Turkey. Although it was originally ANKOS' intention that the new contract be for 2005-2007, this was not realized. For the year 2005 there were twenty-five members, grouped in the same manner as for 2004, with the same percentage price increase for each group.

Although ANKOS members have had subscriptions to EBSCOhost databases for a number of years at ANKOS negotiated prices, 2005 marks the first time a formal license agreement had been drawn up. Members were divided into groups paying different amounts for the same databases and a multi-year contract has been signed with yearly price increases agreed upon. There was a moderately successful attempt to make ANKOS subscriptions more uniform (i.e., to have all members subscribe to the Premier version at a favorable price rather than some to the Elite version). This was accomplished only for Business Source Premier.

In 2005, the ANKOS Steering Committee members involved in contract negotiations experienced difficulties due to the lack of experience of some member libraries' directors. Not realizing the importance of confidentiality, certain details were made available more widely than should have been the case, which set off a fierce competition between vendors' local representatives in an attempt to wrest ANKOS members from each other. From the eventual decisions of the ANKOS members, however, favoring one product over another appears to be more a matter of habit than anything objective since although there were many subscriptions dropped from and added to each, only one library appears to have dropped one of these products in favor of the other.

During the past year, one publisher which has been the subject of much discussion and controversy in the international library community is Elsevier, and ANKOS was not an exception in finding the early negotiations difficult. ANKOS members have had agreements with Elsevier for Science Direct (including Academic Press, since there had already been an ANKOS agreement for those journals before the publisher was taken over by Elsevier) since 2001, when a one-year contract was signed. That was followed by a three-year contract which ended on December 31, 2004. The earlier contracts were based on each member's prior print subscriptions, with an added value for cross-access to all Science Direct subscriptions whether subscribed to by an ANKOS member or not.

For the new contract Elsevier presented ANKOS with an extremely complicated formula by which it charged members according to prior print holdings or lack of them with several add-on fees, which resulted in an unacceptably large increase over the 2004 fee. ANKOS presented a counter-offer which, although based on the 2004 "total spend," brought about some important changes in addition to reducing the price significantly. Based on prior print holdings, it was pointed out that seven members of the sixty-two were paying 64.5 percent of the total

ANKOS fee paid to Elsevier. This meant that their fee per use of the database was much higher than the average of the other fifty-five members. After examining the fee distribution details, the ANKOS Steering Committee decided to reduce the seven members' share of the total to 54 percent and distribute the difference among the other fifty-five members. The fee for accessing ANKOS non-subscribed titles was split equally between all sixty-two members. Fifty-eight of the former sixty-two members accepted the new contract and four new members signed on. Because the new contract could not be finalized by the end of 2004, an interim short-term agreement was signed to allow time to complete the negotiations for the three-year license agreement.

Kluwer Academic, and its new owner Springer, had also been ANKOS vendors with their respective one-year contracts ending December 31, 2004. Despite the fact that their merger had been announced a year ahead, and an early request from ANKOS for a merged three-year renewal contract, the new Springer was unable to propose such a contract until early December. Due to the unacceptability of its terms, ANKOS chose to make a one-year contract in the hope that a more reasonable agreement could be achieved during 2005 for later years.

Other contracts have also been renewed for 2005 (ACM, Blackwell Synergy, Bowker, ebrary, Emerald, Gale, MathSciNet, Ovid, Oxford University Press, Taylor & Francis, Wiley InterScience). Some of these are straightforward and some less so and will be the object of intensified efforts by ANKOS for more favorable conditions in subsequent years as negotiators have more time available from not having to renew every contract each year.

REFLECTIONS ON OUR EXPERIENCES

In the four years of working with the consortium, we have acquired knowledge in negotiation and licensing as well as greater awareness of the emerging digital environment for libraries and issues of scholarly communication. The process of selection and licensing of electronic collections is now fairly well defined. Negotiations and licensing are still carried out by a small number of librarians, but we plan to enlarge this working group. Similarly, more librarians need to be involved in user education and evaluation of usage statistics. In this connection we are planning to invite foreign experts to give training workshops for ANKOS member libraries.

Due to the diversity of the libraries, from time to time there has been a communications overload in dealing with access and payment problems of the members. At the beginning, there was little understanding among librarians of the importance of consortial work and the rapidly changing information environment. In time, however, every academic library has acquired one or more of the electronic collections licensed via ANKOS. Besides the many new libraries which were born in the digital age and therefore have predominantly electronic collections, many other libraries are moving to e-only subscriptions; of the sixty-two members of ScienceDirect, only eight libraries continue to have print subscriptions.

Although library budgets are better than they were four years ago, many libraries have funds that are disproportionate to the size of their institution. Another factor which complicates the licensing process is the direct involvement of university administrators in decisions for the libraries, which causes an additional workload for ANKOS.

Since ANKOS became a member of SPARC Europe, scholarly communication and open access have been discussed more intensively in Turkey. On its agenda for the future, ANKOS plans to give attention to stimulating institutional repositories, management of electronic resources, and supporting research and reference work.

CONCLUSION

ANKOS has gained valuable experience which has helped to shape its expectations from and approach to working with vendors. As the number of members and vendor contracts grew, the importance of having a clear and comprehensive license agreement became more obvious. Thus, while ANKOS is managed and operated by volunteer library directors and their staffs, a few of those volunteers have the ongoing responsibility of negotiating contracts. They have attempted to reduce this workload over time by preferring three-year agreements when possible and advantageous.

Fee distribution is another subject which has gained importance with the expansion of the consortium. Whereas the fee distribution in early contracts was dictated by the vendors, more recently ANKOS has agreed on a global figure with distribution of the costs being the province of the consortium. At this point in time, ANKOS has five main types of contractual arrangements: (1) "e-only plus consortium fee"; (2) "print plus consortium fee"; (3) "population (FTE)-based"; (4) "scaled" (price decreases depend on increase in number of members); and (5) "ANKOS-imposed groupings" by FTE, collection budget, level of English and usage. Only one vendor applies a fixed fee for all institutions within the consortium.

Only three vendors have been dropped by ANKOS. Ten ANKOS members subscribed to Safari E-books in 2003. Because of the limitation on concurrent users and complications with swapping book titles, the database was not used efficiently and ANKOS decided not to continue with it for 2004. In late 2004 the vendor offered a new trial and relaxed the concurrent user restrictions a little, but this time there was not sufficient interest among the institutions to reach an agreement. ANKOS had included E-Village in its subscription list in 2002. Originally this database was subscribed to by a group of universities with the same fixed price for each institution. Despite our warnings, the vendor arranged three-year contracts with libraries ending in different years. From 2002-2004 we observed big differences in the usage by member institutions, and we proposed that the vendor take the size and usage of the institutions into account and work out a differential pricing. Due to the vendor's resistance to changing its practices and pricing policy, ANKOS decided not to have a contract with E-Village for 2005. ANKOS had an agreement for 2002 with Micromedex, but it was not renewed due to insufficient interest.

While early contracts covered print and electronic versions of journals, as of 2004 ANKOS has left print subscriptions to the individual libraries to handle while the consortium makes agreements only for e-access. It is to be hoped that a means will eventually be found to give ANKOS legal status, to enable it to obtain external funding, and to allow ANKOS to collect fees from its members in order to deal with the vendors as a single customer.

Library users and librarians realize that the consortium has achieved access to resources undreamed of in Turkish academe just four years ago. It is the hope of the ANKOS librarians that this will be acknowledged in a way that will lead to its permanence as an institution.

NOTES

1. Bulent Karasozen and J. A. Lindley. "The Impact of ANKOS: Consortium Development in Turkey," *Journal of Academic Librarianship* 30 (2004): 402-409.
2. *Official Gazette* 28 December 2003 (supplement, no. 25330) and personal communications of the directors of the private universities.

3. Council of Higher Education webpage. Date last accessed: 14 January 2005. (http://www.yok.gov.tr/istatistikler/istatistikler.htm). Personal communications of library directors.

4. *2004 ÖSYM Yükseköğretim Programları ve Kontenjanları Kılavuzu* (Student Selection and Placement Center Guide to Higher Education Programs and Quotas).

5. (http://www.heal-link.gr/SELL/index.html) Date last accessed: 10 January 2005.

6. (http://www.ankos.gen.tr/index.php) Date last accessed: 14 March 2005. The ANKOS web site lists licensing firms and participant institutions with information such as the time periods of the licenses and the ANKOS member libraries in each contract, a description of the ANKOS structure, and a list of member libraries, their directors, contact details, IP ranges and ANKOS liaison librarians.

7. Jane Ann Lindley. "The Turkish National Site License (TRNSL)," *Serials* 16(2003): 187-190.

8. Kari Stange, Kristiina Hormia-Poutanen, Karin Bergstrom Gronvall, and Eeva Laurila. "Cost division models in BIBSAM and FinELib consortia," *Serials* 16(2003): 285-292.

9. Lluis Anglada and Nuria Comellas, "What's fair? Pricing models in the electronic era," *Library Management* 23(2002): 227-233.

10. Council of Higher Education web page. Date last accessed: 14 January 2005. (http://www.yok.gov.tr/istatistikler/istatistikler.htm). Personal communications of library directors.

11. Council of Higher Education web page. Date last accessed: 14 January 2005. (http://www.yok.gov.tr/istatistikler/istatistikler.htm). Personal communications of library directors.

Library Advisory Boards:
A Survey of Current Practice
Among Selected Publishers and Vendors

James R. Fries
John R. James

SUMMARY. This article reviews publisher and vendor use of library advisory boards. While they are not new to the information industry, library advisory boards have assumed new importance. From the industry perspective, library advisory boards provide valuable market feedback concerning products and services. For librarians, membership on library advisory boards is an opportunity to learn about new products, provide feedback on existing products, and better understand the information marketplace. Recent literature is reviewed and a number of publishers and vendors are surveyed. The uses and organization of advisory boards and their value to both companies and the library community are presented. *[Article copies available for a fee from The Haworth Document Delivery Service: 1-800-HAWORTH. E-mail address: <docdelivery@haworthpress.com> Website: <http://www.HaworthPress.com> © 2006 by The Haworth Press, Inc. All rights reserved.]*

KEYWORDS. Advisory boards, library-vendor relations, library-publisher relations, market research

James R. Fries is Feldberg Business Engineering Librarian (E-mail: james.r.fries@dartmouth.edu); and John R. James is Associate Librarian (E-mail: john.r.james@dartmouth.edu), both at Dartmouth College Library, Hanover, NH 03755.

[Haworth co-indexing entry note]: "Library Advisory Boards: A Survey of Current Practice Among Selected Publishers and Vendors." Fries, James R., and John R. James. Co-published simultaneously in *Journal of Library Administration* (The Haworth Information Press, an imprint of The Haworth Press, Inc.) Vol. 44, No. 3/4, 2006, pp. 85-93; and: *Library/Vendor Relationships* (ed: Sam Brooks, and David H. Carlson) The Haworth Information Press, an imprint of The Haworth Press, Inc., 2006, pp. 85-93. Single or multiple copies of this article are available for a fee from The Haworth Document Delivery Service [1-800-HAWORTH, 9:00 a.m. - 5:00 p.m. (EST). E-mail address: docdelivery@haworthpress.com].

Available online at http://www.haworthpress.com/web/JLA
© 2006 by The Haworth Press, Inc. All rights reserved.
doi:10.1300/J111v44n03_08

INTRODUCTION AND BACKGROUND

Library advisory boards are a unique source of information for vendors, publishers, and librarians. They provide valuable insights and perspective from customers and help vendors and publishers better understand how their products are used and perceived. For librarians, advisory boards are an opportunity to provide critical assessment and feedback; better understand the applicable company, its industry, product development; and also learn from and interact with colleagues. Further, the advice given has a direct impact on the development and improvement of products and services that librarians provide to their end users.

Advisory boards are not new to the information industry. A 1992 survey of the use of advisory boards among database producers and search services found that "some information industry companies have had advisory boards for a long time, and that it appears that a growing number of companies are starting to use this way of keeping in touch with their customers." The article noted that advisory boards had existed since at least 1976.[1] Though written some thirteen years ago, the observations made in this thorough examination of the use of advisory boards are very relevant to the current scene.

Advisory boards can help companies build stronger relationships with customers. In a more recent paper, Tony Carter, a professor of Sales and Marketing Management at Columbia University, observes:

> Many larger firms have a customer advisory board or its equivalent. Fortune 500 firms such as IBM, Merck & Co., and The Equitable have them and have found them to be extremely helpful in their customer relationship building process. . . . Customer advisory boards allow a company to listen and keep in touch with their customers, a very effective way to build trust and promote retention. The board will obviously never replace talking to customers during sales calls, but boards do provide a formal interface where the relationship is based on honesty, not negotiation.[2]

Customer advisory boards are a powerful tool often used in the corporate sector to target special needs and provide insight and advice that goes beyond the typical focus group or customer survey. The customer advisory board mechanism allows for a continuing dialogue between customers and companies, offering a greater benefit than typical market research, and the opportunity to quickly explore new ideas or act on negative feedback. In a paper examining the use of advisory boards in corporate settings, Susan Stautberg of the Corporate Board notes that companies such as CIGNA, The Financial Times, Swissotel and Avis successfully use customer advisory boards, emphasizing that "advisory boards are not a one-time focus group, but a continuing dialogue with experts who are current or potential customers."[3]

A 1992 study showed that of approximately seventy Fortune 500 companies surveyed, twenty-one had customer advisory boards; nineteen found them to be an "extremely or somewhat effective tool in the customer relationship building process."[4] Advisory boards help 'think outside the company,' strengthen customer relationships, better understand the customer's perspective and opinions, and gain timely feedback on business performance.[5]

Fisher described the recent history of relationships among publishers, vendors, and libraries. He cited accelerating change and increasingly complex operating environments as factors contributing to poor communication between librarians and vendors. He comments that "there is little doubt that the way all publishers, vendors and libraries conduct their business has dramatically changed over the last 20-30 years. While some of these changes have been beneficial and fostered a sense of cooperation . . . other developments have only served to heighten the tension among the three."[6]

Publishers and vendors face a hypercompetitive marketplace and business environment characterized by rapid economic and technological change, and continual product development and innovation. To remain competitive, they must understand and respond to customer needs, wants, and expectations. They must continually scan their environment to monitor competitors' moves and assess evolving customer preferences. Their market knowledge helps librarians better understand and gain perspective on the changing landscape of professional, scholarly, and commercial publishing.

For librarians, the information marketplace can be complex and often confusing. An array of products, business models, license terms, lease or purchase decisions, and other factors occupy attention on a daily basis. Librarians maintain frequent contact with vendors and publishers to stay abreast of seemingly continuous change in the marketplace as well as to provide feedback on products and services. Through their direct work with ultimate end-users and their understanding of how information products are actually perceived and used, librarians are in a unique position to influence publishers and vendors, and ultimately can help to improve the product development process. Librarians, publishers, and vendors together bring expertise and knowledge to advisory boards, enriching the experience for all.

In today's complex and competitive market, advisory board members who bring non-traditional viewpoints to the table are highly valued for their ability to build the partnerships that incubate new ideas and products to meet customer needs and market demands. In a 1999 article on advisory boards, Stautberg discussed the fact that they tend to draw "out of the box thinkers."[7] In a 2000 discussion of advisory boards, Stautberg described board members as "off the grid thinkers" who can afford to be open and forthright.[8] Information industry companies today are seeking input from cutting-edge thinkers with new perspectives and ideas to fuel product design and innovation.

USE OF ADVISORY BOARDS IN THE INFORMATION INDUSTRY

We surveyed twelve information industry companies and librarians to better understand the role and value of library advisory boards. Through our sampling we attempted to gauge opinion from both perspectives–the publisher or vendor maintaining a board, and the librarians serving on a board. The questions asked of publishers and vendors (see Appendix) were intended to provide a general picture, not a comprehensive assessment.

From the responses, a set of core activities emerge as playing a part–to one degree or another–in everyone's use of advisory boards. These include:

- product development
- product improvement
- market strategy
- market research
- market trends analysis
- customer feedback
- standards compliance
- unmet needs and gaps

Depending on companies' priorities and needs, the emphasis on or importance of any of these activities could vary from board to board. In addition, companies using multiple boards segmented by market or product may work on a range of specific tasks and activities that may differ at the detail level. For example, one firm reported using sixteen advisory boards for different purposes, including tasks such as software and thesaurus development.

Over the last decade, the use of advisory boards has matured. In the Van Camp article,[1] it appears that the main focus of most companies was on new product development and product enhancement. Developing, enhancing, and refining products in response to market demands were noted as important tasks. While in a broad sense this remains true, many companies are realizing the board can add value in novel ways. Companies' boards now play a broader and more complex role, even helping companies set business, product, and market strategy. One firm reports that the focus of advisory boards has shifted from a purely product-focus (product development, improvement) to activities such as identifying future directions and strategy for the publishing enterprise. Another company has involved its board in developing and recommending product philosophy and policy as well as in specific activities such as production procedures and recruitment. Yet another firm has engaged board members and their organizations in joint product conceptualization and development.

Advisory boards today are doing more than providing input, opinion, and comment on product development and enhancement. They are engaged in providing advice on a broad range of activities that surround product development, including:

- Business/corporate strategy
- User education
- Interface design (look and feel)
- Software development (functionality)
- Technology trends analysis
- Role of faculty, librarians, end-users in the research process
- Futures and futurizing
- Platform development (users, interface, software, and how they interact)
- Joint product development and development partners
- Product conception

These new board roles and responsibilities reflect the seemingly continuous pace of technological change, the potential impact and influence of new and emerging information technologies on products and customers, and constant economic and cost pressures. Nevertheless, the bottom line remains a focus on customer needs, wants, expectations, and satisfaction.

As advisory board member roles and responsibilities mature, they are evolving in new directions. Beyond offering opinions and providing feedback on particular products, board members are contributing at a strategic level. Publishers and vendors are seeking high-level strategic assessment, perspective, thinking, as well as development partnerships–all this in addition to input on product development. Traditional and emerging roles and expectations for library advisory boards are simultaneously unfolding in response to the seemingly continuous pace of technological change, a more complex business environment, new and emerging information technologies and their potential impact and influence on products and customers, and economic and cost pressures. An important outgrowth of advisory boards are the individual partnerships with board members and their institutions to develop new products for the marketplace.

VALUE OF ADVISORY BOARDS

Ultimately, an advisory board's value is determined by the quality of its advice and counsel and its impact on a company's product and market strategy. A successful advisory board depends on: (1) board members who are knowledgeable, informed, and enthusiastic contributors, and (2) board operating processes, structure, and organization that work efficiently and foster a collegial working environment open to new ideas and thinking. Through their knowledge and insights, board members provide expertise that the vendor would otherwise not have, or could gain only through costly market research.

Board composition (who serves on the board, what organizations and institutions they represent, members' network of colleagues and contacts) is an essential ingredient for board success. The board's work plan should be designed to elicit board member ideas and best thinking. It should also encourage open communication and candid feedback, a team approach to problem identification and problem solving, a climate fostering a long-term working relationship among board members, and a partnership with the company. Board structure should be designed to provide non-binding advice with no legal or financial authority or responsibility. Such a structure should also be flexible regarding both composition and life span of the board itself.

Carefully considered board composition, effective board process, and efficient structure can produce the ultimate value of an advisory board–bringing superior products to market, thereby helping companies build and maintain competitive advantage. One or more of the firms surveyed listed the following benefits of an advisory board, which were seen as being of real importance and major factors in assessing the value of an advisory board:

- faster product development cycle time
- continuous product and process improvement
- up-to-date market and customer knowledge
- "big picture" views on industry direction and trends
- strategic thinking and analysis from customers
- candid, unfiltered feedback
- input on effective marketing messages and strategies

Across the board, vendors surveyed found advisory boards to be invaluable to their company's work. Vendors discussed benefits such as being able to draw on a network of experts beyond the board itself, the development of innovative pilot projects and entirely new products not previously considered, better understanding of industry standards, and deciding to defer a proposed product or direction due to uncertain marketplace acceptance. Advisory boards clearly can help companies maintain a proactive, rather than a reactive, position to better anticipate and meet customer and market needs.

Librarians also see advisory boards as a valuable forum for working and communicating with publishers, vendors, and colleagues. For them, the positive benefits of board service include gaining a better understanding of "how we use and how we want to use" products. One librarian commented that if the advisory board channel did not exist, librarians would be further removed from the range of issues that form the library/publisher or library/vendor relationship. As is the case with publishers and vendors, librarians see many more positives than negatives in serving on an advisory board. Librarians gain a better understanding of the publisher or vendor perspective on customers and the market and have a real opportunity to influence company decisions. Librarians realize that their input and candid assessment are highly desired. Underscoring this view was a publisher comment that librarian feedback through advisory boards has helped avoid costly business mistakes. Librarians have pointed out resources and problem-solving ideas that the publisher might not otherwise have considered. For the publisher, this has provided a much better understanding of both the business aspects of managing libraries as well as the cultural aspects of libraries.

CONCLUSION

The challenge for information companies today is to rapidly innovate in order to meet evolving market needs. In today's competitive business climate, the most successful information companies will be those firms that can create products that provide what customers want and expect. To meet these challenges, many companies and industries are making greater use of different methods to solicit feedback from customers: feedback forums, service quality surveys, and customer advisory boards.[9] In this environment, advisory boards benefit the company (e.g., informing product development, product and process improvement, market strategy) and the library (e.g., greater awareness and understanding of industry and market trends, direct impact on corporate pricing and marketing policies). Our survey results and feedback from publishers, vendors, and librarians show that library advisory boards not only support product development and improvement but also directly contribute to the creation of new products that fill market needs. Taken together, these trends suggest greater use of advisory boards in the future.

NOTES

1. Van Camp, Ann J., "User advisory groups and the online industry," *Online* 16, no. 2 (1992): 40-45.

2. Carter, T., "Customer Advisory Boards," *SalesLobby.com*, http://www.saleslobby.com/OnlineMagazine/0900/features_TCarter.asp.

3. Stautberg, S., "Using advisory boards," *Corporate Board* 20, no. 118 (1999): 21-26.

4. Ross, J., "Why not a customer advisory board," *Harvard Business Review* 75 no. 1 (1997): 12.

5. Lombardo, C., "Customer advisory boards: honoring your customers," *Accounting Technology* 20, no. 4 (2004): 21-26.

6. Fisher, W., "A brief history of library-vendor relations since 1950," *Library Acquisitions: Practice & Theory* 17, no. 1 (1993): 61-69.

7. Stautberg, ibid.

8. Finn, W., "A word of advice," *Director* 54, no. 3(2000): 82-86.

9. Compton, J., "Listening to customers earns CIMCO nearly perfect customer retention," *Customer Relationship Management* 8, no. 8 (2004): 51.

APPENDIX

Questions Asked of Publishers and Vendors Pertaining to Library Advisory Boards

1. What prompted *company name* to create an advisory board?

2. How long has *company name* used library advisory boards?

3. What criteria are used to select and recruit board members?

4. What is the purpose or focus of *company name*'s advisory board(s), e.g., new product development, strategy, marketing, etc.?

5. What has been the value of librarian participation on advisory boards?

6. How has *company name* gained from using a library advisory board(s)?

7. Has there been a down-side to librarian participation? (e.g., violation of confidentiality, agreements, or other problems?

8. How important is an advisory board in terms of its impact on *company name*'s market research effectiveness? In other words, what's the relative weighting and value of the advisory board in comparison to other ways that *company name* does market research (through its sales force, through exhibits and presence at national/regional conferences through its advertising campaigns).

9. Where have advisory boards had the greatest/least impact and contribution?

   a. new product development
   b. environmental scanning/monitoring
   c. understanding/assessing customer satisfaction/dissatisfaction
   d. as one element in setting corporate strategy
   e. insight on user/market needs

10. Are *company name*'s advisory board members compensated and, if so, how?

11. Does *company name* have more than 1 academic advisory board, and if so, what is its purpose.

Library/Vendor Relations
from a Public Library Perspective

Ronald A. Gagnon

SUMMARY. Relationships are key to the success of any library project, and relations with the vendor's staff are too often overlooked or viewed as adversarial. Focusing on automated system and online electronic resource vendors, different functional departments of the vendor's staff are examined with an eye toward the benefits that a good relationship can bring to support the project. The evolving database marketplace is reviewed, particularly in light of the multiple buying cooperatives many public libraries find available to them. *[Article copies available for a fee from The Haworth Document Delivery Service: 1-800-HAWORTH. E-mail address: <docdelivery@haworthpress.com> Website: <http://www.HaworthPress.com> © 2006 by The Haworth Press, Inc. All rights reserved.]*

KEYWORDS. Public libraries, library automation, vendor relations, consortia, electronic resources, databases, innovative interfaces, EBSCO, NOBLE

Relationships are critical to the success of all library projects. While relationships with constituents and funding authorities are easy to un-

---

Ronald A. Gagnon is Executive Director, North of Boston Library Exchange (NOBLE), 26 Cherry Hill Drive, Danvers, MA 01923 (E-mail: Gagnon@noblenet. org).

[Haworth co-indexing entry note]: "Library/Vendor Relations from a Public Library Perspective." Gagnon, Ronald A. Co-published simultaneously in *Journal of Library Administration* (The Haworth Information Press, an imprint of The Haworth Press, Inc.) Vol. 44, No. 3/4, 2006, pp. 95-111; and: *Library/Vendor Relationships* (ed: Sam Brooks, and David H. Carlson) The Haworth Information Press, an imprint of The Haworth Press, Inc., 2006, pp. 95-111. Single or multiple copies of this article are available for a fee from The Haworth Document Delivery Service [1-800-HAWORTH, 9:00 a.m. - 5:00 p.m. (EST). E-mail address: docdelivery@haworthpress.com].

Available online at http://www.haworthpress.com/web/JLA
© 2006 by The Haworth Press, Inc. All rights reserved.
doi:10.1300/J111v44n03_09

derstand and important to address, the role of a library's relationship with its vendors should not be underestimated.

The library's relationship with vendors needs to be considered an important investment, but it is one that is too often overlooked. The investment involves building a relationship between the key library staff and the key people within the vendor's organization to foster understanding, improve service, and identify areas of mutual concern and benefit. Finding a vendor truly interested in such a relationship is key to a successful library implementation of that vendor's resources.

PUBLIC LIBRARIES ARE UNIQUE

Public library needs, while very broad in scope, are often different than those of academic and other research libraries. Vendors must understand and recognize these differences in designing and providing products to public libraries. From a research and development point of view, many products start out as innovations for the academic market. Large academic libraries at prominent, prosperous institutions have specific high-level needs and the operating budget and support staff to aid in development and implementation. There is also more competition among well-known universities and their libraries, as they compete for scholars and students, have a greater willingness to be on the cutting edge of technology, and possess a realization of the need to invest in resources and infrastructure to remain competitive and among the top institutions. "The demand for places in the top 25 schools is so strong that . . . these colleges have an enormous excess supply of students who not only can pay current charges, but also would cheerfully pay even more for a ritzy degree," according to *Forbes*.[1]

While public libraries also have a strong desire for excellence, efficiency, and service improvements, their audience is strictly defined by geography and their budget is more heavily constrained by the vagaries of the local economy which provide the publicly funded support resources through taxes. Increasing community demands for public safety, school improvements, elderly support, roads, etc., within a flat or dwindling pool of funding present priority challenges to budget authorities in counties and municipalities. So, public libraries often have less money to spend, and the average resident has no easily accessible cost-free alternative.

IT'S WHO YOU KNOW

Librarians interact with vendors at many levels at different times in the acquisition and implementation process, and it is their duty to press for the development of products for their constituency. Key members of the project–higher-level administrators overseeing the project as well as the key person running the project–must get to know as many people in the vendor's company as possible. Responsive companies provide many opportunities, often at larger national conferences since those meetings bring together the more active and high-profile practitioners almost automatically. Companies also go beyond conferences as well, inviting selected groups of customers for informational retreats or feedback sessions.

Librarians need to distinguish their library when meeting with company representatives, and make it interesting, memorable, and appealing both to retain a spot in the memories of key personnel and to be seen as the kind of library that will be a shining example of success with the company's products–which may bring opportunities later. Be charming and positive, even if things currently are not quite up to expectations. This will help to get the vendor on the library's side and to see that perspective, for no matter how rosy the current situation, the vendor's help will probably be needed sooner or later.

SALES

The initial point of interaction with a vendor is likely with its sales representatives. Too often, in listening to salespeople, it can seem that everything is possible, available, and included at no extra charge! Particularly at first, view all claims with healthy skepticism and be sure to get it all in writing.

Negotiation is an important aspect of any large project or contract. Negotiation needs to be a win for both sides for a successful project. Negotiations set the tone and define the terms of the relationship for years to come. Neither side will ultimately benefit from cut corners. Shortchanging training, file sizes, server capacity, etc., while saving money initially (and netting the vendor the contract in price competition) may result in a rocky implementation, discord, and additional charges later when funding and institutional support are no longer available. A good project implementation typically results in positive word-of-mouth advertising for the vendor, and a successful project will generate more sales for the vendor in the longer term.

While it is said that a true salesperson could sell anything success-fully, a truly effective salesperson takes the time to understand the needs and issues of the particular institution. The lack of this desire to connect and understand does not bode well if it is representative of the company's attitude. Salespeople's livelihood and employment are contingent on closing sales. But in a relatively small and communica-tive industry such as libraries, a salesperson needs to take the longer perspective and view satisfaction and straightforward dealings as an op-portunity for future sales to the library in question and neighboring in-stitutions.

The long view, however, is often not in favor in corporate America. Corporations, due to stock price pressures, the need to acquire or be ac-quired, and other pressures, often focus only on the short-term and cur-rent quarter. For the salesperson, this can translate into "damn the relationship, sell, sell, sell." There have been examples of this in the li-brary industry, particularly after a company is acquired by a larger cor-poration. Situations like this should be avoided by the library, since the long-term prospects are bleak. As a colleague once observed after a smaller company was acquired by a multi-national corporation, "Have you ever seen this to be a good thing for the customer?" Very often, it is not. "Customers thought they got better service or prices from only 29% of mergers," according to data collected over five years as part of the American Customer Satisfaction Index in an analysis done for *Business Week*.[2]

Interestingly, among library automation system providers, the com-pany with the longest solo history, Innovative Interfaces Inc., led the market in sales in 2003. "In its 25th year of operation, Innovative In-terfaces led the industry in earnings, captured more new-name sales than its competitors, and ranked second in overall sales," according to *Library Journal*'s annual automated marketplace report.[3] Innovative President and CEO Jerry Kline participated in a 2003 panel discussion with CEOs of most of the major integrated library system vendors, and noted that his tenure as Innovative president was 25 years while all the other executives had been in their positions less than three years.[4] Inno-vative and other successful companies focus on the long term, don't overpromise, and listen to their customers and librarians in general.

IMPLEMENTATION AND TRAINING STAFF

To work together toward a successful conclusion, the vendor's staff and the library staff responsible for implementation need to make sure they have a mutual understanding of the project. Consult as soon as possible with implementation and training staff. Make your situation, timetable, and project idiosyncrasies known early so that they can be accommodated in the schedule and researched and resolved as necessary. Try to avoid surprises, and make sure all the facts are known that can affect your implementation.

Ask the vendor for staff who are familiar with libraries of your size and situation to be assigned to your project. Decide early on whether the vendor will directly train all the library staff or only a core set of trainers that will train the remainder of the staff. The latter can often work better, as the local trainers can translate the vendor language into something more useful to the rank and file and eliminate options that the vendor will need to present but that do not apply to your situation.

When training and implementation is wrapping up, be clear that all issues are addressed before signing. The library may never have quite so much attention again. Also, be sure to have a contact for continuing questions and issues that will arise.

If dealing with a situation where training days are purchased from the vendor, libraries should include in the contract or budget for an additional day or two of training and consulting months after the project is released to the public. Only after using a product for a few months can we really find the gaps in our knowledge and the product's performance. Initial training can be overwhelming. After a few months of daily use librarians will be left with practical and philosophical questions on why the product cannot do a certain thing in a certain way. Having an arranged opportunity to explore these issues will be helpful for the promise it provides during the dark days of implementation and for the actual answers that will be provided.

PRODUCT DEVELOPMENT STAFF

The product development staff of the vendor are the most difficult to access because they usually take their input from within the company, not from customers. Conferences and user groups can provide a valuable opportunity to meet and discuss issues with them. If the library has an issue, be prepared with a brief description of needs and the wider application. Changes can happen easily if the right person hears the issue directly.

Be aware that product managers are always looking for libraries to test software and products. To achieve your objectives it is important to work with the company on such issues, and it is a great way to get the software to behave the way your library needs it to behave. But in testing, also keep in mind that you may be considered a typical representative for hundreds of similar libraries and that you do have a responsibility to be serious and thorough in your testing.

CONFERENCES

The library or consortium should be represented at conferences, particularly national conferences. Vendors' exhibits give the opportunity to preview upcoming product improvements, to comparison shop without obligation, to see if a vendor is on the right track, and if the library will be well-served by that vendor.

Conference receptions, lunches, etc., hosted by many vendors must be seen not just as a party or free lunch but as a golden opportunity. It is an opportunity to meet, on a semi-casual basis, with key "bigwigs" of the company, who will likely ask, in a general way, how things are going. This is a social occasion, not a negotiation session, and not an opportunity to pull out the library's punch list of issues. But it is an opportunity to give a strong signal that you have issues or questions and need to meet with someone. Have business cards handy to prompt follow-up. These events are social opportunities, so it should be a mix of business and sociability. Some may think accepting a glass of wine or a free lunch from a vendor somehow compromises one's integrity, but I contend it is an important opportunity to get to know people in the company, to be seen as active in the profession, and to build relationships with a diversity of the vendor's staff.

Vendor conference events are also an important opportunity to network with other librarians who are users of the same product and share concerns. Again, keeping it on a superficial level is appropriate at this kind of venue, but exchange of business cards could lead the way to future contacts on the valuable details.

USER GROUPS

Conferences can also be an opportunity for more organized user-group meetings. These vary widely from company "dog-and-pony" shows of new products to a legitimate opportunity for discussion and interaction with other users.

Large automated system vendors have their own multi-day user group meetings that combine all the good points of the above–presentations by the company and other users as well as opportunities for networking and informal discussions with company folk and colleagues. Most are efficiently run and organized by users with the participation of the company. The highly-focused sessions do incur separate travel and lodging costs but this is a very important opportunity for which serious users need to plan. Being represented is always important and should be regarded as a necessary cost for the successful implementation of the project or product. User groups, while independently organized, also have close ties with high-level company representatives and are also a good venue of mutual benefit, particularly if one is on the steering or planning committee for the meeting or doing a presentation.

Participating in organized discussions with the vendor and other users is often critical to make the product or service work optimally for your type of library or situation. One-time focus groups and standing advisory councils work with higher-level vendor representatives to gauge the product's strong points and gather input about the weak points. While these meetings require time and money for meetings and travel, the amount usually pales compared to what can be achieved by working with the company or the cost of custom development. Further, being willing to work with the company can often make the difference in getting the company to work with you in a crisis, both due to your willingness to participate and the personal contacts made previously.

REGULAR CONTACTS:
HELP DESK AND LOCAL REPS

Librarians should achieve and maintain credibility with service representatives to insure prompt resolution of issues. This level of respect is mostly earned, since often only the high supervisors of service and support attend the conferences. To impress the day-to-day staff who have the solutions to specific issues, library staff must do their homework. Library staff should have a checklist of preliminary troubleshooting before they call, both to establish credibility and to avoid wasting everyone's time. Include things such as verifying network connectivity and power, trying multiple workstations to gauge results, reading and understanding the documentation, and knowing what release (and what product!) you are running.

Even at home, one should stay in contact with local company representatives, meeting with them regularly to update them on specific situations and to find out about new developments within the company. Of course, a good company will also seek out librarians, and it is definitely worthwhile to make time for these meetings, even if nothing new is on the horizon for the library in the near future.

Of course the best participation and contacts in the world only really pay off with a stable company. Companies in a state of flux or closely tied to a conglomerate can see high level people come and go at an amazing rate. The reasons for the turnover include job security fears due to elimination of redundant operations and cost cutting and a change in corporate culture and operations.[5] When this happens, it is time to shop around, because a loss of focus and progress is likely due to merger activities, and a need to achieve promised cost efficiencies may cause service restrictions and cutbacks and a change in personnel on your account. The product will not improve dependably due to differing understandings and changing priorities.

REFERENCE SITES

Serving as a reference site is a great way to help future fellow customers, company sales staff, and yourself. A reference site is a reasonably happy, knowledgeable, and talkative customer similar in size and makeup to a prospective customer seriously considering your vendor. Most often these contacts are arranged by the vendor, but sometimes the customer finds their own contacts to get the "real scoop." For the current customer, serving as a reference site is a way to meet and perhaps begin a relationship with a new customer. It is also an opportunity for all library staff to review how far we've come, which is usually farther than we realize, and offer advice based on experience. The current customer should be frank but positive–our first duty is still to librarianship, not shilling for a company. The *Harvard Business Review* phrased it well in an article on customer satisfaction: "When customers act as references, they do more than indicate that they've received good economic value from a company; they put their own reputations on the line."[6]

A potential opportunity for the current customer can sometimes be found in the questions and the needs of the new customer. Often prospective customers seek a certain functionality which may not quite currently exist in the system but which the vendor could be willing to provide as part of closing the deal. Unless it is a whole new product, incremental improvements such as these generally come to the full customer base in a release or two. Sometimes the new software just misses the mark because the new customer is requesting and designing software for a system they have never used and the company's goal is to meet the letter of the contract. For instance, an automated system contract for a consortium seeking randomization of libraries to be selected as potential providers of needed items probably expected that the pickup point library item would be pulled if it was available. But random means completely random, and copies from 20 miles away are paged to fill a hold for a location with a copy available on its shelf adding to patron service delays, dissatisfaction, and needless handling and transportation costs. Working with the new customer on the issue by explaining or demonstrating the current system and suggesting solutions to fill a common need can result in a better product for all by helping the new customer to craft the solution in the best way.

Word of credible reference site visits will also become known to the company, raising your library's status and visibility in the company which can be helpful later. The company must be aware of the level of satisfaction of the customer before asking them to be a reference site. If they ask a genuinely unhappy customer to be a reference site, the library should make sure that the company knows this when asked. Hopefully the company will take this opportunity to address the library's issues, and probably withdraw the invitation. If the library has made its unhappiness known to the company and it is still asked to be a reference, then the company gets what it deserves. If a librarian is called directly by a library considering a product, without the company's intervention, then the librarian's duty is always to be honest for one's own credibility and to best assist the asking library.

PUBLIC LIBRARIES' DIVERSE AUDIENCE

While academic libraries and special libraries know their strictly-defined constituency and who in the hierarchy to especially satisfy, public librarians face the greatest challenges and opportunities in this regard. Everyone is a potential public library user and critic or supporter. Every possible education level and interest must be credibly covered by the public library. And since everyone in the community contributes to the support of the public library, it must be accountable to all. Toddlers to senior citizens, pre-readers to doctoral candidates, information seekers to escapist pursuits, the on-the-go to the homebound–all depend on the public library.

Almost any service offered by the public library is apt to be used by any of these persons and so requires a multi-level interface, or multiple interfaces, able to be used by nearly everyone. Children's interfaces to automated systems were popular a decade ago, but widespread familiarity with the World Wide Web's standard browser interfaces has somewhat reduced the need for the simplified and specialized interfaces. Access by younger users can be aided by providing ways to limit to specific sub-collections, such as the younger reader's collection in that building, and other limiters to steer users to materials at their level.

The need to access age-appropriate resources is greater now than in previous years since an amazing range of licensed materials is available in electronic format. Periodical database vendors each have their own specific databases geared toward different audiences and research needs. These range from primary school databases and databases limited to popular children's topics (such as animals) to high level research databases dealing with specific research areas (e.g., business, psychology or biomedicine, or historical primary source collections).

If a library has enough money, vendors offer something for every need. Beyond the basic large general periodical database, public libraries must decide the priorities needed by their community. Databases geared to younger researchers as well as business and health databases are frequently selected as they are popular among users and are profitable to families, businesspersons, and average citizens in the community.

Libraries also have the option to configure vendor databases to meet local needs, such as automatically limiting to full-text to expedite satisfying information needs through instant gratification, and limiting youth room workstations to accessing age-appropriate databases.

SO MANY DATABASES, SO LITTLE TIME

When first introduced a decade ago it was extremely difficult to integrate electronic resources with library print holdings; many interim steps have since improved that situation. Initially, database vendors provided libraries the ability to enter their print periodical holdings into the electronic product, so a single search on the electronic database could also uncover titles available only in print format, and provide knowledge about the availability of the print issue for heavily illustrated articles when just the text was not enough.

MARC records for the electronic full-text holdings are provided by some database vendors to participating libraries for loading into local online catalogs. This too improves access by making the complete realm of periodical holdings known and available through a live link to the electronic database for those titles. However, the ongoing content evolution of aggregated databases makes keeping the MARC records correct and indexed a constant requirement.

Web-based periodical list services have grown over the past several years, such as SerialsSolutions and EBSCO's A to Z. These lists are tailored for each library, integrating print subscription lists with individual and database electronic titles, providing links to the online titles. The online lists give a full representation of the library's periodical resources at a reasonable cost with wide accessibility. The databases can also provide useful management information in showing areas of duplicate access and providing usage statistics, and MARC records for loading into the catalog.

Library OPAC vendors have more recently provided the capability for dynamic subject-related linking beyond the catalog. With this capability, a search for a health topic would search the catalog but also provide a direct link to licensed health databases and selected Internet health sites. But these interim steps have not offered the power and appeal of the single federated metasearch. While there is significant initial set-up for the dynamic linking, sharing of lists among users has mitigated the set-up work greatly.

Libraries now have the ability to integrate all their resources through federated searching software. Muse, WebFeat, Follet, and integrated library system vendors all have versions of the metasearch software that, while initially costly, can be highly cost-effective in delivering information to users. Potentially overlooked resources from specialized licensed databases and expert web sites beyond the usual general database are brought to the fore through the federated search, maximizing the significant expenditures already being made for these electronic resources. Combining access to diverse resources can increase database usage and user satisfaction. Many public libraries have taken the lead in implementing federated database searching, since the single interface, single-search program is well-oriented to the quick search public library patron who is much more interested in instant results than a detailed, in-depth research process.

A CONSORTIUM OF CONSORTIA?

In addition to solo purchases of licensed electronic resources, libraries also participate in different groups that provide databases. In Massachusetts, a public library may have databases provided at their own cost through their local automated network, through their participation in the state-funded regional library system, and databases funded by the state library agency (the Mass. Board of Library Commissioners). State-funded college libraries have yet another cooperative purchasing group in addition to the public library resources.

A wealth of combined resources is available including general, academic, health, business, full-text Massachusetts newspapers, biographical and literary databases, e-books, and an encyclopedia. While each of the databases contribute to the general palette of resources available to the residents of Massachusetts, the wealth of resources does accentuate the benefits of metasearching software and the need for librarians to actively promote and explain all the resources available. And due to the variations of state funding which has affected both the regional and state database selection, the menu of resources has been in flux over the past few years.

Fortunately, the major database vendors have been noteworthy in their flexibility in renegotiations to provide reduced packages in financially troubled times within multi-year contracts. In Massachusetts, for example, this flexibility was critical as cuts to state-funded accounts supporting online databases ranged from 24% to 92% over the past few years. The principles of business still do apply to database vendors, however, and for the health of the industry and the profession, librarians must plan to support their database vendors in turn in the better financial times.

WHAT'S IN THE PACKAGE?

The major database packages are on multi-year contracts and librarians participate in the examination and selection of the database packages at renewal. For better or worse, however, inertia is dominant as librarians, accustomed to using databases from a given provider and having trained their patrons in their use, seem to invariably select the same database providers. The rationale is that they are deemed easiest to use, regardless of the merits of the titles and information included in the databases, because the librarians and their constituents already know how to use them.

The major database providers change the holdings of the individual databases and even split or combine databases over time as they compete for exclusives in popular titles to give them a marketing edge. Publishers such as AOL Time Warner are rethinking the marketing of their content, preferring to limit some access to only subscribers. As a result of AOL Time Warner limiting access to content of 13 magazines on their web site to subscribers, "the experiment is a remarkable success" according to the Wall Street Journal. "Subscriptions are up, traffic for most titles is steady despite predictions it would be halved, and ad sales are ahead of predictions."[7]

It is cost-effective for the library and vendor alike to negotiate for packages of databases from a single broad-based vendor. While a vendor may be marketing separate health, business, general, school, and academic databases, there may be a significant amount of overlap of titles across the databases, so the incremental cost of the additional databases from the same vendor is less than databases acquired from different vendors. A single vendor may provide the ability to search across all of their databases if a library decides to configure it that way, improving the odds of instant gratification and minimizing the amount of training required by librarians and patrons.

IMPROVED CONTENT, STABLE COSTS

Over time, the cost of the electronic databases has risen at a reasonable rate relative to other services, while the level of content has increased dramatically. In our consortium, the North Of Boston Library Exchange (NOBLE), we began in 1995 to negotiate with EBSCO Publishing (EBSCO) for 350 full-text titles. Today, we are still with EBSCO and enjoy access to over 4,000 titles in full-text, spread over several databases, with backfiles growing from years to decades, plus image databases and much improved search and linking techniques for a cost only a few percentage points more than a decade ago.

The major database aggregators worked with consortia from the beginning and encouraged group purchases. "Consortia purchases of databases have dramatically improved the quality of databases. There are a lot of new, better titles in the database as a result of competition. And unlike journal subscriptions, the rate of inflation for database prices is not even close. They're negligible,"[8] confirms a Library Journal cover story on "Aggregators." There are many reasons for the relatively stable costs in the mainstream databases, including economies of scale from a rapidly increasing customer base, technology that dramatically lowers the cost of online storage and bandwidth, and competition.

THE NOBLE MODEL

In the Massachusetts model, services acquired at the local consortium level are paid from the individual library to the consortium, a local non-profit providing an automation system, Internet and database services, and related training. The direct payment from the library, and the library's need to justify the spending to their funding authorities, tend to provide a greater level of oversight and input on consortium services than on services provided by larger entities based entirely on state funding beyond their direct control.

NOBLE provides a standard package of databases to our members, which is approved by a full vote of membership at renewal, with the option of acquiring additional databases from the same vendor, EBSCO, through NOBLE. While the discounts on databases are directly related to the volume of libraries choosing each particular database, the discount on a database taken by only a few libraries is not as significant as the discounts on databases taken by all the libraries. However, the ease of ordering, combined billing, and common interface provide less tangible but still significant cost savings and improved efficiency for less popular databases acquired with a group purchase. NOBLE serves as the first point of support for our libraries with all of our vendors, which also saves time in implementation and troubleshooting. In this way, libraries benefit from having a say in the general selection, being able to tailor a package of databases meaningful to them as funds allow, with a single support point.

We have proven to our members the value of database acquisition through consortia rather than as a standalone library. One library that more recently joined NOBLE saw their database costs decrease by 40% for a comparable package.

As a non-profit, NOBLE is able to negotiate directly with vendors and not subject to strict bidding laws of statewide contracts and even some local contracts. The smaller size of our consortium, 28 members, allows for more flexibility and customization when compared to regional and statewide contracts with hundreds of members.

Consortia purchases have allowed libraries to get into database projects earlier than they would have on their own. While needing to agree on a package can result in a selection that does not meet each library's needs exactly, the service benefits have been great. "Consortia are actually raising the bar as far as library services. I know I've been told by many a librarian, we could never have afforded this if it had not been for the consortium purchase. So I'm sure there are lots of libraries that have materials. It is a homogenization, which sounds negative, but I think it's raising access for libraries, and so it's actually a good thing,"[9] explained Diane Smith, Director, Academic Strategic Initiatives for LexisNexis.

NOBLE also represents our members in meetings with our vendors and we participate in focus groups and ALA conference meetings that individual libraries may not always be able to attend. We learn our members' concerns and issues through conversations, training sessions, and roundtable meetings hosted by NOBLE. We bring these concerns to our vendors through the appropriate channels and take advantage of all opportunities as active and vocal participants.

TOO MUCH OF A GOOD THING?

Our libraries also have the option to acquire products through an even larger consortium, NELINET, the traditional OCLC vendor for much of New England. NELINET provides a valuable service to libraries in securing discounts with a multitude of vendors, but given the large number of products presented and the over 600 affiliated libraries,[10] the perception of NELINET over the years has evolved from a member-driven cooperative to a sales-driven jobber. Despite getting an early jump in the consortia hierarchy, NELINET's early focus on academic and large libraries, due to the OCLC services, left smaller and public libraries to form various levels of consortia in Massachusetts.

The multiple levels of consortia, group purchases, and buying clubs can cloud the issue for both the library and the vendors. Vendors are leery of buying clubs due to the uncertainty of potential volume. In an ideal consortium, a defined membership has decided to commit as a group. The decision is made on known parameters. Buying clubs such as NELINET in New England "want the best price but can't promise membership participation,"[11] explains Ed Roche, Director of Sales for

Canada and Northeastern U.S. for EBSCO Publishing. In some cases large optional consortia can work if not too many other groups are vying for deals. A strong and effective group, established early, can limit the growth of other multi-level consortia. "In New York State, WALDO is a trusted friend of libraries," relates Roche. WALDO, the Westchester Academic Library Directors Organization, is a non-profit consortium representing over 2,500 academic, school, public, and special libraries in New York State and provides support and training. "Even with an a la carte menu, libraries trust WALDO for the best prices,"[12] according to Roche.

True consortia also provide a level of support and training which buying clubs and other decentralized groups cannot, forcing participants to spend more local funds figuring out the intricacies of the product.

BEYOND LICENSED DATABASES

While licensed databases present a relatively safe and vetted research pool, much research is done on the general Internet with sometimes unintended and undesired consequences. Google is often the first source consulted, rather than the library's carefully chosen electronic resources. The Internet is a wonderful example of democracy, free speech, capitalism, and the amazing power of technology. Unfortunately, for library research the Internet has put librarians on the defensive, having to account for electronic resources made available through library workstations that can be wrong or highly offensive. Filters are a popular public library response, and a requirement of Federal E-rate funding to support Internet access. While filters reduce but do not eliminate the problem, they can bring their own unintended consequences and additionally bring acquisition and ongoing maintenance costs and responsibilities.

Filters, in a sense, are the ultimate relationship issue, testing the relationship with staff who vary widely on intellectual freedom and protectionism issues, the relationship with trustees and other governing authorities on how viewing of "improper" sites is handled, and the library's relationship with the public and the media. In light of all those issues, filters can be an imperfect but politically expedient way of handling a very prickly public relations situation.

IT'S ALL ABOUT RELATIONSHIPS

Ralph Waldo Emerson once wrote, "A man is a bundle of relations, a knot of roots, whose flower and fruitage is the world."[13] So it is with public libraries, crafting important and intertwined relations (and some funding) to provide improved and superior access to information and resources for the world.

NOTES

1. Susan Lee and Daniel Roth, "Edunomics," *Forbes*, 18 November 1996, 108.

2. Emily Thornton, Michael Arndt and Joseph Weber, "Why Consumers Hate Mergers," *Business Week*, 6 December 2004, 56.

3. Marshall Breeding, "Migration Down Innovation Up," Library Journal, 1 April 2004, 56.

4. Jerry Kline, Opening remarks, 2004 Innovative Users' Group Annual Conference, Boston, Mass., 3 April 2004.

5. "Firms Strive to Avoid Post-Merger Turnover," *Journal of Tax Practice Management*, May/June 2004, 10.

6. Frederick F. Reichheld, "The One Number You Need to Grow," *Harvard Business Review*, December 2003, 48.

7. Matthew Rose, "More Subscribe After Time Ends Free Web Access," *Wall Street Journal*, 8 August 2003, B1.

8. Andrew Richard Albanese, "An LJ Round Table with the Aggregators," *Library Journal*, 15 March 2002, 38.

9. Ibid.

10. NELINET website (http://www.nelinet.net).

11. Ed Roche, interview by author, January 10, 2005.

12. Ibid.

13. John Bartlett, *Familiar Quotations* (Boston: Little, Brown, 1919), 618.

Government Libraries:
Administering Change
in an Uncertain Future

Bradley E. Gernand

SUMMARY. This paper examines the future of government libraries in an information landscape which increasingly differs from that which preceded it. Several of the changes are discussed, such as the growing prevalence of privatization and outsourcing, as well as the increasing availability of e-books and e-journals, and the impact these have on collection development and composition. The increasing desire on the part of government customers to achieve some method and manner of information security are highlighted, along with ways in which government libraries may meet this need. And, finally, this paper suggests that budgets will continue to be unstable for at least the next several years, and recommends ways in which vendors and government customers may mitigate the resulting effects. *[Article copies available for a fee from The Haworth Document Delivery Service: 1-800-HAWORTH. E-mail address: <docdelivery@haworthpress.com> Website: <http://www.HaworthPress.com> © 2006 by The Haworth Press, Inc. All rights reserved.]*

Bradley E. Gernand (E-mail: BGernand@ida.org) manages library and information services for the Institute for Defense Analyses, serving the Office of the Secretary of Defense and Joint Chiefs of Staff; and the Science & Technology Policy Institute, serving the Executive Office of the President. Both are congressionally-funded nonpartisan research organizations.

[Haworth co-indexing entry note]: "Government Libraries: Administering Change in an Uncertain Future." Gernand, Bradley E. Co-published simultaneously in *Journal of Library Administration* (The Haworth Information Press, an imprint of The Haworth Press, Inc.) Vol. 44, No. 3/4, 2006, pp. 113-125; and: *Library/Vendor Relationships* (ed: Sam Brooks, and David H. Carlson) The Haworth Information Press, an imprint of The Haworth Press, Inc., 2006, pp. 113-125. Single or multiple copies of this article are available for a fee from The Haworth Document Delivery Service [1-800-HAWORTH, 9:00 a.m. - 5:00 p.m. (EST). E-mail address: docdelivery@haworthpress.com].

Available online at http://www.haworthpress.com/web/JLA
© 2006 by The Haworth Press, Inc. All rights reserved.
doi:10.1300/J111v44n03_10

113

KEYWORDS. FEDLINK, government libraries, vendors, e-books, e-journals, outsourcing, privatization, information, Internet, collection development, budgets, security, online resources, databases, information security, collection formats

Historian Francis Fukuyama must not have had libraries in mind when publishing his famous 1992 book, *The End of History and the Last Man*.[1] Rather than finding themselves in the cozy and well-known terrain of librarianship as it has been practiced for decades, or even centuries, twenty-first century government librarians are grappling with developments both large and small, most of which are arriving at a pace defying easy assimilation.

The terror attacks of September 11, 2001 changed many aspects of American life and government, some of them forever. In terms of impact, it has become the Pearl Harbor of the current day, changing how Americans think of themselves, their government and their civil rights, and launching changes which may not fully manifest themselves for years or even decades.

As observers and pundits today appear well to understand, the full impacts of the events launched by 9/11 will continue to unfold. Redrawn borders in the Middle East may be one result; changes in governments there have already occurred. Many in the public library community fear changes here at home caused by the Patriot Act.[2] In what ways have library-vendor relations changed–and what may be expected in the future?

Arthur C. Clarke, a popular science fiction writer who correctly predicted in the 1940s that satellites would one day orbit the earth and change communications completely, has remarked, "The future is a foreign country; they do things differently there."[3] Predicting events–i.e., going where fools dare to tread–is always a difficult exercise, but certain trends are already becoming evident, and bear examining.

If September 11, 2001 ushered in a different and more sober future than many had expected, it also coincided with massive changes sweeping the information industry–the Internet was coming into its own as a legitimate (and in some quarters preferred) information provision tool.

As *The Economist* magazine observed in a recent survey of the information technology industry, what we have experienced thus far in the Internet age is still just the proverbial tip of the iceberg; much more is yet to come. When comparing the Internet as a basic service or utility with electricity–an innovation which continues even now to change the world via the technology it enables–the Internet is still as electricity was in the 1920s, the magazine says.[4] Electricity during the Flapper Era had impacted only major industries and larger factories; many smaller businesses and customers were yet largely untouched by it. But all that was to change.

For government libraries the changes now underway in the information industry and government itself offer welcome opportunities and serious drawbacks. In some cases, the changes caused by September 11 and those caused by the ever-evolving Internet are the same; in others, they are mutually exclusive and comprise wholly separate issues.

ONGOING PRIVATIZATION

Government service once meant stable employment with enviable benefits, but no longer. Although the number of government employees has grown since 9/11, this has mostly been to staff the new Transportation Security Administration, and to buttress homeland security services. Government library operations for the past decade have been subject to outsourcing–as contracting operations to the private sector is known–and this trend continues.

Libraries serving federal departments, agencies, bureaus, and quasi-corporations are increasingly being turned over to the private sector, which competes for and manages them via a series of rolling contracts. Contracts, far from being uncompetitive or static, change with surprising regularity. Government agencies being served must acquaint themselves with wholly new library staffs and methods of operation.

Although outsourced libraries are much more bottom-line-oriented than federal ones, featuring few or no "dead wood" employees, these savings are offset by some of the drawbacks of contracting. In particular, the library spaces of federal department-level libraries were generally designed for larger, permanent staffs, and their sizeable book and journal collections require manpower-intensive maintenance, which contractors are often unable to afford. In some cases, library collections have become more or less uncontrolled and administered poorly as contract employees focus more on the immediate tasks at hand, such as providing daily reference service.

Privatization, long associated with Republican administrations, will become more of a necessity for both political parties through at least the near- and medium-term futures as federal budgets are forced further and further into the red by the potentially declining dollar, overseas military expenditures, and security requirements at home.[5]

Outsourcing should be approached with caution. The concept means many things to many people, and may prove the chief instance in which a process involving library operations is driven by people outside the library, with little understanding of patrons' needs–namely, organizational financial officers.

The view from "on high" may diverge radically from that of the library, at least when outsourcing is concerned. As mentioned earlier, outsourcing may lead to situations in which libraries become understaffed and unable to maintain book and serial collections which, for all practical purposes, become legacy collections dating from an earlier time in which technical staffs were present to control and administer them. The fact that this wastes an organization's previous and substantial investments in library resources may not be grasped by "bean counters"–financial officers with little understanding of how libraries operate.

Outsourcing also represents opportunities. The technical services arena is changing as libraries implement e-books and e-journals. These drive down the rates of interlibrary loan, diminishing that as a stand-alone function. Similarly, journals check-in now takes libraries less time and manpower to accomplish as fewer titles arrive in print format. This revolution frees staff to perform other duties, some of which, ironically, have arisen as a result of the information age! More to the point, it is now more difficult for small and medium-sized libraries to maintain technical staffs of the same size as formerly, without taking steps to enrich staff positions so that the persons filling them have appropriately challenging duties approximating forty hours of work per week.

For libraries unable to achieve this balance within the changed technical services environment, private-sector vendors may provide an answer. If journals check-in, or book ordering, or ILL are no longer full-time jobs, perhaps outsourcing one or more to a vendor is a solution. Blackwell and other companies now cater to libraries for just these sorts of purposes. And others, such as Barnes & Noble, now offer opportunities for fulfilling information requests which did not exist in the past. In this way the previous definition of outsourcing must be expanded. No longer does it mean spinning off duties formerly performed in-house; it now also means taking advantage of developments in the commercial information provision industry which may change the way we do business–for the better.

CHANGING COLLECTIONS

Electronic books, or e-books, which until now generally have fallen short of expectations and failed to win public acceptance, have suddenly begun to impact government libraries in ways unforeseen just a short while ago. The turn-around is due to a broadening variety of access formats, most of which resemble databases, in which the books are full-text searchable and are always available, usually to simultaneous readers. The database-style format is a distinct departure from the NetLibrary-style format espoused by OCLC.

Services such as Ebrary, which offers upwards of 20,000 titles from major publishers for a remarkably low price, are proving popular. Knovel, a database of science and technology books, is gaining ever-more footholds, and CRC Press, a widely respected publisher of science and technology information, has now launched a variety of book databases marketed in broad subject categories.

In terms of platforms, it is difficult to beat the leader, Wiley InterScience. Its platform, which allows its encyclopedias, books, and journals to be searched in a single search, may be limited to any one, two, or more such options. Its search engine is robust, and its search capabilities are highly flexible. Information technology books–long a devil of librarians due to the speed at which they become outdated and must be replaced–are being marketed via Safari and Books 24x7, competitors, which also offer full-text search capability. These two vendors, unfortunately, are examples of business models which are designed for corporate information technology shops, not libraries–they require individual user accounts and are not marketed as site-license flat-fee purchases except to academic libraries.[6]

Safari's and Books 24x7's business models, unfortunately, offer excellent examples of those designed with specific user communities in mind–namely, individual information technology professionals–and do not work well for libraries. Site licenses are generally not available to libraries outside the academic realm. Special, corporate, and other libraries wishing to make these resources available must do so on a user-specific basis. Someone within the library, or larger organization, must administer individual accounts. Rather than making the library's work process more simplified, these two companies offer examples of business models which cause libraries more work. The site-license model is almost always preferable.

All these services furnish MARC records, so that library catalogs remain an important part of the information discovery process. Users may link to these books from individual MARC records, at least when held via site license. And the databases which supply them may be positioned by librarians to appeal to specific groups of researchers–Ebrary, for those with more catholic tastes, as example, and Safari to those interested mostly in information technology.

E-books not only are here to stay, but will also consume ever-large quantities of government library acquisition budgets. Considering the instability represented by outsourcing, this method of book acquisition may now be preferred. Contractors will be more, not less, likely in the future to begin new government library contracts by furnishing book collections at the clicks of a button, rather than by the more human-intensive methods of individually selecting and physically ordering, marking, and shelving books. This ensures the information is available to researchers and on a scale appropriate to the size of the current library staff. Subscribing to an online package of book titles, as example, requires payment of only one invoice and yields immediate access to several hundred book titles. Product selection, invoice payment, and downloading MARC records into an organizational catalog could well be administered by a very small staff–a boon for outsourced libraries. Providing the same resources in print would require a substantially larger staff.

Electronic journals are also proving widely popular, but these met with quicker public acceptance and demonstrated their utility early on. Whereas e-journals resembled, and sometimes are, exact replicas of their print ancestors, e-books have not until recently appeared to resemble their print versions, either in print or usability. And whereas e-journal articles are generally available for downloading or printing in full, e-books are hobbled by the fact their vendors often limit printing to several pages at a time–offering hardly a replacement for a print copy, from which pages may be photocopied in large numbers. As we all know, researchers occasionally ignore copyright laws, and their wish to be able to do so will continue to govern what they think of e-books–despite our wishes to the contrary.

Online journals marketed by certain for-profit publishers will continue to be out of the reach of government libraries, but those published by the learned societies and other not-for-profit groups will be necessary purchases. Open Access publishing, a growing segment of journal publishing, will likely prove a boon to acquisition budgets as impact factors slowly swing from longstanding print journals to the newer open source and inexpensive journals, such as those made available by BioMed Central and Project Euclid.[7]

NEW RESEARCH TOOLS

Google, the world's most popular Internet search engine,[8] is pioneering digital access into the world of print libraries and journals via a series of projects which hold great promise to researchers and the librarians who serve them.

One, a Google initiative to digitize books from the collections of several prestigious American and British universities and public libraries, should do wonders for the process of information discovery. The project aims to make freely available published content from works now out of copyright protection, and snippets of information from works still protected by copyright. All in all, government researchers should be better able to locate relevant books, which may then be obtained via ILL or by purchase.

Another Google initiative, currently finishing a year-long pilot launch, was developed by Google in conjunction with almost thirty major publishers and learned societies. The publishers are allowing Google to enter their proprietary systems and digitize content, which is searchable via a special Google search box. Researchers in organizations holding site-license to content represented in the search hits are able to link directly through to full-text. This may make the use of expensive federated ("single-search") software unnecessary.

However, this initiative will require significant refinement if it is to prove both popular and successful. At present its searching is limited to one box only, without any advanced searching capability. Unlike mainstream Google, it does not offer an "Advanced Searching" capacity. But even so, the promise of searching Google just for the content of major publishers, without searching the broader Internet, should guarantee the eventual success of this project. Before long, those publishers that have resisted this advance (usually for-profit companies), will find themselves required to engage in it, or be shunted to the sidelines.[9]

To some degree this ability is already available to government researchers whose libraries subscribe to online abstracting and indexing databases. Researchers in the government health and medical libraries, as example, searching MEDLINE for relevant abstracts may then link directly into their libraries' site-licenses for *Nature, Science, JAMA, New England Journal of Medicine*, JSTOR, the American Chemical Society, the American Society for Microbiology, or aggregator databases. Google's initiative may draw research business away from the established abstracting and indexing databases–but since searching vast oceans of full-text information is often overwhelming, services such as Inspec, MEDLINE, Web of Science, and Elsevier's new Scopus product will likely continue to be a staple of the government's science and technology libraries.

Web of Science and Scopus are not cheap, however. Cash-strapped government libraries may instead elect to rely on the abstracting/indexing provided by aggregator databases, such as ProQuest and EBSCO. Both abstract and index many more journals than they carry in full-text, allowing scholars significant breadth and depth of view into available research for a relatively cheap cost. The drawback of these two vendors is that their abstracting and indexing generally begins in the 1990s. While broad in scope it is shallow in depth. EBSCO also licenses subject-specific indices, such as ERIC, MEDLINE, Inspec, and others, which currently take coverage in these respective fields back to the 1950s for MEDLINE, 1968 for ERIC, and 1898 for Inspec. Searching and linking is seamless, providing quite a lot of research bang for relatively few bucks. No vendor or publisher has yet offered access via abstracting and indexing to the huge information trove represented by the journals included in JSTOR. And Google, by the nature of its arrangements with participating publishers, does not access JSTOR.

INFORMATION SECURITY

One unforeseen consequence of the Internet revolution in government libraries has been an increasing discomfort on the part of researchers, librarians, and security experts concerning the query data accumulated by search engines accessed by researchers within a library's site license. This discomfort stems from different quarters for different reasons.

JSTOR reports increasing requests by university researchers for anonymous searching–that is, the ability to enter search requests which cannot be attributed to any specific university, campus, or research institution. Many university or government scientists, as example, engaged in time-sensitive or competitive research, do not wish their research interests made known to anyone else. This question has grown as courts have ordered such information providers as cell phone companies and Internet service providers to provide customer usage records. The government's Patent and Trademark Office is one example of an agency which considers the question of sufficient importance to spearhead discussions with major online vendors as to ways in which the potential negative consequences may be averted.

Lexis Nexis already offers government customers the ability to establish encrypted links to and from its servers, and also pledges not to collect search query data for agencies requesting this special step. Dialog offers similar options.

Some libraries have resorted to local loading of tape data provided by vendors, so that the libraries themselves control all record of search activity. This also allows for a certain comfort in guaranteeing that information bought only from online sources, and not in print, will always be available to an institution, come what may with the original information provider.

One example of this concept in practice is the highly successful approach employed by the Los Alamos National Laboratory. The Laboratory library downloads many hundreds of journals produced by numerous publishers and vendors. In this manner, the Laboratory's scientists may direct their queries to the Laboratory's servers and not via the open Internet to the publishers themselves. In this way, confidential or security-sensitive queries may still be made of the data, but directed to a secured source. Such an endeavor requires a large technical staff, but–such is the cost of security.

The security of information will undoubtedly remain an important consideration for certain government institutions, such as the Patent and Trademark Office cited here, and vendors should expect continuing and increasing requests from government customers for anonymous searching and for more sensitive handling of the accumulated search query data.

What may vendors do to empower government libraries to access their data safely and securely? Arrangements such as the one at Los Alamos may be key, at least for journals and conference proceedings. Information contained in less mainstream databases is not included in utilities such as that of Los Alamos, however, and will require separate, stand-alone arrangements.

Government customers tend to be enthusiastic customers of JSTOR, as example. JSTOR's holdings may not be downloaded into locally-hosted utilities due to the nature of JSTOR itself, which involves a host of arrangements with individual publishers, and also due to technical limitations. And military offices tend to utilize the daily updates appearing on the web sites of the Defense Daily Network and "Inside Defense."[10] Much of the value of these sites is from information which is updated daily and is not packaged within the confines of a standard journal title. In all these instances publishers should be willing to consider agreeing to host encrypted links between customers and the vendors' servers, to allow for site-to-site transmission security, and also make changes in processes and procedures by which their systems stop logging query data from government customers. EBSCO and JSTOR are two vendors which have indicated to various customers a willingness to engage in these unorthodox–but increasingly necessary–arrangements.

Whatever the method of customer access, usage statistics will be vital for government libraries if they wish to continue or expand use of online resources. The need to purchase certain online print resources is often an open-and-shut case. But funding large-scale online purchases is, for many government agencies, still an exotic venture. Providing tracking data to a library manager's superiors, particularly if it helps make the case for renewal or purchase, will be utterly necessary. Publishers not yet doing so should get on the "COUNTER-compliancy" bandwagon or offer tracking data of similar scope and characteristics.

FLEXIBLE PAYMENT OPTIONS

Federal libraries are plagued by insecure and untimely financial arrangements, and these will continue. The dreaded "continuing resolution," by which federal agencies often find themselves financed by Congress on an ad-hoc basis, force libraries to withhold payments for services until monies become available in a more permanent fashion. This sometimes strains the letter of procurement contracts, which occasionally call for payment within a fairly short time frame.

Vendors need to institutionalize the continuing resolution in their planning. Government libraries will experience this need on what will likely be a recurring basis, as the federal budget deficit and contested spending priorities in Congress cause budgeting to be a highly politicized process for at least the next several years. Payment options should be lengthened and designed to be more elastic than they are at present.

Some vendors already cater to this need by planning in advance, even if informally, for government libraries to require more time than private-sector customers to generate payment. Vendors should give government libraries ample wiggle room, and not penalize them for lack of prompt payment. Chaotic budgeting may be the lot of government libraries for years to come. Crystal balls are notoriously murky, but ours should prove accurate on at least this point!

CONCLUSION

Arthur C. Clarke, cited earlier for his thoughtful remark that the future is a different country with different customs, habits, and circumstances, has made the future of information and its impact on society one of his life's interests. Even he, however, would likely concede that no sage with his crystal ball will be able to predict what the future holds for government libraries. Certain trends seem guaranteed to wreak changes, either for better or worse.

The difference will depend on whether government libraries seize the day–*carpe diem*–or allow themselves to be buffeted by these changes, and forced into a reactionary mold. Government librarians often appear to assume they are powerless to influence and shape events, but this is not true. Examples of government libraries which are successfully shaping the environments in which they operate are those of Los Alamos National Laboratory, cited here, and the Naval Research Laboratory. Both libraries have shifted their collecting focus, engaged in visionary electronic initiatives, and been proactive in working with publishers to ensure their needs are met.

Privatization, so often imposed upon libraries from on high, may prove beneficial to a library's health. By outsourcing certain aspects of work the scarce dollars in a government library's budget may be stretched, often with gains in efficiency, and without the declines in morale which many assume will automatically occur. Of all the changes occurring in the library world this is the one in which libraries have the least ability to manipulate–but even so, this is by no means guaranteed, particularly if they initiate selective outsourcing rather than waiting for cost-conscious financial officers to do it.

Government librarians should never wait for patrons to drive or suggest changes to the composition of their collections. By planning for and initiating the switchover from print to online resources, they will earn the respect of their users and be proactive in making the changes occur. Anticipating users' needs is key, but certain tools help. Journal citation rankings allow government librarians to focus on key titles or packages, and reviews of online packages and vendors allow very educated guesses to be made as to which may prove the most popular.

Similarly, taking advantage of the new research tools such as those offered by Google or the publishing industry need not be a reactionary process. Some government libraries actively participate in fashioning or refining these new research tools by providing the vendor with helpful and welcome feedback.[11] Shouldn't yours?

Information security will be an ever-expanding watchword during upcoming years, particularly for government research and development libraries. Here, there is strength in numbers, and by allying with agencies with similar needs, libraries may approach vendors as part of a united front. Certainly, vendors will profit from this approach as it allows them to resolve issues just once, and apply the solution across a larger swath of customers.

Likewise, there is strength in numbers in arranging with vendors for flexible payment options. But here a library's good relations with vendors come in handy, too. Approaching the issue via purchasing consortia such as FEDLINK or regional and local consortia may do the trick–but arranging in advance with vendors may prove equally effective.

Change may be a vehicle for bettering the research environments in which government libraries and librarians work–but only if the libraries take a role in advancing the changes.

Carpe diem!

NOTES

1. Francis Fukuyama, *The End of History and the Last Man* (New York: Free Press, 1992).

2. Librarians' opposition to certain provisions of the Patriot Act has received extensive coverage in the national media. However, with the Act up for renewal, two articles are helpful for framing and discussing the overall debate in the library community: Paul T. Jaeger et al., "The USA Patriot Act, the Foreign Intelligence Surveillance Act, and Information Policy Research in Libraries: Issues, Impacts and Questions for Libraries and Researchers," *Library Quarterly*, April 2004, vol. 74, no. 2, pp. 99-121; and Zara Gelsey, *Humanist*, Sept./Oct. 2002, vol. 62, no. 5, pp. 38-39.

3. Arthur C. Clarke, *Profiles of the Future* (New York: Warner Books, 1984, p. ix).

4. This article cites earlier research by Robert Gordon of Northwest University and Paul David of Oxford University, both of whom found that productivity gains and other economic, industrial and social impacts of electricity took years to realize. Their research indicates today's Internet has not yet by any means equalled the impact that motor cars and electricity had at a similar time in their development and popularity. *The Economist*, Sept. 13, 2003, vol. 368, no. 8341, "Special Report."

5. Some of the positive and negative aspects of library outsourcing are covered by Herbert S. White in his article, "Why Outsourcing Happens, and What To Do About It," *American Libraries*, Jan. 2000, vol. 31, no. 1, pp. 66-71. The most widely available book on the subject appears to be Arnold Hirshon and Barbara Winters' *Outsourcing Library Technical Services: A How-To-Do-It Manual for Librarians* (New York: Neal-Shuman, 1996). Hirshon and Winters detail only case studies of successful outsourcing projects; anecdotal evidence in the library community suggests many in-

stances in which the outcome was much less rosy. As this book makes clear, however, outsourcing is here to stay, and looks certain to expand.

6. Readers may access the Wiley and CRC Press search interfaces at www.wileyinterscience.com and www.crcnetbase.com. The best view of the CRC Press interface may be found at www.engnetbase.com.

7. BioMed Central and the Public Library of Science have made well-known inroads by helping establish Open Access as a functional alternative for scientific publishing. Less well known is an online resource serving the mathematics and statistical sciences disciplines, Project Euclid, which brings together journals from university of not-for-profit organizations whose goal is to offer a lower-priced alternative to the more expensive for-profit publishers. See www.projecteuclid.org for more information.

8. "How Google Works," *The Economist*, Sept. 18, 2004, vol. 372, no. 8393, "Technology Quarterly" section; "The Ranking," *Business Week*, April 4, 2005, vol. 3927; "Google–Innovation Under Fire," *PC Magazine*, June 8, 2004, vol. 23, no. 10.

9. Participating publishers currently number over 40 and include for-profit publishing giants Taylor & Francis and John Wiley & Sons, as well as many of the world's chief scientific publishers, including the American Institute of Physics, the Institute of Physics, and the Nature Publishing Group. Prominent university presses represented include those of Cambridge, Oxford and the universities of California and Chicago. The Google initiative is a partnership with CrossRef. See http://www.crossref.org/crossrefsearch.html for more information.

10. Defense Daily Network, owned by PBI Media, Inc., is found at www.defensedaily.com. It features 11 publications. "Inside Defense," owned by Inside Washington Publishers, Inc., is found at www.insidedefense.com. It features 7 publications. Both sites are updated daily and offer a host of collateral data in addition to their flagship publications.

11. Some vendors utilize library advisory boards. Those that do, profit from receiving valuable feedback and input from customers. Many, however, do not employ such boards, and for them the communication flow is entirely between customers and account representatives.

Library-Vendor Relations
in the World of Information Standards:
A View of a Partnership That Improves
Research, Information Access,
and Revenue Opportunities

Pat Harris

SUMMARY. In all business communities, standards development is a collaborative activity that requires the participation of all players in the value chain. This article looks at how NISO's current work, supported largely through a collaboration of vendors and libraries, relates to trends and innovations in library services management. It also gives insights into how the information community accomplishes its standards goals through multiple channels. Featured sections include historical perspectives on information standards and discussion of major influences on the development of next-generation standards affecting library management. *[Article copies available for a fee from The Haworth Document Delivery Service: 1-800-HAWORTH. E-mail address: <docdelivery@haworthpress.com> Website: <http://www.HaworthPress.com> © 2006 by The Haworth Press, Inc. All rights reserved.]*

Pat Harris is Executive Director, National Information Standards Organization (NISO) (E-mail: pharris@niso.org).

[Haworth co-indexing entry note]: "Library-Vendor Relations in the World of Information Standards: A View of a Partnership That Improves Research, Information Access, and Revenue Opportunities." Harris, Pat. Co-published simultaneously in *Journal of Library Administration* (The Haworth Information Press, an imprint of The Haworth Press, Inc.) Vol. 44, No. 3/4, 2006, pp. 127-136; and: *Library/Vendor Relationships* (ed: Sam Brooks, and David H. Carlson) The Haworth Information Press, an imprint of The Haworth Press, Inc., 2006, pp. 127-136. Single or multiple copies of this article are available for a fee from The Haworth Document Delivery Service [1-800-HAWORTH, 9:00 a.m. - 5:00 p.m. (EST). E-mail address: docdelivery@haworthpress.com].

KEYWORDS. NISO, standards, standards development

WHY STANDARDS?

Information is one key ingredient for success in business and scholarship today, and standards are the foundation of all information systems. Many people think of standards as the "plumbing" that supports the system. However, technical standards provide more than plumbing–they provide the infrastructure that makes information systems and databases less expensive to develop, easier to use, and universal in value. Just as a house would collapse if its infrastructure were weak, an information system cannot remain standing or evolve without an extensible and robust support structure.

This understanding has led many professional and business communities, profit and non-profit organizations, consumers, government agencies, producers, and manufacturers to set common standards for their respective communities. The National Information Standards Organization (NISO) is the nationally accredited, and internationally recognized, standards developer that works closely with the library and information technology and publishing communities to set the standards needed by this important sector of the educational and business world. NISO is just one of four-hundred standards developers accredited by the American National Standards Institute (ANSI), the leading federation of standards developers in the U.S. These standards setters have disparate agendas, but share a desire to solve specific technical problems by achieving a level of uniformity that is supported across their respective communities. For vendors, this means customers can count on them for reliable products that consistently meet expected performance levels. For users or consumers, this means "friendlier" systems that give them predictable results.

In the library and information sector there are a number of organizations that complement NISO's standards reach. The International Coalition of Library Consortia (ICOLC) is one example. First convened in 1997 as the Consortium of Consortia (COC), this group remains an informal, self-organized network of about 150 library consortia worldwide. ICOLC was formed to facilitate the discussion and the sharing of information among consortia with regard to common interests such as the pricing practices of electronic information providers, the selection and purchasing of electronic content (books, e-journals, etc.), and information concerning new electronic information resources.[1] ICOLC

guidelines help ensure that customers of electronic information resources will have accurate and reliable usage statistics.

Another organization concerned with the development of standards for
statistical reporting by electronic information vendors is COUNTER
(Counting Online Usage of Networked Electronic Resources). Orga-
nized in 2002, COUNTER was formed by the Publisher and Librarian
Solutions (PALS) group, and is based in the United Kingdom.[2] COUN-
TER's standards for statistical measurement have won it global recog-
nition and support from other professional organizations such as the
Association of American Publishers (AAP), Association of Research
Libraries (ARL), and the United Kingdom Serials Group (UKSG).

The Digital Library Federation (DLF), chartered in 1995, is also concerned about standards. The fundamental aspiration of DLF is the development of a globally accessible digital library comprised of electronic
information collections garnered from a multitude of libraries and other
sources on an international scale. The DLF's Electronic Resource Management Initiative is developing common specifications for managing
the license agreements, related administrative information, and internal
processes associated with collections of licensed electronic resources.

NISO has much in common with these organizations but is different
in three important ways:

- NISO is accredited by the American National Standards Institute
  (ANSI)
- NISO makes its standards freely available on the Web
- NISO has seventy years of practical experience in serving the information community and its evolving priorities–from archiving
  words on paper to transforming research with computer technology[3]

NISO HISTORY

NISO grew out of a collaboration of the library and publishing communities and was launched in 1935 to "standardize" serial publications.
Libraries were challenged to catalog, collect, and provide access to the
growing body of serials and journal literature. There were few common
practices to support the production of serials and journals–everything
from page numbering, to issue numbering, to gutter size was done in an
ad hoc, "non-standard" way. Formally accredited by ANSI in 1941,
NISO set out to solve these problems. It did so with its first standard

Z39.1, Periodicals–Format and Arrangement. Interestingly, many of the problems confronted in the print world still exist in the digital information environment.

NISO's mission and program expanded with the onset of digital information exchange. Commercial forces began influencing timetables and agendas as it became clear that "library standards" could do more than make libraries more valuable and efficient–they enabled and improved information exchange and created commercial opportunities.

This is reflected in NISO's membership. Thirty years ago, NISO's members were mostly corporate libraries and professional associations. Today, NISO's eighty-five member organizations are content consumers, such as libraries, and information dependent businesses including publishers, content aggregators, and the companies that provide software and technology services. NISO serves the needs of many kinds of organizations, including libraries, whose business model depends on content, whether in a profit or nonprofit environment. For this entire community, NISO provides a neutral zone to explore common needs and solutions.

BREAKTHROUGHS IN STANDARDS DEVELOPMENT

The technical issues that engage NISO members in standards-setting encompass a wide range of information-related needs, including retrieval, re-purposing, storage, metadata, and preservation. The process of addressing these issues involves face-to-face and online meetings to gather and consolidate information on best practices, innovations, and emerging challenges. Participants develop and vet proposed solutions and combine the best available theoretical information with practical applications. The procedures NISO follows encompass three cardinal principles common to all consensus standards developers: due process (there is an established process to address questions and concerns from any interested party); openness (the development process is transparent and all stakeholders can participate); and balance (a variety of viewpoints are deliberately engaged).

Ironically, formal standards bodies such as NISO have long been the target of criticism as some contend that the consensus-building process takes too long. In response, NISO has adapted by streamlining its processes and offering new standards products. This response has resulted in the following strategies.

First, NISO has collapsed its standards development cycle. A convergence of factors has made that possible. NISO is selective in recruiting technical experts who have the expertise to produce superior standards, and the capacity to use technology for collaborative authoring and review. They grasp the potential of standards to reshape the information landscape and know that this will not happen if they rely on the old model of a three-to-five year development cycle.

Second, NISO's standards agenda has become more sharply focused on shaping an interoperable and linked information environment. NISO's recent work, driven by library and business needs, includes:

- The OpenURL standard–*The OpenURL Framework for Context-Sensitive Services* (NISO Z39.88-2004), now used by Google Scholar, takes context into account in web-based service environments. For example, a student searching for a scholarly information resource can obtain immediate access to the most appropriate copy of that resource. "Appropriateness" reflects the user's unique situation, such as the user's location, or the contractual or license agreements the user's library has negotiated with information suppliers.[4]
- Virtual reference–NISO has made significant progress in shaping protocols to support networked reference systems, one of the fastest growing new areas of library service. A proposed new NISO standard (Z39.90), now being tested, defines a method and structure for data exchange to support online reference services. While the service may be delivered via real-time chat or asynchronous e-mail, the essential characteristic of the service is the ability of the patron to submit questions and to receive answers via electronic means.[5]
- Circulation Interchange Protocol–The NISO Circulation Interchange Protocol (NCIP) enables a library to link its local circulation system to self-check machines, to other circulation systems in a regional or statewide resource-sharing consortium, and to traditional interlibrary loan systems. NCIP supports two-way conversations between systems, potentially offering unlimited interoperation. Patrons and staff benefit because NCIP services are robust and automated, offering self-service features and more immediate results for patrons.[6]

NISO has also forged productive relationships with organizations working on similar problems. For example, the Joint Working Party NISO formed in 2004 with EDItEUR (an international organization supporting the implementation of Electronic Data Interchange standards) is developing new standards to simplify the complex nature of serials data interchange.

NISO's standards development procedures have also been expanded. The Registration Process, launched in 2004, enables other communities to partner with NISO to share their guidelines, best practices, and other benchmark documents with the larger circle of potential users in NISO. The NISO Registration Process offers a lighter-weight review and accreditation to existing specifications developed outside the formal standards process. The newest NISO registration is the ARK (Archival Resource Key) Persistent Identifier Scheme, a collaborative effort with Internet Engineering Task Force (IETF) members and the California Digital Library. ARK facilitates the persistent naming and retrieval of information objects and does not require a proprietary resolver.[7]

NEXT-GENERATION PROJECTS AND ISSUES

NISO's current work is focused on enabling better solutions to support library services and library management; projects now in development include the following.

Metasearch Initiative

In 2004, NISO launched the Metasearch Initiative to frame technical solutions to the challenge of providing aggregated search services. A typical academic library licenses more than two hundred different electronic resources. To support efficient research, libraries need to provide search services that can seamlessly move across all of the aggregated resources that are licensed or unlicensed, provide complete bibliographic citations, and exclude extraneous sources. The vendors and librarians participating in the Metasearch Initiative are focusing initially on solving problems related to access management, collection description, and search and retrieval.

Digital Rights Expression

Rights expression languages and enforcement technologies are emerging in the commercial sector and the entertainment industry. However, these commercial solutions appropriate to the entertainment industry do not effectively address the needs of libraries and other content providers. A NISO sponsored pre-standards workshop held in May 2005 defined a set of tactical proposals to help resolve problems related to digital rights expression. Part of the solution will be to build on the DLF's progress with ERMI, referenced earlier in this article.[8]

Information Identifiers

One of NISO's longstanding and most successful core program areas is the identification of print and digital information. NISO was a leader in the development and use of the ISBN standard and ISSN identifier. Most recently NISO took the lead in supporting the revision of the ISBN expanding the ISBN identifier to 13-digits. The transition to the ISBN-13 will begin officially on January 1, 2006. However, as information delivery methods evolve, so do the need for identifiers. In 2005, NISO will bring together publishers, content aggregators, vendors, libraries, and others to explore the challenges in identifying digital content and collections.

Planning for the Future

NISO's Board of Directors understands that success in standards setting can only continue with a strategic plan of the highest calibre. Supported in part by a Mellon Foundation grant, the NISO Board launched a comprehensive planning effort in 2004. With the advice of an external Blue Ribbon Panel composed of thought leaders from various sectors of the information community, a redefined Strategic Direction was released June 2005.[9] This new Direction sets a roadmap for NISO's work and tasks NISO to create a framework to identify new areas of opportunity, gaps, and potential partnerships.

CONCLUSION

NISO has drawn participation from libraries, library vendors, publishers, content aggregators, technology vendors, and companies providing web-based information services–in other words: all parties engaged with the organization and distribution of information. This inclusive collaboration distinguishes NISO in the standards world. The results of that collaboration, in the form of pre-standards investigations, best practices, guidelines, standards, and registrations, are meeting the commercial needs of vendors and the service needs of libraries.

NISO VOTING MEMBERS

NISO's voting membership of eighty-eight organizations reflects the ongoing collaboration of libraries and vendors in the process of developing information standards. Many more organizations participate on an ad hoc basis, or in specific technical work.

3M
American Association of Law Libraries
American Chemical Society
American Library Association
American Society for Information Science and Technology (ASIS&T)
American Society of Indexers
American Theological Library Association
ARMA International
Armed Forces Medical Library
Art Libraries Society of North America (ARLIS/NA)
Association for Information and Image Management (AIIM)
Association of Information and Dissemination Centers (ASIDIC)
Association of Jewish Libraries
Association of Research Libraries
Auto-Graphics, Inc.
Barnes & Noble, Inc.
Book Industry Communication
California Digital Library
Cambridge Information Group
Checkpoint Systems, Inc.
College Center for Library Automation (CCLA)
Colorado State Library
Copyright Clearance Center
CrossRef
DAISY Consortium
Davandy, L.L.C.
Dynix Corporation
EBSCO Information Services
Elsevier
Endeavor Information Systems, Inc.

Ex Libris, Inc.
Fretwell-Downing Informatics
Gale Group
Geac Library Solutions
H. W. Wilson Company
Helsinki University Library
Index Data
INFLIBNET Centre
Infotrieve
Innodata Isogen, Inc.
Innovative Interfaces, Inc.
International DOI Foundation, The
Ithaka/JSTOR/ARTstor
John Wiley & Sons, Inc.
Library Binding Institute
Library Corporation, The
Library of Congress
Los Alamos National Laboratory
Lucent Technologies
Medical Library Association
MINITEX
Modern Language Association
Motion Picture Association of America (MPAA)
MuseGlobal, Inc.
Music Library Association
National Agricultural Library
National Archives and Records Administration
National Library of Medicine
National Security Agency
NFAIS
OCLC Online Computer Library Center
Openly Informatics, Inc.
OpenRFP, Inc.
Paratext
Polaris Library Systems
ProQuest Information and Learning
Random House, Inc.
Recording Industry Association of America
RLG
Sage Publications
Serials Solutions, Inc.

SIRSI Corporation
Society for Technical Communication (STC)
Society of American Archivists
Special Libraries Association (SLA)
Synapse Corporation
TAGSYS, Inc.
Talis Information Ltd.
The Cherry Hill Company
Thomson Scientific
Triangle Research Libraries Network
U.S. Department of Commerce, NIST, Office of Information Services
U.S. Department of Defense, DTIC (Defense Technical Information Center)
U.S. Department of Energy, Office of Scientific & Technical Information
U.S. Government Printing Office
VTLS, Inc.
WebFeat
Zone & Zone Co. Ltd.

NOTES

1. ICOLC Web site–http://www.library.yale.edu/consortia/.
2. COUNTER Web site–http://www.projectcounter.org/about.html.
3. NISO Web site–http://www.niso.org.
4. More information and a free copy of the standard are available at: http://www.niso.org/standards/standard_detail.cfm?std_id=783.
5. More information and a free copy of the draft standard for trial use are available at: http://www.niso.org/standards/standard_detail.cfm?std_id=804.
6. More information and a free copy of the standard are available at: http://www.niso.org/standards/standard_detail.cfm?std_id=728.
7. For more information on NISO registrations and URL for the electronic copy of the ARK scheme, visit: http://www.niso.org/registration/registration_approved.html.
8. For more information on the Initiative and discussion of the tactics proposed at the workshop, go to: http://www.niso.org/news/events_workshops/RE-workshop.html.
9. More information is available at: http://www.niso.org/members/secure/StrategicPlan.html.

Integrated Ecommerce in the Library: A Software Development Partnership Between Innovative Interfaces and the Westerville Public Library, Ohio

Jerry Kline
Don Barlow

SUMMARY. This article describes the opportunities, challenges, and results of a vendor-library development project to create an ecommerce[1] tool as an integrated facet of Innovative's Web OPAC. Westerville Public Library was engaged with the software development process from the outset, communicating administrative, technical, and service issues and needs while also testing the product with its customers. The project culminated in early 2004 with the installation of Innovative's Ecommerce product and resulted in the collection of large payments online and an increase in total fine revenue collected. Most notably, the team found that Ecommerce gathered nearly a quarter of all fines collected in 2004,

Jerry Kline is Chairman and CEO, Innovative Interfaces, Inc. (E-mail: jkline@iii.com).

Don Barlow is Executive Director, Westerville Public Library (E-mail: barlowd@westervillelibrary.org).

The authors would like to thank Kristen Hewitt of Westerville, as well as Dinah Sanders and Spenser Thompson at Innovative Interfaces, for their help in preparing this article.

[Haworth co-indexing entry note]: "Integrated Ecommerce in the Library: A Software Development Partnership Between Innovative Interfaces and the Westerville Public Library, Ohio." Kline, Jerry, and Don Barlow. Co-published simultaneously in *Journal of Library Administration* (The Haworth Information Press, an imprint of The Haworth Press, Inc.) Vol. 44, No. 3/4, 2006, pp. 137-155; and: *Library/Vendor Relationships* (ed: Sam Brooks, and David H. Carlson) The Haworth Information Press, an imprint of The Haworth Press, Inc., 2006, pp. 137-155. Single or multiple copies of this article are available for a fee from The Haworth Document Delivery Service [1-800-HAWORTH, 9:00 a.m. - 5:00 p.m. (EST). E-mail address: docdelivery@haworthpress.com].

and almost one-third of fines collected in the first half of 2005. The participants reflect on the nature and history of the partnership, outcomes, best practices, and future plans. *[Article copies available for a fee from The Haworth Document Delivery Service: 1-800-HAWORTH. E-mail address: <docdelivery@haworthpress.com> Website: <http://www.HaworthPress.com>* © *2006 by The Haworth Press, Inc. All rights reserved.]*

KEYWORDS. Ecommerce, commerce, OPAC, public libraries, software development, library fines, library circulation, integrated library system, partnerships, library management system, Innovative Interfaces, Inc., Westerville Public Library

INTRODUCTION

The following describes a software development partnership between Innovative Interfaces, Inc. and the Westerville Public Library, Ohio. The agreement arose from a mutual desire on the part of both organizations to see electronic buyer-seller transactions come to the digital library. During a period of two years, Innovative's Ecommerce product was conceptualized, tested, and implemented in a development partnership. The formal development phase began in January 2003.

What Is Ecommerce?

"Ecommerce" is a financial transaction conducted over the Internet between a buyer and a seller. Making transactions successful and secure requires the coordinated effort of a complex network of financial institutions and processors. Merchants must connect their store to this network of banks, processors, and other financial institutions so that payment information provided by the customer can be routed reliably, and confirmation of the availability of funds can be obtained in real time.

Demand on the Rise

This chain of instant, secure financial communication is now well established and in widespread use by retailers around the world. There are many providers for the necessary services, and the costs can be reliably predicted. The popularity of Web sites such as Amazon, eBay, and

Expedia have increased the average person's awareness of and comfort with paying with credit cards online. In fact, a 2004 data memo released by the Pew Internet and American Life Project found that 65 percent of all Internet users have shopped online.[2] Just as the growing use of credit cards for in-person retail transactions led to patron requests to "charge it" at the library circulation desk, so has the growth of ecommerce created patron demand for a convenient online method of paying library fees and fines.

In "Service Please! Rethinking Public Library Web Sites," Australian librarian Ian Hildebrand made the strong assertion that "the absence of ecommerce facilities reduces the ability of a public library Web site to act as a true virtual branch."[3] Demand for public library services, as well as the credit payment method, is also on the rise. Unfortunately, while library usage, population, and urban density continue to increase, libraries are not seeing a parallel increase in staff to deal with the usage.[4] For these reasons, self-service functions are increasingly beneficial. The time seems right for ecommerce in the library setting to handle fee-based library services.

Challenges

Despite early interest in the idea from librarians, only recently has the time become right for implementation. The delay was due to a widespread perception that per-transaction costs were too high. Because many fines are quite small, libraries faced the same conundrum as commercial entities wishing to collect micropayments: how to deal with the costs of accepting credit card payments on the Web. In some cases, the costs would be more than the money collected.

During the "dot-com" boom, libraries began to feel increasing pressure as the popular acceptance of paying online grew. It became clear to libraries that they had a growing number of patrons who were willing and eager to take that self-serve step and type in their credit card number. Patron demand for the library to provide this convenient service, just like any other business in the community, increased.

Since ecommerce solutions for retailers were not designed to access patron records, libraries wishing to offer this convenience have had to create additional processes and technical solutions to achieve this goal. The Las Vegas-Clark County Library District was a pioneer in early ecommerce development in the library, reporting at the 2004 ALA Annual Conference their efforts towards creating an ecommerce system outside their integrated library management system.[5] The Library District's solution took advantage of a programmatic interface allowing real-time data exchanges with the patron files in their legacy system. This implementation required an additional server to the one used for the library management system.

THE PARTNERSHIP FORMS

What has been missing in the past is a solution in which ecommerce fully integrates into the software systems already in use by the patron and the library, does not require a separate server, and does not require extensive research and development for each library wishing to implement it. At the beginning of 2002, after many face-to-face discussions with librarians to understand the desired workflow, Innovative began research into the current offerings of the service partners required for ecommerce. Along with assessing the technical requirements for integration, average cost of use was determined and presented to advisory groups of library staff members who had expressed interest in online credit card payment for library fees. Ecommerce began to be seen as a basic part of good customer service. If you could pay for a cup of coffee at Starbucks with a credit card, why couldn't you pay library fees the same way?

Over time, libraries had found their way over the hurdle of transaction costs. The true costs of handling cash payments, particularly the procedural overhead required whenever cash is involved, were found to be not significantly less expensive than online processing. Along with this change in perception from the library management side, the public view of paying online as a highly appreciated, even expected, convenience had reached a tipping point.

In 2002, Innovative and Westerville staff noticed that integrated ecommerce in library systems was beginning to make the transition from "an interesting idea" to "part of our roadmap for the next few years." Each organization recognized in the other the potential for making bold ideas a reality, and so began discussions about an ecommerce solution in the fall of that year. Active development began in early 2003 (see Table 1). The overall development strategy for Ecommerce was one of partnership, as is traditional at Innovative. The recent development of Electronic Resource Management with Glasgow University, Ohio State University, University of Washington, University of Western Australia, and Washington State University was a stand-out partnership that brought an industry-first product to market in 2004.[6]

TABLE 1. Sofware Development: A Timeline

Innovative Begins Exploring Ecommerce Options	January, 2002
Westerville Staff Contact Jerry Kline	Fall, 2002
Development Phase with Westerville Begins	January, 2003
Testing Phase Begins	October, 2003
Ecommerce Launches at Westerville	January, 2004
Ecommerce Available to Millennium Libraries	July, 2004
Westerville Looks Back on the First Year	December, 2004

Innovative first analyzed the requirements for integrating ecommerce with a library automation system and decided on the following:

1. A patron interface, analogous to the shopping cart in traditional retail ecommerce for the selection of fees to be paid and submission of payment information
2. A payment gateway software for management of communication with the secure gateway provider[7]
3. A mechanism for approved ecommerce payments to be logged immediately in the patron record and any reporting logs in the same ways in which in-person payments are logged
4. Facilitation of secure financial transactions without requiring additional physical security for library servers

It became obvious in initial discussions between Innovative and Westerville that an off-the-shelf ecommerce solution was insufficient to meet library and patron needs. Providing a familiar, trusted interface, which would allow easy adoption of the new feature was a high priority. This would not be achieved by simply grafting a shopping cart to the public catalog. Since patrons already have the ability to log in and view their record to see details of fees and fines in Innovative's Millennium Web OPAC, this interface was the logical place to introduce the user experience of an online payment.

Westerville and Innovative also identified data consistency as an important factor in Ecommerce development, which would only be possible through integrating the product with Millennium. Because the online payment is managed from the library management system, libraries using Ecommerce are able to ensure this consistency. When the transaction is sent for approval, the patron's record can be locked for a moment until an approval or denial code is returned from the processor.

If approved, the payments can be immediately entered in the patron record and any other reporting logging can be done along with any actions, such as clearing blocks created because of a debt, which prevent the patron from using certain services such as accessing full-text databases or requesting materials.

Together, Innovative and Westerville concluded that it is unnecessary and undesirable for the patron's credit card number to be stored anywhere on the library's server. Because of this, the number is transmitted from the patron's browser to the credit card processor without logging it. Therefore the additional security required is purely for the browser session and the transmission of the data. This is achieved through the use of SSL[8] and the design of the Ecommerce product, which does not offer a payment screen unless the session is secure. Extra protection of the library's physical server is not needed since it does not contain credit card numbers.

PARTNERSHIP: LIBRARY PERSPECTIVE

The Westerville Public Library, an independent library located near Columbus, Ohio, serves a population of approximately 80,000 residents. The library maintains approximately 67,000 registered borrowers and welcomes around 60,000 walk-in visitors monthly. Last year, the library reached the 1.5 million mark for total annual circulation.

Staff found the opportunity to partner with Innovative an exciting one. The Westerville places a great deal of emphasis on implementing new and improved library technology. The underlying attitude of library staff is that the benefit of progress is very much worth any "bumps" along the way. Westerville staff members knew that ecommerce would be an important service to offer. They shared the same enthusiasm for the product and the self-service concept in libraries and agreed that an ecommerce product would benefit many libraries. Shortly after the initial discussion, they agreed that Westerville and Innovative were an ideal combination for developing and testing the new Ecommerce solution.

The alternative to an integrated ecommerce solution was placing stand-alone credit card transaction units at all circulation points in the library. This approach would not have the benefits of an integrated solution and would discourage self-service. A development partnership was chosen in order to more seamlessly integrate Westerville's service offerings. This would allow fine payment through a Web browser, as a part of the existing self-service functionality offered by Innovative (placing holds, renewing items, etc.).

Administrative Issues

There were four key administrative issues involved in the initial software partnership decision. Library staff had to first decide if Innovative's Ecommerce product would provide a service that would fit into the Westerville's service model. The library has a business model, which highly values the patron experience and envisions library users as customers. Ecommerce was a perfect fit with this philosophy, considering that it would be available day and night, could be patron-initiated, and would provide the familiar experience of shopping online at other Web sites. Library staff also had enough anecdotal evidence through contact with patrons (in person and online) to suggest that they would accept an ecommerce solution.

The second key administrative issue involved in the software partnership was financial. The nature of ecommerce, regardless of how it is implemented, requires third-party accounts. In addition to the one-time cost of the Ecommerce software, reoccurring costs for an SSL certificate, secure gateway service, as well as transaction fees paid to an Internet merchant account provider all had to be considered. Library staff decided that considering this, a better service could be developed with Innovative for comparable funds.

The third key administrative issue concerned the allocation of necessary staff time to make the partnership successful. Staff time initially involved software set-up, testing, and staff training. To be successful in development partnerships, library staff need to report issues in a timely manner to the vendor to keep quality high and make sure the product will work for other libraries in the best way possible. Once the Ecommerce was "live," library staff time was spent reporting issues to Innovative staff and training the public how to use the new service.

The last key administrative issue had to do with being able to effectively market the new software in order to maximize visibility and usage. Management selected a team with the technical, library, and marketing skills necessary to move the project forward without involving too many hours or too many staff in the process.

Key staff involved in Ecommerce set-up at Westerville included Kristen Hewitt, manager of support services, as well as webmaster Tonya Taylor. Kristen Hewitt handled acquiring the SSL, setting up the Internet merchant account, as well as closely monitoring the beta testing period. Tonya Taylor handled the customization of the HTML forms to maximize usability as well as aesthetics. Usability was not a major obstacle in the process, because ecommerce had become a somewhat straightforward and familiar process on the Web, which now was being incorporated into the library management system. The process took several hours per week from involved staff members. Kristen Hewitt was the main testing and troubleshooting staff person for whom the task required "constant vigilance" at first. As the project got underway and workflow was established, the workload went down. For the first three to four months, Hewitt spent about five hours a week on the Ecommerce development project.

Starting the Process

Good communication with Innovative was in place from the beginning of the development process. Initially, much of the communication took place with e-mail. As the project progressed, an electronic discussion list was created and periodic teleconferences took place. The Ecommerce development electronic discussion list came together as a place for all Ecommerce libraries to discuss implementation questions and experiences. This list continues to be an invaluable resource for Ecommerce libraries. One particularly useful thread concerned trading tips on the reporting tools offered by VeriSign's Web-based management system.

Westerville submitted a basic list of requirements to Innovative in 2002. Staff wanted customers to be able to pay fines and fees online. Customers would be empowered to remove service blocks from accounts, thereby restoring remote access to licensed databases, and presenting the ability to reserve materials. In this way an unintentional barrier to continuous library service would be removed.

Testing

Once the beta software was loaded and all of the third-party subscriptions were secured, testing commenced. The Ecommerce software was loaded for beta testing in early October 2003 and went live to Westerville customers on January 5, 2004. The software went into general release to other Innovative customers in July 2004 as an optional product with Innovative's Millennium Silver. Testing of the Ecommerce product relied on the beta release of the Web OPAC software, which also had to be loaded and tested simultaneously. During the testing process, software updates took place on a weekly basis.

The library staff time involved in testing the Ecommerce product was significant. However, Westerville staff were very motivated to get this product "off the ground," so allotting the necessary staff time was not a concern. Having participated in several other beta tests with Innovative, the process was very familiar and consistent with past testing.

Results

Gathering statistics is made possible with the VeriSign Manager from Westerville's secure gateway provider. The VeriSign Manager is a Web-based management tool that allows administrators to search, process, void, and credit transactions. It additionally generates statistics on a given period of time. From January to August 2004, the Ecommerce product successfully processed 2,090 transactions totaling $25,832.22. The number of transactions processed each month continues to grow. For example, the total amount of fines collected in the same period (January to August) rose 4.5 percent from 2003 to 2004.

Month-end reconciliation of new online transactions has proved to be a minimal change in workflow. It takes the library's account clerk approximately 30 extra minutes each month to reconcile this information against the library's bank account. Even though customers pay fines with credit cards from different providers, there is no need to reconcile accounts with banks separately. This is handled as part of the service provided by Merchant Solutions, the Internet merchant account provider.

Staff at the circulation desk currently use the Ecommerce product as well. The software was designed to be self-service, but can also allow library staff to process payments on behalf of patrons when they are in the library. Library staff are poised to demonstrate the process, which has been an effective method of making customers comfortable enough to make their first online payment. This unexpected use of an online solution for in-person processing was a solution originating at Westerville. This kind of "on-the-ground" creative thinking is one of the biggest benefits of development partnerships.

Besides offering "24/7" convenience, the Ecommerce product provides a sense of anonymity to customers who have excessive fines and need to clear their account. Westerville staff heard a customer say that this new service would help other patrons "avoid the embarrassment of a face-to-face transaction like this." In fact, the Westerville team has noticed a number of large fine payments, which may have occurred for a similar reason. Customers are paying both small and large fines with the Ecommerce product. In 2004, the smallest single payment was $2.00 and the largest was $114.92. It appears that some families may be making use of Ecommerce to clear a larger combined total of fines from their separate patron accounts.

In 2003, before the implementation of Ecommerce, Westerville collected $159,988.73 in fines. In January 2005, after Ecommerce was "live" for a year, staff calculated fines totaling $166,568.30. It is a reasonable expectation that ease of service and customer demand caused this number to go up. The most clear and impressive result, however, is that over 23 percent of the 2004 fines were collected online with the new Ecommerce product, over $38,000. This percentage only rose in the first half of 2005. From January 1 to June 30, Ecommerce processed 2,448 transactions totaling $29,014.13–almost one third (32 percent) of all fines collected by the library. It is worth emphasizing again that there has been minimal publicity for the service, so this is most probably observing a natural progression where Ecommerce takes a larger and larger percentage of fine amounts each month. Kristen Hewitt notes that circulation desk staff is definitely feeling the positive impact of almost one third of revenue collection efforts now being handled without staff intervention. More time is now available to provide additional assistance to patrons and doing other administrative tasks.

By embracing opportunities for service, Westerville serves increasingly technology-savvy customers. These patrons have been requesting ecommerce features for several years. Ecommerce empowers customers to take charge of their account. If it is 1:00 a.m., and a customer cannot gain access to the library's licensed resources because of excessive fines, ecommerce allows that customer to immediately rectify the situation.

Westerville is extremely pleased with the development process and remains eager to participate in additional tests of new development, should the opportunity arise.

INNOVATIVE'S ECOMMERCE: ANATOMY OF A TRANSACTION

The Innovative Ecommerce experience is familiar to library users because it starts from a known point (their usual view of their patron record), follows standard interface practices familiar to them from other online shopping experiences, and makes use of library-customizable

Web pages which permit preservation of the library's "look and feel" throughout the payment process.

What happens during an Innovative Ecommerce transaction? The patron selects fines/fees to be paid or an amount to donate and enters required billing information (e.g., name, postal code, credit card number, and expiration date). A page is displayed requesting the patron to confirm that the amount to be charged and the entered information are correct. Once confirmed, the transaction is submitted for authorization.

Authorization is the process by which a customer's credit card is verified as active and has the credit available to make a transaction. In the online payment processing world of "card not present" transactions, an authorization also verifies that the billing information the customer has provided matches up with the information on record with their credit card company (see Figure 1).

If authorization is not received, a customizable error message is displayed to the patron, usually encouraging the patron to double check that information has been entered correctly or to make the payment in person at the library. No fines/fees are cleared from the patron record in this case.

If authorization is received, the payment can be logged in the system just as if it had been paid in person, and any blocks preventing the patron from using certain services can be lifted in real-time. A customizable success message is displayed along with receipt information, which the patron is encouraged to print for his or her record. Each successful transaction includes a unique reference number, which can be matched by library staff against the activity logged in the secure gateway's Web-based reporting tool, VeriSign Manager. After a successful payment, funds are moved from the patron's bank account to the library's bank account automatically (see Figure 2).

A New Business Model

Two pieces of information have frequently come as a surprise to customers with whom Innovative has discussed ecommerce: (1) that they must establish business relationships with outside service providers; and (2) that there are both per-transaction costs and regular service fees charged by the gateway providers and Internet merchant account providers.

The model for Ecommerce is unlike other library software products; it is not simply installed by the library management system vendor. A key element of its functionality is the ongoing business relationships,

FIGURE 1. The Authorization Process

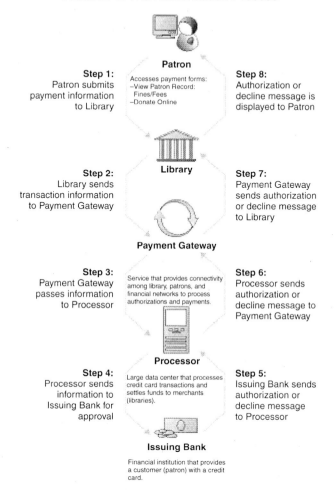

Patron

Step 1:
Patron submits
payment information
to Library

Accesses payment forms:
–View Patron Record:
 Fines/Fees
–Donate Online

Step 8:
Authorization or
decline message is
displayed to Patron

Library

Step 2:
Library sends
transaction information
to Payment Gateway

Step 7:
Payment Gateway
sends authorization
or decline message
to Library

Payment Gateway

Step 3:
Payment Gateway
passes information
to Processor

Service that provides connectivity
among library, patrons, and
financial networks to process
authorizations and payments.

Step 6:
Processor sends
authorization or
decline message to
Payment Gateway

Processor

Step 4:
Processor sends
information to
Issuing Bank for
approval

Large data center that processes
credit card transactions and
settles funds to merchants
(libraries).

Step 5:
Issuing Bank sends
authorization or
decline message
to Processor

Issuing Bank

Financial institution that provides
a customer (patron) with a credit
card.

which the library must maintain with a secure gateway provider (such as VeriSign) and a bank (often called an Internet merchant account provider). One advantage which integrated ecommerce solutions like Innovative's solution can have over a "do it yourself" approach is that the library management system vendor will carry more weight with these providers than a library approaching them alone.

Due to their strong reputation as an industry leader and their presence in many countries worldwide, Innovative selected VeriSign as the first

FIGURE 2. The Transaction Process

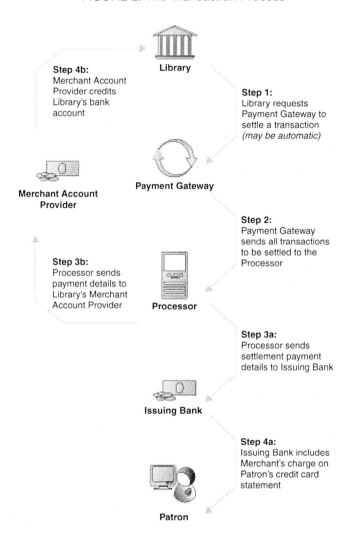

Step 4b:
Merchant Account
Provider credits
Library's bank
account

Library

Step 1:
Library requests
Payment Gateway to
settle a transaction
(may be automatic)

**Merchant Account
Provider**

Payment Gateway

Step 2:
Payment Gateway
sends all transactions
to be settled to the
Processor

Step 3b:
Processor sends
payment details to
Library's Merchant
Account Provider

Processor

Step 3a:
Processor sends
settlement payment
details to Issuing Bank

Issuing Bank

Step 4a:
Issuing Bank includes
Merchant's charge on
Patron's credit card
statement

Patron

secure gateway provider for integration using their Payflow Pro API (Application Programming Interface).[9] This payment engine was also used in the Las Vegas Library District's ecommerce solution. One of the biggest advantages to starting with Payflow Pro is the large number of Internet merchant account providers who can work with this API.

By choosing a very popular vendor, Innovative was able to leave the selection of an Internet merchant account up to the libraries. In many cases, existing business relationships can be maintained in managing this new service. Westerville and Innovative selected Merchant eSolutions as the merchant account provider for the development partnership. Additionally, a SSL had to be obtained to provide 128-bit encryption for all transactions. VeriSign was selected as the SSL vendor. This product mix offered the library a best combination of products for the first implementation of Ecommerce in terms of security, maintenance, and price.

Innovative established a relationship with VeriSign U.S. to help them understand the needs of libraries and how they differ from VeriSign's usual retail customers. This partnership has allowed Innovative to streamline the secure gateway account application process and minimize the effort required for that aspect of implementing an ecommerce solution. Innovative was also able to build a relationship with an Internet merchant account vendor, Merchant eSolutions, and, again, teach them about library needs for ecommerce. Such providers now understand that libraries are not a high-risk market–payments for lost books are not likely to be prone to the same fraud rates as, for example, the purchase of car stereos online. Because of Innovative's efforts, this provider offers customers of Innovative's Ecommerce very competitive fees. Even if Innovative customers do not choose to work with this provider, they can take these rates to another provider and use them to negotiate a better rate.

The cost of adding Ecommerce solutions, even an integrated one like Innovative's, will vary. Pricing for the software itself is dependent on institution size. Base monthly service costs will depend on the service providers chosen, but in the United States have tended to fall between $100 (Innovative solution) and $200 (SSL certificate costs are not included in this statistic since many libraries already purchase these to meet other security needs). To these base costs must be added transaction fees of approximately 35 cents plus 2-3 percent for each successful payment.

BEST PRACTICES AND OUTCOMES OF VENDOR-LIBRARY SOFTWARE DEVELOPMENT

From Westerville's experiences as a software development partner, a set of best practices can be put forth. A fundamental guideline is the assignment of a software development partnership leader at the library. In the case of the Westerville, this person is also the Innovative site coordinator who is already very familiar with other Innovative software modules.

Secondly, library staff members need to have the ability to quickly report as accurately and as thoroughly as possible issues that need to be addressed. It is important to be able to clearly articulate what is happening with as much supporting information as possible. Strong communication channels between the library and the vendor are essential. E-mail is most valuable because it allows busy people to communicate asynchronously, but a good working relationship which allows for informal phone calls to discuss an unclear issue or a problem as it is occurring helps to streamline the process. Because Innovative works on a weekly update schedule during testing, frequent communications prevent the situation of having to wait too long for a software fix to be completed.

In the future, Westerville hopes to be considered for future beta tests as well as new product development. The process is very beneficial for staff as well as customers. Staff and customers benefit by being able to utilize enhancements six to nine months before they are otherwise generally available. The benefits of entering into a partnership earlier rather than later are clear. The ability to offer new and exciting services more quickly is a significant motivator for staff. It is exciting to be able to offer services that add value to a user's experience. Another benefit to a software partnership is the ability to help shape the final product for other libraries.

To other libraries considering a partnership, Westerville would recommend a couple of things to consider. The first consideration would be to allocate appropriate staff time for a partnership of this type. A partnership like this takes considerable time away from normal day-to-day functions. Second, a partnership relationship takes patience and understanding. Libraries must understand that there will be bumps along the way. While these bumps may be inconvenient at the time, they are the cost and progress is the reward. Third, knowledge of the vendor's software is important. In this case, knowledge of the Web Options that control the "look and feel" of the Web OPAC was particularly helpful. Basic knowledge in the library of web design and HTML forms was necessary to customize the user experience for Westerville patrons based on the starting examples provided by Innovative, but no programming at all was done by Westerville staff. Lastly, consider that development partnerships become easier the second time around as relationships and communication patterns are established.

LOOKING TO THE FUTURE

In today's public library, the timeline between "I've never heard of it" and "I can't believe you don't have it" is declining exponentially. In order for the organization to remain responsive and relevant, staff of public libraries must embrace this challenge and avoid natural tendencies to fall into a maintenance stage and become idle. The future is dependent on the ability to change rapidly in order to anticipate and address customer needs. This can only be accomplished by partnerships between imaginative companies such as Innovative and pioneering libraries such as Westerville. In fact, Westerville had been a beta test site for Innovative's WebBridge, a smart linking solution for resources internal and external to Millennium, and MetaFind, a federated searching solution.

Westerville is often referred to as "a cutting edge library" by many public librarians who visit the site or e-mail after seeing the Web site. It was the first Ohio library to provide public Internet access, the first to have a Web-based catalog, the first to implement self-check machines, etc. However, these were new technologies for *libraries*, not the marketplace. The fact remains, these initiatives were reactive to customer demands first established in other industries. Westerville's partnership decision was based on anticipating customer needs rather than the old paradigm of simply responding to customer demands.

Public libraries simply do not have the resources or ability to influence the development of new technologies, but they can form creative partnerships with vendors to realize their goals. Public libraries do have some influence from serving on vendor advisory boards. But all too often the boards are asked to provide advice or comments after the fact–meaning after a product or service has been designed. Very rarely are libraries engaged at the development or design stage of the process, which is where development partnerships come in.

Westerville's contribution to this software development partnership is based on the staff's desire to embrace new technologies and implement new products and services quickly and efficiently. The philosophy is simply to provide customers with what they want, when they want it, and in the manner they desire. Westerville staff like to say: "We must always remember that to accomplish what we have never done, we have to do things we've never attempted." For example, Westerville's future includes expanding usage of Innovative's Ecommerce to include online book purchasing, online purchasing of items from the Gift Shoppe, and online classes.

Similarly, libraries must understand that mobile phones are much more than a communication device–they are a fundamental part of daily life. In fact, a study by the Pew Internet and American Life Project (2005) found that 134 million American adults have these devices and 34 million use them to send SMS (Short Message Service) messages.[10] Westerville will move forward with text messaging for reference services, "*49" for quick phone access to the library, scanning and sending documents to cell phones and palm pilots, etc. As Westerville moves to reducing or eliminating reference desks by untethering librarians with the use of tablet PCs and AirPAC (Innovative's small screen interface to the Millennium online catalog) to enhance customer services, Westerville remains focused on the belief that the customer and not the librarian must define information delivery. This is the new service paradigm for public libraries and Westerville staff are excited by these opportunities and look forward to "Delivering the Future" for customers.

This partnership has been the latest chapter in Innovative's long-term commitment to improving and expanding self-service options for library patrons. This has included the ability to request ILL transactions through INN-Reach systems like LINK + and OhioLINK, My Millennium personalization features such as setting e-mail alerts for when desirable items are added to the library, updating the patron record, requesting renewals and placing holds, as well as viewing currently checked-out items, holds, fines, and bookings. More self-service enhancements will be with Millennium 2005, including patron rating of books on the Web OPAC and Graphical Self Check, which allows patrons to check out materials on a standard PC workstation. The Ecommerce product Innovative developed also reveals the potential for additional self-service capabilities such as making donations to the library directly through the Web OPAC.

On the heels of the Ecommerce project, Innovative will make another partnership-driven product available with Millennium 2005. Program Registration, developed with Westerville and Middle Country Public Library (New York), allows patrons to sign up for library events through the Web OPAC. The benefits of self-service products like Ecommerce and Program Registration to the library are manifold: happier customers, reduced staff workload, increased money collected, and even, it appears, the patrons who would not have paid before willingly paying the charges on their accounts. Another next step may be an attitude change. It may be time to take away the stigma of "fines." What if libraries started using a more positive term such as "Extended Use Fees" instead? Through their willingness to take control into their hands, patrons may be telling us that this too is just another service.

CONCLUSION

Development partnerships, like the one between Westerville Public Library and Innovative Interfaces, are an outstanding way to create library software for all concerned. For the library, it presents the opportunity to get real solutions to the challenges it faces, without overextending staff or arriving at a result that cannot evolve or be supported properly. For the vendor, development partnerships ensure that it remains close to the issues of its customers. These partnerships give the company a chance to provide excellent solutions tailored to the actual environment of the library.

The development of Ecommerce was a great success, as numerous libraries around the world have selected the product. At Westerville, library users have embraced Ecommerce and the percentage of total fines collected online continues to rise. The Ecommerce product sets a high standard because Westerville and Innovative harnessed their collective knowledge to develop a solution in close partnership. Throughout the process, both organizations understood the technical, procedural, and communicative commitment necessary to make such an industry-first product possible.

NOTES

1. For the purposes of this article, please note that "Ecommerce" is Innovative's software product name and ecommerce describes the phenomenon of online buyer/seller transactions.

2. Pew Internet and American Life Project, Pew Internet Project Data Memo, April 2004, <http://www.pewinternet.org/pdfs/PIP_April2004_Data_Memo.pdf> (17 September, 2004).

3. Ian Hildebrand, "Service Please! Rethinking Public Library Web Sites," Library Review, vol. 52, no. 6 (2003): 275.

4. Dick Boss, Joe Ford, David Leung, and Dan Walters, *Implementing eCommerce On-line Transactions at a Public Library*, January 2004, <http://www.ala.org/ala/pla/plaevents/plaatalaannual/danwalters.pdf> (17 September 2004).

5. Ibid.

6. Theodore A. Fons, Diane Grover, "The Innovative Electronic Resource Management System," *Serials Review*, vol. 30 (2004): 110-116.

7. A secure gateway provider is a service that provides connectivity among library, patrons, and financial networks to process authorizations and payments. A merchant account provider is a bank or bank representative (such as a credit card company) that offers a variety of products and services that enables credit card payments from customers.

8. Secured Sockets Layer (SSL) is a protocol that transmits encrypted data over the Web. It is often used to protect consumer credit card information.

9. See: http://www.verisign.com/products-services/payment-processing/online-payment/payflow-pro/Purchase/index.html.

10. Pew Internet and American Life Project, *Thirty-Four Million American Adults Send Text Messages on their Cell Phones*, March 2004, <http://www.pewinternet.org/press_release.asp?r=99> (14 March,2005).

The OCLC Members Council:
A Communication and Governance Forum
for the Global Library Collaborative

George M. Needham
Richard Van Orden

SUMMARY. The relationship between OCLC Online Computer Library Center and its member institutions worldwide is formalized in the Members Council. This body, representing OCLC's constituent networks and service centers, has a key role in helping the OCLC Board of Trustees and management determine the future direction of the cooperative. Its core responsibilities include electing six trustees to the fif-

---

George M. Needham is Vice President, Member Services, OCLC Online Computer Library Center, 6565 Frantz Road, Dublin, OH 43017 (E-mail: needhamg@oclc.org). He has also been the State Librarian of Michigan, the Executive Director of ALA's Public Library Association, Member Services Director of the Ohio Library Association, and Director of Fairfield County District Library in Lancaster, Ohio.

Richard Van Orden is Program Director, OCLC Members Council (E-mail: rich_vanorden@oclc.org). Previous to this decade of service, he was Program Director, Academic and Research Libraries, and Manager, Enhanced Information Planning, OCLC. Mr. Van Orden began his career at the University of Utah Libraries in 1978 as the Assistant Circulation Librarian and later served as Manager, Online Cataloging, until 1987. He has participated in numerous executive education programs including the ARL Management Review and Analysis Program and leadership development courses at The Ohio State University Fisher College of Business.

[Haworth co-indexing entry note]: "The OCLC Members Council: A Communication and Governance Forum for the Global Library Collaborative." Needham, George M., and Richard Van Orden. Co-published simultaneously in *Journal of Library Administration* (The Haworth Information Press, an imprint of The Haworth Press, Inc.) Vol. 44, No. 3/4, 2006, pp. 157-171; and: *Library/Vendor Relationships* (ed: Sam Brooks, and David H. Carlson) The Haworth Information Press, an imprint of The Haworth Press, Inc., 2006, pp. 157-171. Single or multiple copies of this article are available for a fee from The Haworth Document Delivery Service [1-800-HAWORTH, 9:00 a.m. - 5:00 p.m. (EST). E-mail address: docdelivery@haworthpress.com].

Available online at http://www.haworthpress.com/web/JLA
© 2006 by The Haworth Press, Inc. All rights reserved.
doi:10.1300/J111v44n03_13

157

teen-member Board, and approving or rejecting changes to OCLC's
Articles of Incorporation and *Code of Regulations*, the corporation's
founding documents. The Members Council also represents the interests
of libraries to OCLC. While the Board, Council, and management do not
agree on all issues, their relationships are characterized by extensive interaction and mutual respect. *[Article copies available for a fee from The
Haworth Document Delivery Service: 1-800-HAWORTH. E-mail address:
<docdelivery@haworthpress.com> Website: <http://www.HaworthPress.com>*

KEYWORDS. OCLC, Members Council, libraries, membership, networks, governance, strategy

INTRODUCTION

A November 10, 2004, press release from OCLC described the October 2004 Members Council meeting.

The OCLC Members Council met October 24-26, 2004, in Dublin, Ohio, where delegates discussed the library implications of
massively multiplayer online games, e-learning, and extending
services to more libraries in more countries worldwide as part of
its overall theme of "Moving Libraries Beyond Their Comfort
Zones." It was the first of three meetings for the 2004/2005 Members Council that would consider questions and findings from the
OCLC Environmental Scan: Pattern Recognition, a report produced for the OCLC worldwide membership to examine significant issues and trends impacting OCLC, libraries, museums,
archives and other allied organizations, now and in the future.
"The social, technology, learning and library landscapes from
the *Environmental Scan* will frame this year's Members Council
discussions, programs and activities, as delegates explore implications of these landscapes and how best to move beyond their comfort zones," said Charles Kratz (PALINET), Members Council
President and Director, Library and Information Resources, Wein-
berg Memorial Library, University of Scranton.[1]

How did the Members Council assume such an important role in
forging the direction for an international collaborative that serves scores

of nations, tens of thousands of institutions, and, through these institutions, millions of people around the globe? This paper contends that the role the Members Council plays is a result of OCLC's foundation as a membership organization, and that Council's input has helped OCLC to fulfill its vision as the "leading global library cooperative." A brief history of the Members Council (neé Users Council) and an assessment of its impact are the primary purposes of this analysis.

A BRIEF HISTORY OF USERS COUNCIL

The Ohio College Library Center (OCLC) was founded as a non-profit, membership, computer library service and research organization to serve academic libraries in the State of Ohio on July 6, 1967. Interest in the project grew rapidly in other states. Beginning with the Pittsburgh Regional Library Center (PRLC), OCLC began to contract with existing U.S. networks to offer system access to libraries beyond Ohio. As David Brunell, the executive director of the Bibliographic Center for Research (BCR) noted, not only did this expansion give OCLC additional revenue, it saved money by allowing OCLC to pay interstate telecommunications fees rather than higher in-state rates.[2] Working in partnership with these networks also meant that OCLC could extend its mission of "furthering access to the world's information" without having to create a large technical support and sales staff, and could collaborate with people who understood local library environments and knew the key players.

By the mid-1970s, less than ten years after OCLC's founding, the majority of its users were located outside of Ohio. Users sought a role in determining the directions this new service would take. In response, the Board of Trustees hired the consulting firm Arthur D. Little, Inc. to assist in planning a new structure that would permit broader representation in OCLC governance.

The A. D. Little consultants recommended a three-part governance structure: a Board of Trustees with fiduciary responsibility for the cooperative, a Users Council composed of elected representatives of the regional networks, and general members (libraries that contributed to the OCLC database and voted for Council delegates). The "members" of the cooperative for purposes of the elected council would be the networks that supplied OCLC services to their local libraries. Therefore, three categories of members–members of the Board of Trustees, network members of Users Council, and member libraries–would comprise the governance structure of the not-for-profit corporation to be chartered under Ohio law.

The Council would be composed of sixty delegates, elected by "general members" (in this case, the libraries) in each network. Representation on the Council would be allocated proportionately by the amount of activity in cataloging (and later resource sharing) that each network brought to the cooperative.[3] These recommendations were adopted in December 1977. (OCLC service centers, which are owned by OCLC but provide services in areas unserved by networks, were included later as members in the allocation of delegates for the Users Council.)

The first meeting of the OCLC Users Council was held in June 1978 at the Holiday Inn in Columbus near Ohio State University. The minutes of that first meeting report Board Chair H. Paul Shrank Jr. stating that the creation of the Users Council could have a significant impact on OCLC. His comments proved prescient.

ROLES AND RESPONSIBILITIES OF USERS COUNCIL

Under the new *OCLC Code of Regulations*, the Users Council would have three primary roles: elect six of the fifteen members of the Board of Trustees; approve or reject without modification any changes to the *Articles of Incorporation* and *Code of Regulations* proposed by the Board; and represent the interests and concerns of the membership to OCLC management.

The Council set about these tasks diligently. The first six Council-elected OCLC Trustees were Hugh Atkinson, Miriam Drake, Glyn Evans, Kaye Gapen, Anthony Martin, and Russell Shank, all well-respected, national library leaders. The quality and experience reflected in this first group of Members Council-elected trustees reflected the ongoing importance that Council has placed on this responsibility.

The *Code of Regulations* has been amended from time to time in the twenty-six years since its adoption. In some cases, the amendments were editorial changes such as updating the corporation's legal name.[4] The *Code* also included such details as what would be counted in the delegate allocation formula (the "delegate algorithm" for apportioning Users Council delegates) and how each type of activity would be weighted in the algorithm. In contrast to these administrative stipulations needing adjustment occasionally, major changes such as expanded purposes of the Council and delegate certification requirements also required official approval of both the Board and Council.

It was in the third responsibility of the original OCLC *Code of Regulations*, representing the interests and concerns of the membership, that discussion sometimes became charged. Council reacted heatedly in the early 1980s when the Board of Trustees authorized copyrighting the OCLC Online Union Catalog, the cooperative's database of cataloging records and holdings input by libraries. At issue was libraries' ownership of the records they input into OCLC and the copyrighting of the database would impede or advance the continued growth of the Online Union Catalog. In voicing the concerns of the membership, the Council partnered with the Board to find an equitable resolution. This debate culminated in the passage of protocols and guidelines for the appropriate use of the database in 1985, but significant revisions were made over the next two years. The current version of the document, "Guidelines for the Use and Transfer of OCLC-Derived Records," was produced by a Board committee, including Council delegates, in 1987 and remains in effect today.[5]

The Council frequently addressed the importance of membership and contribution to the cooperative throughout its history. In 1996, delegates unanimously approved "WorldCat Principles of Cooperation," which set out the underlying value of contributing to and sharing the database that library staff so carefully built for three decades.[6] Six years later, as the World Wide Web offered the ability to pluck catalog records from a variety of sources without sharing holdings information, the Council responded by noting that member libraries have a responsibility to protect OCLC WorldCat against unauthorized use and by re-emphasizing the Principles of Cooperation. The "Statement on Principles of Membership of the OCLC Collaborative" adopted by the Council in February 2002 includes such member commitments as:

- Share collections, metadata, best practices, and expertise without expectations of parity
- Promote internationally accepted standards to facilitate resource sharing and information exchange
- Participate in and work to enhance the governance structure of OCLC through Members Council and the Board of Trustees
- Promote the responsible use of OCLC-derived records by approved users.[7]

The Council also recommended new services to OCLC staff and management. For example, it urged OCLC to implement what is now the ILL Fee Management (IFM) service, which simplifies the transfer of small payments among libraries to reimburse each other for resource sharing. A long debate among the membership and within the OCLC staff had ensued about the advisability of OCLC facilitating the capability of libraries to charge one another for ILL. The Council finally passed a resolution encouraging the company to go forward with this service which saves libraries hundreds of thousands of dollars each year in institutional staff costs to process inter-library payments.

FROM "USERS COUNCIL" TO "MEMBERS COUNCIL"

By the late 1990s, the need for change in the structure and composition of the Users Council had become obvious to many of the varied stakeholders in the OCLC cooperative. Two key problems with the existing structure were apparent. First, the Council had almost no international representation at a time when OCLC was expanding its service centers for Europe, Asia, and Canada, and establishing a new base in Latin America. Second, some of OCLC's newest services were not counted in the algorithm for allocating Council delegates to the regional service providers. Since the governance structure had been adopted in 1977, the only activities that counted toward allocating delegates were contributing or enhancing cataloging records (original or copy cataloging, online or batch-load) or adding holdings to the Online Union Catalog, and resource sharing through the OCLC Interlibrary Loan subsystem.

In November 1999, the Board of Trustees commissioned "a study to determine how OCLC can best organize its governance to achieve (its) global vision."[8] The study would examine the environmental factors likely to have an impact on OCLC; identify possible roles for OCLC in the evolving global library and information infrastructure; review and evaluate alternative governance forms for OCLC; and recommend a governance structure appropriate to the roles OCLC would play in the 21st century.

OCLC Board Chair William J. Crowe asked Nancy Eaton, the dean of university libraries at Pennsylvania State University and a veteran member of the Board of Trustees, to chair the Strategic Directions and Governance Advisory Council.[9] The Board gave the Advisory Council one year to issue its report. Arthur D. Little, Inc., which had written the 1977 report proposing the structure that moved OCLC from being an Ohio-centric association to a national organization, was hired to consult with the Advisory Council. Having the same company help move OCLC into the international sphere seemed to close the circle.

The study was nearly derailed before it began. The first meeting of the consultants with the Users Council in February 2000 was less than successful. The consultants floated several trial balloons that betrayed a deaf ear for OCLC's traditions of working with the regional networks and for its nonprofit status. Under Ms. Eaton's direction, the Advisory Council managed to put the study back on track.

Ms. Eaton ensured that the Users Council would be part of the deliberations of the Strategic Directions and Governance Council. She wanted the delegates' ideas and input early in the process, so that they would not feel blindsided by the recommendations that would come forward. At both the May and October 2000 Council meetings, plenary sessions on the governance structure resulted in the consideration of many new ideas. To keep the dialogue going, the Users Council held an unprecedented meeting at the ALA Annual Conference in Chicago in July 2000. Members of the Board of Trustees, at the encouragement of Dr. Crowe, also attended these sessions and actively engaged in the dialogue. Members of the Advisory Council and OCLC staff participated in more than a dozen network and service center meetings to discuss the progress of the study and gather ideas from members.

The Advisory Council submitted its final report to the Board on December 21, 2000. It recommended changing the name of "Users Council" to "Members Council" and establishing a "Standing Committee on Membership" to review the meaning of contribution and membership as circumstances warrant. The study established roles for the Board, the Users Council, the staff, and a new "Strategic Directions and Governance Advisory Council."

The Council also recommended the addition of six delegates from nations in which OCLC was planning to increase its activity: Japan, China, Mexico, France, the Netherlands, and South Africa. These "transitional delegates," so named because they would help to transition OCLC from a national organization to a global cooperative, would have full voting rights, be eligible for election to Council office or the Board of Trustees, and serve three-year terms on the Members Council. The transition delegates took office at the October 2001 Council meeting.[10] In 2003 the transition period was extended for three more years, from 2004 to 2007. Two new transitional delegates would be elected for this second period from each of three OCLC international service centers: OCLC Asia Pacific, OCLC PICA, and OCLC Latin America and the Caribbean. (OCLC Canada already had an elected delegate to Members

Council based on its usage of the system.) The report of the Advisory Council concluded:

> OCLC must become a more agile, global organization. Fundamental to this strategy must be the encouragement of and adherence to technical standards that assure interoperability across technical platforms that accommodate multiple formats, scripts, languages, and cultural materials. OCLC management, the Board of Trustees, and Users Council have validated these new directions and show strong evidence that they have the will and the talent to meet these challenges. The recommendations of the Advisory Council are intended to expedite these changes. With these changes, the OCLC governance structure is "fit for purpose" for the digital age.[11]

To implement the recommendations, the Board and Council appointed a second group, named the ad hoc Committee on Membership, to review the *Articles of Incorporation*, the Council Bylaws, and the OCLC *Code of Regulations* and propose amendments in accordance with the Strategic Directions and Governance Committee's recommendations. Mary-Alice Lynch, the executive director of NYLINK, the New York regional OCLC network, chaired this committee.[12]

The committee returned with a number of recommendations for altering governance and purpose. It recommended changes in the membership structure and proposed a new document, "The Membership and Contribution Protocols," that would codify the ground rules for OCLC membership and define what constitutes "contribution" for membership purposes. The document would be monitored on a regular basis by a "Standing Joint Committee on Membership," comprised of three Trustees, three Members Council delegates, and the director of an OCLC regional network or service center. The OCLC Vice President for Member Services would serve as an ex-officio member of the group. The proposals were submitted to the newly-christened Members Council and the Board, and approved in May and June 2002.

Bureaucratic restructuring can be of limited interest and provide little opportunity to challenge and engage people in dialogue, but it sometimes has far-reaching consequences. Another idea that arose from the study of governance and strategic directions was that the Members Council needed to be more active in its interaction with OCLC management and the Board. This was a concept that simultaneously sparked support and caution.

Both the Advisory Council and the Committee on Membership had noted that Members Council was becoming more of a reactive body, as the insights and experience of the delegates were not being substantively solicited during or between meetings. As a result, delegates were not fully engaged.

Each of the Members Council presidents since the adoption of the new rules has sought to change the nature of the group's deliberations from reacting to OCLC decisions already made to providing advice during early planning stages. Delegates, the Board, and management alike refer to this approach as "moving the Council upstream."

Larry Alford (SOLINET), President of the Members Council in the transition year of 2000-2001, championed the effort to move the Council upstream in deliberations among the delegates. However, he also cautioned delegates and OCLC management that opening the meetings to greater interaction could create situations in which OCLC management may be confronted by ideas they may not like. He reminded the stakeholders of the controversies over copyright and ownership of the database in the 1980s, to ensure that all parties entered into the enhanced relationship with their eyes open. Appropriately warned, the Council accepted its strengthened role with gusto.

Jerry Stephens, also representing SOLINET, was the first president of the Members Council under the new regulations. During his term, discussion focused on OCLC's new strategic plan, providing an opportunity for delegates to provide input on implementing the idea of "Weaving libraries into the web, and the web into libraries," the central objective of the plan. Dr. Stephens began the movement to provide additional time in small group discussions to allow greater dialogue between staff and delegates. There are two types of group discussions at each Council meeting. The "interest groups" discuss important aspects of library activity such as cataloging and metadata or reference. "Library groups" are organized around the various types of libraries.[13] In 2003, the former "type of library" advisory committees that had existed outside of the Council structure were disbanded in favor of giving more emphasis to the library groups, a further vote of confidence for the Council.

Jerry Stephens also presided over the first web cast of an OCLC Members Council meeting.[14] This web cast was intended to allow greater participation and awareness of the Council, although attendance was not as great as desired. Rather than live web casts, selected plenary sessions of subsequent meetings were videotaped and made available on streaming video from the Members Council web site.[15]

Mr. Stephens reported, in his closing comments at the May 2002 meeting, that the transition from "Users Council" to "Members Council" had been a success.

> I view the change from Users Council in May of 2001 to today as the difference between "may" and "can". . . . We replaced, in our minds and in the culture of OCLC, the word "may," a question, sometimes a timid request for permission to participate, with the word "can," an enabler, a declaration, a proactive willingness to contribute, based on our inherent knowledge that the whole is greater and stronger than the sum of the parts.[16]

In the plan for the Members Council for her presidential term in 2002-2003, Kristin Senecal noted, "This year we want to continue the push to a more global viewpoint, and intend to do that by gaining a better understanding of the environment in which libraries operate in a variety of geographic locations. We intend to take a look at the opportunities and the constraints under which libraries function at a national level, a regional level, and a local level."[17] These discussions contributed to the 2004 publication of *Pattern Recognition: The 2003 OCLC Environmental Scan.*[18] Ms. Senecal, a delegate from PALINET, also focused on staff development during her term. She appointed a task force, chaired by SOLINET delegate Charlene Hurt, to look into the role of OCLC in assisting libraries in preparing their staff members for the changes in the library environment. The task force made several recommendations that have since been adopted by OCLC, including:

- Creation of a web site that brings together the learning opportunities offered by OCLC and its regional networks[19]
- Evaluation of the effective use of digital collections and user behavior in the realm of digitized information[20]
- Creation of a web site that lists standards activities in which OCLC is engaged, to help promulgate such standards in the library community[21]

An aspect of Council deliberations that particularly concerned Ms. Senecal was that each meeting's discussions seemed to be hermetically sealed; discussions had little continuity from one meeting to another. She suggested a framework to remedy this which has become known as the "Significant Issues" report. Each interest and library group is expected to record any important issues that come up in its meetings which should receive further attention from OCLC management and/or the Council's own Executive Committee. The collected and de-duplicated list of issues is then forwarded to the appropriate units within OCLC for a response from management. These responses are then returned to the groups before the next Council meeting for further discussion or to make specific recommendations for action. Thus, Members Council and OCLC management have created a virtual circle of communication that keeps both groups informed.

Amigos Library Services delegate Bob Seal served as President of the Council in 2003-2004. His term included a focus by the Members Council Executive Committee on developing better communications within the cooperative. He appointed the Committee on Communications for the Cooperative (CCC), chaired by SOLINET delegate Emma Bradford Perry, which reviewed the various ways OCLC and the regional networks communicate with members. The committee reported on survey findings that had indicated that the top two ways in which members find out about what OCLC is doing are e-mails from the networks (favored by 61 percent of respondents) and the OCLC *Newsletter* (favored by 58 percent).[22] These results led to changes in the *Newsletter*, making it more news-oriented and colorful. It also led to a revitalization of the weekly e-mail publication called *OCLC Abstracts* that focuses on new products and services from OCLC, services from the regional networks, lists new members, and highlights news from the rest of the information environment that affects libraries.[23]

In the 2004-2005 Council year, PALINET delegate Charles Kratz assumed the presidency. His term has been marked by the explosion of online information being made available both through library sources and through commercial entities such as Google, Yahoo, Amazon, and MSN. In 2004 during Mr. Kratz's administration, and following much discussion with delegates, OCLC made the sixty-million record WorldCat database available for harvesting by commercial search engines, and these records became the vital link for Google in its project to digitize library holdings. This tectonic shift in how libraries interact with their users and their own collections has sparked intense discussion of the future of libraries, their relationship with OCLC and the networks, and how to add value in the "Amazoogle"[24] environment. Mr. Kratz shaped the three meetings of the Council during his term around the landscapes set out in the *OCLC Environmental Scan*, the growth and importance of e-learning, and OCLC's global strategies.[25]

In the middle of 2004 during the transition from Mr. Seal's to Mr. Kratz's terms as president, volunteer Members Council delegates worked in the OCLC exhibit booth during the ALA Annual Conference. This show of support reflects the result of 30 years of cooperation and accumulated trust between the members and the staff. The delegates were not in the booth to sell products or services; instead, they were there to show that OCLC is the collective contribution and collaboration of thousands of librarians in thousands of libraries around the world.

CONCLUSION

Assessing the impact of the Members Council, Bob Seal, who served as the Council's President for the 2003-2004 term, stated in his closing remarks at the May 2004 meeting

> The minutes of the first Members Council meeting noted that the board chair said the creation of the Council could have a significant impact on OCLC. In looking back at my six years on Members Council, my observation is that we are, indeed, making excellent progress in strategically planning together and communicating more effectively with the stakeholders in this worldwide cooperative.
>
> I salute the more than 400 delegates who have contributed their time and voluntarily served the OCLC Members Council including the 25 Council presidents who have preceded me. Using an estimate of 100 hours per delegate each year, that totals more than 100,000 hours of knowledgeable, experienced, and devoted members' and institutional time as a critical contribution to the collaborative. We, the members, OCLC and libraries around the world are much more productive, cost-effective, and of service to our users because of this expertise and time donated by delegates to the world's largest library cooperative. On behalf of librarians everywhere, I tip my hat to you our delegates and those before you over these 25 years who have faithfully trekked to Ohio three times annually in the service of libraries and their patrons.[26]

OCLC has been organized as a members' cooperative from its beginning in 1967 through its transition to a national, and now global, library service. Despite this, there is a continuing tension between the library members and OCLC as an organization to charge enough for its products to allow it to survive, and the need to offer services which individual libraries would be unable to provide. Because it must operate in a business-like manner, OCLC is sometimes considered "just another vendor" by its members and users.

The Members Council is a refutation of this argument. Delegates bring their concerns, their aspirations, and their insights into the future landscape to the meetings, and OCLC management takes this input very seriously. The delegates have real authority in electing their peers to the Board of Trustees, and the power to approve or reject changes to the foundation documents of the cooperative.

In expanding the role of the Council in February 2004, Members Council Bylaws were restated to incorporate these purposes: "Members Council shall: (i) serve to reflect and articulate the various interests of Governing Members and Members; (ii) advise the Board of Trustees and OCLC management of emerging, critical issues that require OCLC tracking, planning, or other responses so that OCLC's own strategic planning is informed by this input; (iii) provide feedback to the Board and OCLC management on OCLC's strategic directions."

The OCLC regional networks and service centers, responsible for elections to the Council, consistently send library leaders of knowledgeable professionalism and extensive experience to the forum. From this melding of many disparate perspectives comes a proactive collaborative that is stronger than any of its cooperative parts.

NOTES

1. OCLC. "OCLC Members Council explores social landscape of infosphere." (News release) OCLC, 2004. http://www.oclc.org/news/releases/200415.htm.

2. David H. Brunell. "The Strategic Alliance between OCLC and Networks: Partnerships That Work." Co-published simultaneously in *Journal of Library Administration* 25, no. 2/3 (1998): 21, and *OCLC 1967-1997: Thirty Years of Furthering Access to the World's Information* (edited by K. Wayne Smith). The Haworth Press, Inc., 1998, page 21.

3. Arthur D. Little, Inc. *A New Governance Structure for OCLC: Principles and Recommendations*. Metuchen, NJ: Scarecrow Press, 1978.

4. "In 1977, the Ohio members of OCLC adopted changes in the governance structure that enabled libraries outside Ohio to become members and participate in the election of the Board of Trustees; the Ohio College Library Center became OCLC, Inc. In 1981, the legal name of the corporation became OCLC Online Computer Library Center, Inc." "About OCLC: History of OCLC." OCLC, undated. http://www.oclc.org/about/history/default.htm.

5. OCLC Board of Trustees. "Guidelines for the Use and Transfer of OCLC-Derived Records." OCLC, 1987. http://www.oclc.org/support/documentation/worldcat/records/guidelines/.

6. OCLC Users Council. "WorldCat Principles of Cooperation." OCLC, 1996. http://www.oclc.org/worldcat/contribute/principles/.

7. OCLC Members Council. "Statement on Principles of Membership of the OCLC Collaborative." OCLC, 2002. http://www.oclc.org/memberscouncil/documents/membership.htm.

8. "OCLC will be the leading global library cooperative, helping libraries serve people by providing economical access to knowledge through innovation and collaboration." (Adopted in 1999 as OCLC's vision. The mission, vision, and quality policy statements of OCLC are available at http://www.oclc.org/about/mission/default.htm.)

9. The other members of the advisory council, and their positions at the time of their appointment, were: Larry Alford, senior associate university librarian, University of North Carolina, Chapel Hill, and president-elect, OCLC Users Council; Min-min Chang, director, Library of the Hong Kong University of Science and Technology; Christine Deschamps, president, International Federation of Library Associations and Institutions, and member, OCLC Board of Trustees; Brian Follett, vice chancellor, University of Warwick, United Kingdom; Maurice Glicksman, professor, Division of Engineering, Brown University, and member, OCLC Board of Trustees; Martín Gómez, director, Brooklyn Public Library, New York; Deanna Marcum, president, Council on Library and Information Resources; Kate Nevins, executive director, SOLINET, and chair, Regional OCLC Network Directors Advisory Committee; Sara Ann Parker, state librarian, Missouri State Library; Winston Tabb, associate librarian, Library of Congress; and Jonathan Zittrain, executive director, Berkman Center for Internet & Society, and lecturer, Harvard Law School. Due to irresolvable scheduling problems, Mr. Zittrain left the Council in April 2000.

10. The delegates were Wim van Drimmelen (the Netherlands); Françoise Lemelle (France, who resigned before the end of her term due to changes in the relationship between French libraries and OCLC); Huanwen Cheng (China); Michitaro Urakawa (Japan); Alvaro Quijano Solis (Mexico); and Jan Hedrik (Hennie) Viljoen and Norma Read (who split the term from South Africa).

11. Nancy Eaton. *OCLC Strategic Directions and Governance: Report of the Advisory Council.* OCLC, 2000.

12. The other members of the ad hoc Committee on Membership and their affiliations at the time of their appointments were Maurice Glicksman, member, OCLC Board of Trustees, and professor of engineering (Research) and provost emeritus, Brown University; Victoria Hanawalt, member, OCLC Board of Trustees, and college librarian, Eric V. Hauser Library, Reed College; Ian Mowat, member, OCLC Users Council, and librarian, Edinburgh University Library; Kristin Senecal, OCLC Users Council, and acting director, Waidner-Spahr Library, Dickinson College; Jerry Stephens, OCLC Users Council vice president/president-elect, and librarian and director, Mervyn H. Sterne Library, University of Alabama-Birmingham. Ex-officio members were Larry Alford, OCLC Users Council president, and deputy university librarian, University of North Carolina-Chapel Hill; William J. Crowe, chair, OCLC Board of Trustees, and Spencer Librarian, Kenneth Spencer Research Library, University of Kansas; George Needham, OCLC vice president for Member Services, and Richard Van Orden, Program Director, Members Council.

13. OCLC Members Council. "2004-2005 Directory" OCLC Members Council, 2004. http://www.oclc.org/memberscouncil/delegates/members_council_directory.pdf. This annual directory lists the interest and library groups and their rosters.

14. Richard Van Orden. "Minutes of the May 19-21, 2002 Members Council Meeting." OCLC Members Council. OCLC Members Council, 2002. http://www.oclc. org/memberscouncil/meetings/2002/may/minutes.htm.

15. Streaming video presentations of past Council meetings may be found at http://www.oclc.org/memberscouncil.

16. Richard Van Orden. "Minutes of the May 19-21, 2002 Members Council Meeting." OCLC Members Council. OCLC Members Council, 2002. http://www.oclc.org/ memberscouncil/meetings/2002/may/minutes.htm.

17. OCLC Members Council. "Members Council 2002/2003 Annual Plan." OCLC Members Council, 2002. http://www.oclc.org/memberscouncil/documents/2002_2003. htm.

18. Cathy De Rosa, Lorcan Dempsey, Alane Wilson. *The 2003 OCLC Environmental Scan: Pattern Recognition. A Report to the OCLC Membership*. OCLC, 2004. http://www.oclc.org/membership/escan/default.htm.

19. "Online training from U.S. regional service providers." OCLC, 2004. http:// www.oclc.org/education/regional/usa/default.htm.

20. OCLC Office of Research. "Sense-Making the Information Confluence: The Whys and Hows of College and University User Satisficing of Information Needs." OCLC, 2004. http://www.oclc.org/research/projects/imls/default.htm. This is an IMLS-funded project between OCLC's Office of Research and The Ohio State University.

21. OCLC Office of Research. "Standards Activities and Bodies that OCLC Supports." OCLC, 2005. http://www.oclc.org/community/oclc/involvement/standards.htm.

22. Ad Hoc Committee on Communication for the Collaborative. OCLC Members Council. "Final Report, May 2004" Unpublished. A summary of the May 2004 Members Council meeting, including a summary of the Committee's report is available at http://www.oclc.org/memberscouncil/meetings/2004/may/summarydetailmay.pdf.

23. Subscriptions to *OCLC Abstracts* are available at http://www.oclc.org/news/ abstracts/subscribe.htm. Other OCLC publications may be viewed at http://www. oclc.org/news/publications/default.htm.

24. Dempsey, Lorcan. "Libraries in the Age of Amazoogle: Some Issues and Responses: The Example of Open WorldCat." Presentation at JISC/CNI Meeting 2004: The Future of Scholarship in the Digital Age, July 9, 2004, at Brighton (UK). http://www.oclc.org/research/presentations/dempsey/brightonowc.ppt.

25. OCLC Members Council. "Annual Plan 2004/2005." OCLC Members Council. http://www.oclc.org/memberscouncil/documents/2004_2005.pdf.

26. Bob Seal's closing comments to Members Council's May 2004 meeting are not published. These notes were taken from the detailed agenda maintained by Richard Van Orden.

Business, Science, and the Common Good

René Olivieri

SUMMARY. Librarians, as the scientific community's purchasing agent, seem to be in a no-win situation: they do not entirely trust their providers and their customers want more for less; they are caught between the cultures of commerce and science. The historical traditions of these cultures are explored at length. The differing opinions on the 'Big Deal' demonstrate the problem but we are now seeing signs of cultural emergence. There are also signs of a rapprochement, and this can be furthered by taking a fresh look at concepts of 'value' and 'cost.' Librarians and publishers can work together for a common cause using new technology and new commercial models to help advance science. *[Article copies available for a fee from The Haworth Document Delivery Service: 1-800-HAWORTH. E-mail address: <docdelivery@haworthpress.com> Website: <http://www.HaworthPress.com> © 2006 by The Haworth Press, Inc. All rights reserved.]*

KEYWORDS. Business ethics, impact factor, open access, peer review, pricing, publishing

INTRODUCTION

The scientific community's confidence in publishing has been undermined by reports of monopoly pricing and profiteering. Under the banner

René Olivieri is President, Blackwell Publishing Ltd., Oxford, England (E-mail: Rene.Olivieri@oxon.blackwellpublishing.com).

[Haworth co-indexing entry note]: "Business, Science, and the Common Good." Olivieri, René. Co-published simultaneously in *Journal of Library Administration* (The Haworth Information Press, an imprint of The Haworth Press, Inc.) Vol. 44, No. 3/4, 2006, pp. 173-185; and: *Library/Vendor Relationships* (ed: Sam Brooks, and David H. Carlson) The Haworth Information Press, an imprint of The Haworth Press, Inc., 2006, pp. 173-185. Single or multiple copies of this article are available for a fee from The Haworth Document Delivery Service [1-800-HAWORTH, 9:00 a.m. - 5:00 p.m. (EST). E-mail address: docdelivery@haworthpress.com].

of 'Open Access,' some are calling for the overthrow of the traditional publishing model, the subscription-based journal.[1] At the same time, scientific use of and dependence on published literature has never been greater.[2] Librarians, the scientific community's purchasing agents, find themselves in an impossible position, having to deal with providers they may not entirely trust and with customers who want them to acquire more for less. How did this no-win situation come about and what can be done about it?

The historical origins of this conflict can be traced back to the Enlightenment. A review of the ethical traditions of business and science demonstrates that the two cultures started from radically different positions. The author suggests that the successful business of the future will have to behave more like a university and that the successful university will have to behave more like a business. The common good can best be served by publishers and librarians emphasizing and building on their shared views and aims rather than remaining in entrenched positions. There is a need to come to a new definition of what constitutes 'value' in publishing. If we can make common cause for a common purpose, new technology and new commercial models provide us with the opportunity to advance science in ways never before possible.

THE EVOLUTION OF BUSINESS ETHICS

The Ancient Greeks were much concerned with ethical questions. They took a holistic view and found it harder than we do today to reconcile private vice and public virtue. For them business was a dubious personal activity as its principle ends were divorced from civic duty and the good life. A good life was one informed consistently by understanding and virtue, not narrow self-interest. The Christian tradition put more emphasis on emotion than thought with selfless love as the ultimate standard for personal decision-making.

Of course, businessmen through the ages have been as adept as those in politics and the professions at using religion and philosophy to justify selfish actions. It remained for Adam Smith in the Enlightenment to turn private vice into public virtue. Smith's *The Wealth of Nations* was widely interpreted by entrepreneurs and industrialists as a licence to 'print money,' i.e., to pursue their individual gain without regard for others. Indeed, Smith's followers argued that the 'invisible hand' made greed good. The implication was that efforts to take the interests of others into account would ultimately prove counter-productive. Later, science itself inadvertently underpinned this world view. Darwin's *Origin of the Species* with its image of nature 'red in tooth and claw' was employed in support of a new vision of unfettered competition as the engine of social and economic progress. The Scottish philosopher Herbert Spencer transformed scientific hypothesis into political economics when he coined the phrase 'survival of the fittest.'

The ruthless robber barons of the late 19th and early 20th century Industrial Revolution spoke for themselves. Many took the sting out of criticism of their business practices by becoming great philanthropists. Carnegie and Rockefeller were well known as much for their generosity as for their toughness. In the first half of the 20th century the chief opposition to the pursuit of the profit motive came from socialism. But socialism in practice became discredited because of its failure to deliver the economic goods and because of its poor track record with democracy. By comparison, the evils associated with unbridled capitalism seemed easy to swallow.

In the Reagan-Thatcher era, Milton Friedman and others insisted management had a moral and legal duty to ensure every business decision was justified solely in terms of maximising shareholder value.[3] By the pragmatic 1990s, a more concrete interpretation of private enterprise's role and obligations began to emerge, couched in terms of 'stakeholders.' This approach rejected the idea that only shareholders mattered but it broke the 'common good' into an array of sectoral interests. In this view, shareholders constitute only one of a number of different classes of interests, each with a legal and moral claim on corporate resources and attention. This approach, adopted by many business schools and even some governments, requires boards and management to be accountable for the specific effects their actions have on employers, customers, the community, the natural environment, and even competitors.

Companies today ignore this broader context at their peril, not just for fear of legal action. Stakeholders themselves are proactive, showing more interest in 'who' they do business with. Investors and customers may blacklist products from companies known to exploit staff, pollute the environment, or earn levels of profits they consider excessive. Even large investors, particularly charities and pension funds, have developed ethical investment policies. The London Stock Exchange, for example, has recently introduced what it calls FTSE4Good,[4] a social responsibility index, requiring companies to demonstrate that their suppliers are not using employment practices involving discrimination, child labour, or forced labour. The rapid growth of corporate governance as an area of study and practice demonstrates how seriously many businesses now take their social responsibility. In a recent example, C. K. Prahalad, whose principle contribution to management studies is the notion of core competency, has proposed a consumer 'bill of rights' to which multi-nationals would have to commit before they would be allowed to do business in developing countries.[5]

As a firm's circle of ethical responsibility widens it should naturally extend to include those on whom it depends most–its customers and suppliers. For commercial publishers, this entails a much closer identification with the aims and values of the scientific community. Indeed, as we shall see later, this is what is already happening.

THE EVOLUTION OF SCIENTIFIC ETHICS

If business is as old as civilization, universities and scholarly societies flourished when economic progress (and business) provided a sufficient surplus for some members of society to spend their time in contemplation and disinterested investigation. The advancement of science for its own sake or for the benefit of others, rather than for personal profit, was one (if not the only) motivating force for knowledge acquisition in the ancient world. Knowledge preservation, as opposed to creation, became the chief aim of the university in the Middle Ages; the Church set the ethical and intellectual boundaries on permissible scientific research and publication.

Vesalius, Copernicus, Gallileo, and Bacon all breathed life back into science during the Renaissance. In England a religious revolution and a civil war really got science moving again. Most intellectual historians date the birth of modern science to the foundation of the Royal Society in Britain.[6] Publishing was central to this enterprise. Even at the time scientists referred to this new world as 'the Republic of Letters.' The notion of a 'republic' signifies a break with established authority and received wisdom; all citizens of the republic had an equal right to engage in the scientific enterprise and, most importantly, to criticize the scientific work of other citizens. Despite the importance of public debate at society meetings, it was in the written record that battles were eventually won and lost. Just as authority in matters of state passed from the monarch to the Commons, so authority in matters of science passed from the church to the community of scholars. The rule of law meant 'peer' rule by Parliament. Its counterpart in science was equally revolutionary: peer review. Both have withstood the test of time.

With authentication and discovery came the expansion of publishing: letters, articles, and books. "The citizens of this imaginary realm understood it as an international society of men, and later women, dedicated to the pursuit of knowledge rather than of personal gain. They organized collective inquiries, sent each other news of discoveries, and published constantly, always, they insisted, in the hope of establishing the simple truth."[7]

Despite its emphasis on collective endeavour, the Republic was not without its prima donnas. Some early idealistic authors withheld their names from their publications, but the majority, foremost among them the great Sir Isaac Newton, were not so modest. In this new marketplace each scientist became an entrepreneur, promoting his own reputation and career. Even in these early days professional advancement and personal egos led to some bruising and not altogether honest exchanges. "In these debates a basic principle of modern science took shape: what matters is not simply arriving at the truth, but arriving there first."[8] It was precisely this kind of competitive pressure two centuries later which compelled the reticent Charles Darwin to finally publish his *Origin of the Species*: he needed to stake out his intellectual claim ahead of Alfred Russell Wallace.

Today, publishing qualified by peer review drives the scientific process. With competition and the pressure to achieve greater than ever, there is a great temptation to conduct dishonest science, to fabricate results, or take credit for the discoveries of others.[9] One of the great strengths of the scientific method, however, is that it uncovers cheating. Results that are not corroborated eventually become found out. Irreproducible results, sloppy analysis, and cheating all provide perfect opportunities for someone else to be published by exposing the flaws of a previous article. It is clear why publishers, journal editors, and tenure committees need peer review. What is less clear is why individuals who are themselves being pushed to publish should be prepared to spend precious time reviewing the work of others without being paid for it. The published article is the tip of the scholarly iceberg, the bit that is visible to the outside world. By way of illustration, assume that the typical journal has a twenty-five percent acceptance rate and that each article is subjected to at least two peer reviews, so the number of readers reports relative to articles published may be as much as eight or ten. If a million peer reviewed articles are published each year each requiring, say, three hours of effort to review, then the total number of highly skilled, unpaid man hours going into the system each year may be as many as 30 million.

Why is this sustainable? For a scientist, only the view of another scientist matters. But few expect to win tenure, let alone a Nobel Prize, on the basis of the quality or quantity of their peer reviewing. The advancement of science is the answer given by most scientists today, but personal advancement remains a strong motivation.[10] Reviewers may see peer reviewing as a way of keeping up with the literature. Some seem to have a particular talent for reviewing and simply enjoy it. Others may find it satisfying to exercise power over their colleagues who are also their competitors. The scientist who engages in peer review does so partly out of a sense of civic obligation and partly out of a desire to control his discipline. As a citizen of the Republic of Letters, the scientist wants to maximize his influence. Selection as a peer reviewer legitimises the scientist's claim to be an authority on that subject. In sum, it seems reasonable to suggest that peer review today is motivated by something more than personal aggrandizement and something less than pure altruism.[11] "It [Science] is a real community with leaders, laws, fellowship and history. Amazingly, it has held together for centuries without formal government, without inherited privilege and without violence, police or prisons. It is sufficiently tolerant to actually invite dissent. Its heretics are not burnt at the stake but hailed as heroes. This is not, of course, a society of angels. Personal ambition is a major driving force. But to a substantial degree this force is harnessed to a shared goal. That goal is not a venal or cruel one, but the humane goal of understanding."[12]

Knowledge is power, and increasingly it is the basis on which companies and nations compete. Science today is both big business and big politics. The greater importance of intellectual property brings with it greater potential for corruption and conflict at all levels. Modern science is resource-hungry. Funding for research is growing at a tremendous rate globally. Medical research in America is dominated by a single government organisation, the National Institutes of Health, on the one hand, and pharmaceutical companies on the other. Government-funded science research in the UK is slated to increase by thirty percent in real terms over the next three years.

Peer review is the ethical guardian of science because it sets and maintains the standards for quality and objectivity. Although it still has the general support of the scientific community, the legitimacy of peer review has recently come under attack from a number of quarters. Published results from clinical trials and medical research for example, can make or break a new drug that has cost billions of dollars to develop. To guard against possible bias, journal editors have imposed new rules on authors and reviewers, demanding full disclosure on funding sources and conflicts of interest.[13]

Is there a case for more formal regulation? There is a fear that the introduction of formal standards might lead to systematic bias, especially if these were manipulated by organizations and governments with motivations other than the advancement of science. This is one of the legitimate concerns raised about suggestions for a wholesale move to centrally funded peer-reviewed repositories as a replacement for the current decentralised system of peer review.

WHERE SCIENCE MEETS BUSINESS

The typical scientist is at least as competitive as the typical businessman.[14] The difference, and it is an important one, is that businessmen compete for a financial return whereas the gains from scientific success are principally 'honorific.'

If each scientist is an entrepreneur, each journal is a small business. As in any business, poor service and poor quality are punished eventually with poor sales and a decline in the value of the goodwill and equity associated with that brand. Authors act in some senses like consumers. They are highly aware of a journal's reputation for quality.[15] The Impact Factor is the most widely accepted independent measure of influence and scientists like the concreteness it implies. To advance in their discipline they need to collect impact factors and prestige; the greater the number of highly cited papers, the more highly regarded and 'marketable' is the scientist.

Scientists accept that the journals in which they publish compete for readers and subscriptions just as they themselves compete with other authors. What they sometimes object to is what they perceive to be the publisher's obsession with revenues and profits. Where the publisher is a non-profit learned society, researchers may have fewer qualms about donating their work as author and reviewer for free but they may feel differently where a commercial publisher is involved. This feeling of inequity is reinforced where scientists suspect that electronic-only publication over the Internet would dramatically increase access and decrease costs if prices were not kept artificially high by traditional publishers.

Some scientists want dramatic revolutionary change. They propose alternative publishing models which would limit what they see as the monopoly pricing power of the publisher. One manifestation of this dissent is the so-called Open Access movement. In one form of Open Access, the 'author-pays' model, readers are given a 'free ride' while exposing the system to new strains and potential abuses. Will publishers, editors, and societies be able to resist the temptation to apply double standards for quality and originality in peer review and acceptance, when the author of the first has no access to publishing funds while the author of the second stands ready to cut a cheque? Will the successful author be happy to subsidize the peer review of unsuccessful submissions? Will peer reviewers continue to work for free when they know the author is now paying to be published? These are important unanswered questions.

The position of learned societies in this is ambivalent. They are run by scientists on a not-for-profit basis and they are important players in publishing. Two-thirds of the top journals ranked by Impact Factor and half of the 20,000 peer-reviewed titles listed in Ulrich's Periodicals Directory are published by non-profits, the majority of which are learned societies.[16] Even though society officers do not personally benefit financially from publishing, they do often rely on it to generate a surplus to support other loss-making activities. Societies spend their income, which includes surpluses from publishing, on all kinds of non-profitable activities: public and professional education, lobbying, research grants, scholarships, conferences, membership subsidies, etc.

WHERE FORCES MEET

If the society officer is an agent acting on behalf of a discipline-specific community, then the librarian is an agent acting on behalf of a faculty-based community. Librarians engage with both learned societies and commercial publishers. If any rapprochement between science and commerce is possible, it must start here.

Librarians are the modern equivalents of medieval laybrothers who lived in the monasteries but were not ordained and therefore were not formally bound by the same strict vows. They went to the marketplace to shop for the community they served. It would be surprising then if librarians did not have some reservations about commercial vendors for it is easy to see publishers and intermediaries as the odd ones out in the enterprise of science and scholarship, the only ones who are explicitly 'in it for the money.'

Today librarians enter the fray with additional grounds for dissatisfaction. Their budgets have not kept pace either with the rate of increase in scientific publishing or the concomitant rate of increase in the prices of scientific journals.

In the developed world, the proportion of the typical university's total budget spent on the library has declined from around four percent to around 2.5 percent over the last twenty years.[17] Serials account for about a third of this spend. Can we interpret from this that what the library provides to the university is less important today than it was in the past? How can we agree about what the right level of expenditure for a library on 'new journal acquisitions' should be as a percentage of the total library budget?

BACK TO BASICS

If we are to move beyond recriminations in private and public debate, we need to take a fresh look at some of the traditional values, particularly the vexed issues of 'value' and 'cost,' which lie at the centre of any discussion of equity and fairness.

Value is a difficult concept to come to grips with. It is bandied about in phrases such as 'value added,' 'value for money,' and 'marginal value.' The Oxford English Dictionary defines *value* as the 'relative status of a thing or person; the estimate in which it is held according to its real or supposed worth, usefulness or importance.'

How can we reach a consensus about the 'added value' publishing makes to original research? In both private negotiations and public debates, librarians and publishers resort to 'relative' quantitative measures of value. Libraries point repeatedly to rises in individual journal prices. Publishers respond with measures of price-per-use or price-per-article. Both focus on 'incremental' change without critically assessing the base point of comparison. Did that starting point represent fair value to begin with? Are we comparing apples and oranges? Might the print product of yesterday be inferior to today's electronic product in terms of what can be done with it?

Tommy Kågner, librarian at the Karolinska Institute in Sweden and a member of the Blackwell Library Advisory Board, puts it this way: "The main problem here is that all publishers and librarians start with the assumption that paper journals and electronic journals are of equal value. Maybe it's just me, but in my opinion the e-version provides that much more value, therefore it should be priced differently. Your biggest mistake was to start pricing it in accordance with the price of a printed journal."

If we want to arrive at an agreement about price based on relative value, why restrict comparison to an individual journal or the journals of an individual publisher? Surely a more fruitful analysis would take account of price-per-use or price-per-article across publishers and would recognize relative changes in the number of pages or the number of titles in a publisher's list from one year to the next.

So much for value. There is, however, another side to the pricing equation, namely costs. For their part, publishers need to admit that marginal costs decline with increasing online access. One of the great things about electronic delivery and site licensing is that it makes it possible to provide wider access to a greater quantity of content at very low additional cost. The Big Deal (purchases of an entire publisher's list by a library or library consortia) is indeed a 'big deal' for both parties. The publisher receives slightly increased revenue (or a guarantee on existing subscriptions) and, in theory, a more satisfied customer. The presence of low 'marginal costs' makes the exchange possible because 'fixed' and 'average' costs are presumed to be covered by core full-price subscriptions, which Big Deal purchasers have agreed to retain. Nevertheless, some librarians complain that the 'extra content' is accessed less than the 'core,' forgetting that the price per unit on the core is many times higher than that for the 'extra' content. It has even been suggested that the marginal cost should be extended to cover the core collection as well. This argument completely ignores the high fixed costs of publishing. A recent study in the UK shows cost per use falling dramatically as a result of Big Deals.[18]

The resulting negotiations can reach a stalemate, fuelled by misunderstanding and mistrust, with librarians sometimes assuming that Big Deals are more profitable than they are and publishers remaining inflexible in the face of demands for cancellations on 'core' subscriptions which threaten to eat away at the contribution to their high fixed costs. A similar dilemma relates to third party database publishing which is only financially viable for the publisher on the basis of marginal costing.[19]

CULTURAL CONVERGENCE

Fortunately, the emergence of electronic journals and the consequent changes in the way scholarly information is produced and disseminated have coincided with fundamental changes in the cultures of all those who participate in the process, not just librarians and publishers, but also the scientific community of authors and readers. Journal authors recognize that peer review is no longer sufficient in order for them to gain them the recognition they need to succeed in the scientific marketplace. Publishers increasingly provide authoring tools, promote usage and encourage citations, acting as the author's coach as well as PR and marketing agent. Readers expect the publisher and librarian to provide an online environment which leads them pro-actively to the content they want.

Librarians too are becoming more business savvy. Would a librarian of ten years ago have been so critical of his own profession as Rick Anderson at the University of Nevada?

> As librarians, we're all keenly aware of our potential as agents of social improvement. That's great, but I think we need to make sure we also give due consideration to our role as economic agents in the marketplace. Most of us are managing a tremendous amount of public money in trust, and it behoves us to understand the marketplace in which we are spending that money. I'm dismayed when I hear my colleagues talk about "celebrating inefficiency" or expressing facile anti-corporate sentiments. If we really want to serve our patrons well, we will work hard both to minimize waste and to foster appropriate and constructive relationships with our vendors and publishers. Sometimes it seems as if our profession as a whole devotes more energy to expressing the proper sentiments than to figuring out how to work most effectively in the real world.

For their part, publishers recognize that they now live in a different world. Would an STM publisher of ten years ago have produced a mission statement with the following reference to values?

> Just as we support the advance of knowledge and learning, we are constantly developing our own professional skills too.
>
> We strive to align our goals and values with those of our clients and customers. In partnership with them we are making an important contribution to society.[20]

For a company, social responsibility can become a competitive differentiator, not just in terms of public relations but in forcing it to identify with the wider aspirations of customers and clients. Indeed, it may make good business sense for the CEO to take a direct interest in ethical issues to the extent even of writing articles on the subject in scholarly journals! In what other industry and at what other time would a commercial company like Blackwell take pride in being described by a major funding publishing body, the Wellcome Trust, as an 'honorary not for profit'?[21]

Nearly all successful modern companies talk about themselves as service-providers rather than product-makers. In describing themselves they use phrases such as 'customer-centric,' 'research-driven,' and 'externally-facing.' Success depends on narrowing the gap between the mind-set of clients and customers on the one hand and staff and management on the other. During the past year alone Blackwell has conducted detailed surveys of every customer or client group with which we work: librarians, authors, society officers and editors, society members, students, researchers, and teachers.

But there is no substitute for persistent direct contact. It is easier to misinterpret or disparage those you don't know. Decision-makers need to be more accessible; organizations need to be more permeable. A key objective of every dynamic organization has to be maximizing personal contact with customers and clients. Blackwell's own Library Advisory Board meets twice a year and gives us detailed feedback on prices and pricing models, archiving, digitizing back issues, licensing terms, e-books, open access and institutional repositories. At our executive seminars, which are also held twice a year, librarians and society officers engage with each other, often for the first time. Blackwell also contributes time and resources to such public service initiatives as LOCKSS, COUNTER, Open Archiving and PatientInform, HINARI and AGORA. We make our decision to participate on the basis of their intrinsic merit (are they likely to succeed?) and the support they have or are likely to receive within the scholarly and scientific community. We could call it altruism or enlightened self-interest but we prefer the explanation of Daniel Mattes Durrett, another member of the Blackwell Library Advisory Board and a librarian at Universidad Anáhuac, México, "The more I see, the more I am convinced that libraries and publishers are partners (albeit sometimes unwillingly!) in a larger social process."

NOTES

1. The Wellcome Trust in Britain published its 'Economic Analysis of Scientific Research Publishing' in January 2003. Public Library of Science: 'Publishing Open Access Journals,' www.plos.org. The Berlin Declaration on Open Access to Knowledge in the Sciences and Humanities 2003, Bethesda statement on Open Access in Publishing 2003.

2. The Wellcome Trust *op.cit.* page 2.

3. Milton Friedman, 'The social responsibility of business is to increase its profits.' New York Times, September 13, 1970.

4. www.FTSE.com/ftse4good/index.jsp.

5. Pralahad, C.K., *The Fortune at the bottom of the Pyramid.* Pearson 2005.

6. Anthony Grafton reviewing the Newtonian Movement: *Science and the making of modern culture*, an exhibition at the New York Public Library.

7. Anthony Grafton *op.cit.*

8. Anthony Grafton *op.cit.* p39 New York Review of Books, December 2, 2004.

9. Anthony Grafton *op.cit.* p39 New York Review of Books, December 2, 2004.

10. Mulligan, A. *Is peer review in crisis?* Perspectives in Publishing No. 2. Elsevier, August 2004.

11. Coles, B (1993), STM Information System in the UK, Royal Society, British Library, ALPSP London and Mabe, M and Amin, M (2002), Dr Jekyll and Dr Hyde, Aslib Proceedings, Vol 54, No 3, Pages 149-157.

12. Polanyi, John, *Science and Conscience*, p24, New Perspectives Quarterly, Fall 2004, published by Blackwell Publishing.

13. One of several organisations which set ethical guidelines for reviewing is the committee on Publication of Ethics (COPE).

14. James Watson was one of the first to expose this in his book The Double Helix, 1968.

15. Unpublished research results by Alma Swan, Key Perspectives Ltd., for Blackwell Publishing and by Michael Mabe for Elsevier Science.

16. Morris, S., Olivieri, R., *The Secret Life of STM Publishing*, Serials Vol. 17 No. 2, July 2004.

17. U.S. Department of Education.

18. http://www.jisc.ac.uk/uploaded_documents/nesli2_usstudy.pdf.

19. Sam Brooks "Integration of Information Resources and Collection Development Strategy" published in the *Journal of Academic Librarianship* Volume 27 Issue 4 (July 2001).

20. Extract from Blackwell Publishing mission statement. www.blackwellpublishing. com.

21. *Economic analysis of scientific research publishing*–a report commissioned by the Wellcome Trust 2003.

Community College Library/Vendor Relations: You Can't Always Get What You Want . . . or Can You?

Sarah Raley
Jean Smith

SUMMARY. Community colleges serve a large and diverse student population. Vendors and community colleges would be well served by smaller database packages with focus on non-traditional studies. Untapped key elements vendors should consider in promoting sales with community colleges include: timely responses, practical license structures, and consistent database offerings. Fostering positive vendor/community college relationships is assisted by strategies to address current economic realities, customizing database contents, focus groups and other forums to communicate mutual needs and capabilities. Proactive librarians should assist vendors in understanding the unique needs of community colleges. *[Article copies available for a fee from The Haworth Document Delivery Service: 1-800-HAWORTH. E-mail address: <docdelivery@haworthpress.com> Website: <http://www.HaworthPress.com> © 2006 by The Haworth Press, Inc. All rights reserved.]*

Sarah Raley is Electronic Resources Consortium Director, Community College League of California (E-mail: sarahraley@ccleague.org).

Jean Smith is Periodicals Librarian, San Diego Mesa College (E-mail: jesmith@sdccd.edu).

[Haworth co-indexing entry note]: "Community College Library/Vendor Relations: You Can't Always Get What You Want . . . or Can You?" Raley, Sarah, and Jean Smith. Co-published simultaneously in *Journal of Library Administration* (The Haworth Information Press, an imprint of The Haworth Press, Inc.) Vol. 44, No. 3/4, 2006, pp. 187-202; and: *Library/Vendor Relationships* (ed: Sam Brooks, and David H. Carlson) The Haworth Information Press, an imprint of The Haworth Press, Inc., 2006, pp. 187-202. Single or multiple copies of this article are available for a fee from The Haworth Document Delivery Service [1-800-HAWORTH, 9:00 a.m. - 5:00 p.m. (EST). E-mail address: docdelivery@haworthpress.com].

Available online at http://www.haworthpress.com/web/JLA
© 2006 by The Haworth Press, Inc. All rights reserved.
doi:10.1300/J111v44n03_15

KEYWORDS. Community colleges, California, collection development, library consortia, database selection, electronic resources

INTRODUCTION

Community colleges have a multi-faceted mission to provide quality postsecondary education opportunities regardless of income, background, or prior academic experience. They prepare students for transfers to four-year institutions through programs of lower division and general education courses. At the same time, community colleges provide workforce development through vocational programs geared to community needs. "Community colleges not only hold the key to success for millions of our citizens, but also the key to a workforce prepared to compete in a global economy, and the key to an educated citizenry that serves as the stable basis for a strong multicultural democracy."[1] For the community college library, acquiring and maintaining a collection to support these diverse programs is a challenge made difficult by dwindling funds and, in some areas, the lack of suitable resources to fit the needs of community college-level programs. Online resources in particular pose a set of challenges for community college librarians in areas from availability to pricing to access.

Nationwide, there are over 1,100 community colleges serving over ten million students and conferring more than 490,000 associate degrees and nearly 235,000 two-year certificates each year. These numbers represent 46 percent of all undergraduates in the United States. Community college students can range in age from sixteen to eighty with the average age (nationwide) being twenty-nine.[2] There are vast differences in what these students bring to the table academically, socially, and technologically. Those who fall into the "Tidal Wave II"[3] demographic possess advanced computer skills but not always the ability to distinguish between legitimate information resources and inaccurate, misleading, or false information from questionable web sites. Many are older students returning to school after a lengthy hiatus to complete a degree or to train for new professions. The majority are employed either full or part-time and many have families to support. Those whose studies require some form of library research universally prefer full-text resources with remote access. While users consider usefulness and quality of information as important, convenience looms large.[4] This is especially true for the students enrolled in the growing number of courses offered online through distance learning programs.

California community colleges are as diverse as the vendors with whom they work. The colleges are publicly supported two-year institutions. They serve a variety of student needs and offer classes for transfer to a four-year college, vocational education programs, remedial programs, and continuing education classes to enhance lifestyle and emphasize technology. Students are not required to have a high school diploma to attend a community college if they are over eighteen years of age and can attend while still in high school, under certain conditions. There are 109 colleges in seventy-two districts located throughout the state of California. The campuses range from rural to urban, small to large, and serve from 2,200 to 26,000 students on respective campuses. Altogether, the community colleges of California serve over 2.9 million students. Half of the students in California's community colleges are twenty-four years old or younger and approximately fifty-six percent are female. The majority attend classes in the daytime. Seventy-two percent are considered part-time students and one eighth of them take non-credit classes.[5] Of the 61,712 undergraduate degrees granted to students graduating in 2003 from the California State University system, slightly more than 35,000 were transfer students from the California Community Colleges.[6]

Students attend community colleges for diverse reasons. It can be a way of taking basic classes for a student who wants to later transfer to a four-year college. Students save money because costs per class are much lower than at four-year institutions. In 2004-2005, the average cost for tuition and fees at a four-year public college was $5,132, while the community college cost was $2,076.[7] Associate degrees and certificate programs are available for many fields. Many areas of occupational training are offered in community colleges. Vocational training is offered in the health occupations, electronics and computer sciences, police and fire science, agriculture, business support, and more.

With successful library consortia in place in the University of California and the California State University systems, the path to follow was clear for the California Community College System. The Community College Library Consortium was created in 1998 in partnership with the California State University system to allow California community college libraries to purchase electronic products at a discount.[8] This was a joint effort between the California Community College Council of Chief Librarians[9] and the Community College League of California.[10] The project has grown from five electronic offerings in 1999 to over 115 product offerings to community colleges in California and surrounding states. Although some of the offerings are in partnership with the CSU system, the majority are community college-only arrangements.

COLLECTION NEEDS

Aggregator databases are the primary resources that most libraries, including those in the community college system, purchase. The cost of getting access to the thousands of journals packaged by aggregators would be phenomenal if libraries tried to arrange access on a one-by-one basis. Publishers worry about the financial impact on their print subscriptions when they allow their journals to be included in an aggregated database but library users tire of having to search a multitude of interfaces to find appropriate resources. The growth of federated search engines and link resolvers speaks to the disdain users have for trying to decipher whether a journal is in an aggregated database, an e-journal package, or some other format. The breadth of coverage offered in products by EBSCO, Gale, ProQuest, and Wilson allow community colleges access that was previously limited only to larger research institutions.

Some vendors admit that community colleges often fall through the cracks in sales of online products. Databases geared to public libraries and those geared to academic libraries are fairly well-defined but community college needs, especially for vocational programs, are often overlooked. Community college students at various points in their studies will need the basic-level materials, as well as some of the scholarly literature that online vendors tout in their offerings. Vendors frequently employ one of two sales approaches with community colleges. Some lump them in with the K-12 market and have the same sales representatives handle the community colleges. Others assign them to their academic representative, who also handles four-year colleges. The community college market is a bridge market designed to accommodate students between these two areas. Community colleges have a more diverse population than a K-12 school and products/services that are appropriate for the lower level don't meet most community college students' needs. Neither do their needs exactly match those of the four-year academic population as most community college students are working on either basic classes or technical education.

The community colleges have been slow to move into purchasing publisher packages of electronic journals, such as those offered by Elsevier, Wiley, and others, as students rarely need the in-depth research publications offered in those packages. What are lacking are practitioner-level materials. For example, the major health databases are designed to serve the consumer on one end, or the M.D. or medical student on the other. Nursing is covered fairly well, but certificate programs like medical assisting, dental hygiene, radiologic technician, and veterinary assistant are seldom covered in any depth.

One area of promise is the online publication of technical manuals and standard reference works. Titles such as the Merck Manual of Diagnosis and Therapy, the Diagnostic and Statistical Manual of Mental Disorders, and several titles for nurses, physician's assistants, and medical assistants are available from StatRef on a subscription basis. If vendors price these products within reach of community college budgets, the potential market could be quite large. The community college library database wish list continues with subject coverage in specialized areas such as forestry, landscape architecture, culinary arts, and real estate. Another welcome addition to the market would be the online availability of industrial codes and standards in a user, and budget-friendly product. This would include subjects like building, plumbing, electrical codes, time-saver standards, and so on.

In a report published in the *Monthly Labor Review* entitled "Occupational Employment Projections to 2012,"[11] several of the fastest growing occupations are in areas of study offered in community colleges including computer support and allied health occupations such as home health care workers, medical assistants, medical records technicians, and physical therapy assistants.

Products like Safari Tech Books Online, available from Proquest, give libraries the opportunity to select ebooks from hundreds of available titles to suit their students' needs. In addition to works geared to technical specialists, basic guides to popular programs such as Microsoft Office® and Adobe® are available for a broader student population. The Greenwood Publishing Group also offers an ebook collection that allows libraries to customize their collection, a service that is becoming increasingly important as community colleges push to expand distance education but want to select books to meet their needs.

The American Psychological Association publishes a number of the core journals in psychology online in a product called PsycARTICLES®, but only allows online licensing of a package of all fifty-plus of their journals, many geared to practicing professionals. Their pricing structure includes a category for community colleges and technical schools with costs reduced by half over those for higher education institutions–baccalaureate level or above. Unfortunately, only ten or fifteen of the titles in the package are appropriate for community college students and the cost of the full package is still high in proportion to the number of students who would use it. Only one-tenth of the journals in PsycARTICLES® are available as true electronic journals so ordering just the appropriate titles as ejournals is not a choice available in this particular case. A subset of journals created by the American Psychological Association for the community college level and offered at an affordable cost would surely attract many subscriptions for this underserved market. As with other electronic publisher journal packages, most community college libraries cannot afford to subsidize the higher level, more specialized publications.

DATABASE SELECTION

California's Community College Library Consortium selects databases to offer its colleges based on in-depth reviews by its Electronic Access and Resources Committee. Eleven librarians representing areas around the state evaluate products based on several criteria. Title lists are reviewed for overlap, embargoes, and currency. The ability to utilize an administrative module for customization is important, as is the ease and availability of usage statistics. Reviewers look at e-mailing, printing, and computer and browser configurations required to operate a product. Users are concerned about customer support, documentation, ease of use, and ADA compliance. The value of the database to the specific community is critical. Is the database at an appropriate level for community college students and will it support the curriculum? This is typically how the value of a resource has been evaluated. As budgets have shrunk for libraries, librarians are becoming more selective about whether a resource is worth the cost.

As many faculty introduce their students to scholarly, peer-reviewed journals at the community college level but without the cutting edge research required at four-year and research institutions, titles with modest embargo periods are sufficient. With a few exceptions, extensive backfiles of journal content are not as critical to community college students. Vendors who add considerable value through retrospective conversion projects should consider pricing options that separate current and older content with one-time funding for older content and reduced ongoing subscription costs. CQ Press is one vendor that currently offers this option for several of its databases. Also, those vendors of aggregated products who are able to maintain core collections of titles in support of the lower-division liberal arts curriculum (e.g., English, history, sociology, political science, speech, psychology, anthropology, etc.) at reasonable costs will continue to gain support among community college libraries.

REMOTE ACCESS

As colleges evaluate resources for their libraries, off-campus access has become a larger issue. Traditional resources that require a student to be physically present on the campus are not the product of choice. Community college students are non-residential commuters and, either through preference or by necessity, must do much of their research from home or another off-campus location. Students want full-text included in the database. Inter-library loan or searching for a print holding is not practical for the needs of a non-residential student. This has created a challenge of making access work for off-campus students. To serve a population made up of commuters, a majority of who are employed, remote access to online resources provides flexibility not possible ten years ago. Community colleges, like their four-year counterparts, have stepped up to offer remote access but often face technological obstacles.

Lacking the integrated, campus-wide computer portal available at some colleges and universities, many community colleges do not have the ability to centrally and electronically authenticate their users. Without access to an account on a campus computer or through a proxy server, many community colleges must administer sets of passwords for remote access to their subscription databases. Most of the major vendors who are familiar with and market to the library community are aware of this limitation and support user name and password authentication. There are some, however, who require libraries to authenticate via IP address or other electronic means. One vendor includes in their license a statement indicating that they won't guarantee successful implementation of remote campus access, although they will try to help a subscribing institution set it up. A recent tour of exhibits at an ALA conference turned up a test preparation database and a car repair database that did not allow password authentication for remote access. These are clearly products that would benefit community college programs but some librarians are hesitant to commit funds if remote access is not possible. With the explosion of online courses offered by community colleges, there is even more pressure to provide distance learners with the same resources that are available to the campus-based population.

Access issues have been complicated by the introduction of wireless technology into our library buildings. Some of our libraries are establishing areas where students can pick up a wireless signal to connect to the Internet. There are advantages for both the students and the library. Students are able to use their own laptops to access library services and libraries don't have to purchase more hardware to serve the needs of their students. Using a hotspot model keeps students from connecting to the college's infrastructure, which cuts down on the possibility of hackers accessing the colleges' sensitive data. This model takes us back to the password issue, however, for students accessing campus databases. These machines are not authenticated within the libraries' IP ranges and students are denied access to material because of authentication issues.

Access issues are also compounded by budget constraints. Recent cuts caused a reduction in the hours California community college libraries are open. The libraries are open from forty-six to seventy-five hours a week, with most closed on Sunday and some open only part of the day on Saturday. Students cannot get into the library and must have access to resources from other locations. With some vendors slow to embrace off-campus accessibility, a whole market of products has been developed for libraries to make gateways into the databases from off-campus. Many of the colleges are embracing services that will set up the access for their students or make searching easier. Proxy servers, access management platforms, and link resolvers are starting to make their way into our community but vendors need to remain flexible in terms of supporting the various authentication methods.

VENDOR SUPPORT

The smaller community college library budgets, compared to those of four-year colleges, pose a dichotomy. Vendors will spend less time soliciting and servicing accounts with lower price tags and yet it is the community colleges with limited materials budgets and staffing that could most benefit from vendor assistance. Larger vendors may provide personalized assistance through account services representatives who, on a regional basis, periodically visit their library customers and are on call to assist with issues that may require follow-up. However, such support may not be offered to the smaller or more isolated colleges. Most vendors can and do offer free trials of their online products and many offer training materials with product demonstrations and the opportunity for questions and answers. As the librarians' time is stretched to the limit, they are looking for more help from vendors to utilize the products. Vendors who are accustomed to working with four-year and graduate institutions that have large systems and technical services departments may not realize that a comparably sized community college may have one or two people responsible for all technical support functions. Large vendors such as OCLC, EBSCO, and ProQuest, all offer web-based training sessions. This allows the librarians to stagger their training time around other duties and receive training on a schedule convenient to them. Support documentation and promotional materials are available for libraries to publicize the various products. Vendor representatives need to not only sell their product, but also train librarians and staff on the intricacies of the database. A recent study by Cambridge Information Group indicated that librarians want vendor reps to be less sales focused and more knowledgeable.[12]

Librarians also seek help from the vendor with the technical aspects of database set-up. Conflicts between IPs, shared IPs at multiple locations, referring URLs, and other authentication issues create many concerns for libraries that do not usually have a technical person devoted to authentication in a library. Community college librarians may give more favorable consideration to vendors who provide assistance with database set-up and ongoing technical support when needed. A growing and disturbing phenomenon is the inability to obtain immediate technical support because the vendor requires that all technical support questions be e-mailed. Being unable to get immediate phone assistance can be a major problem for a college that is without access to their purchased databases. Whereas a four-year college may have full-time technical services and systems librarians and staff, many community college librarians are required to cover their technical support areas along with reference, teaching, and collection development responsibilities. Vendor technical support at time of need is critical. Several of the larger database vendors have developed web-based support services with context-specific help, research strategies, and citing guidelines as well as administrator manuals and teaching tips for librarian-instructors. A recent and welcome addition to the suite of vendor support services is the "webinar," a real-time online session with a vendor representative "pushing" a presentation to the campus-based workstation of the individual librarian. All are linked via a live phone connection, which allows for questions and answers.

PRICING AND BUDGETS

Pricing is a major consideration and one that is surprisingly complicated. Vendors package products in many ways. Some will package similar databases together (for instance, all their health resources in a package). This allows the libraries to select some complementary databases at a lower price. Some will offer one database at the regular price and then discounts on any additional databases. Pricing discounts have also been given for early renewals. In the consortium arrangement, pricing will often be lower if more campuses subscribe.

The pricing structure is as different as the companies who offer products. Prices are often based on FTE, as they are for four-year educational institutions. Some companies base prices on total student population, which can be out of reach in an institution with a majority of part-time students. Many vendors do not consider whether all of these students are involved in the discipline that might use the database. Some will set prices based on seats or simultaneous users (a limited amount of licenses). This model can work as new licenses can be purchased as the demand grows and students become aware of the resource but it can be difficult to judge at the beginning of the contract term. Allowing multiple campuses to access purchased seats is a good way for colleges to lower prices while still maintaining access to a resource. This model would only work for a specialty product that would see limited use by a campus. Flat rate pricing, regardless of student population, can be a hardship for smaller colleges. Many community college students attend for technical/vocational instruction only and rarely use a library's resources. Although the number of vocational, electronic offerings presented to the colleges is increasing, the pricing has not been creative enough to allow a sampling of the resources by our community. Colleges are hesitant to commit to a high cost product without knowing what the demand from students will be.

Funding levels for community colleges often fall far below those for four-year and graduate-level institutions. Recent record deficits in California brought to light the vast differences in funding between the University of California system, with its nine research and doctoral level campuses; the California State University system, with twenty-three campuses offering bachelor's and master's level programs; and the 109-campus California Community College system. "The state pays far more to educate students at UC and CSU than at community colleges. According to the Legislative Analyst's Office, the state spends about $14,300 annually on each UC student, $7,200 per CSU student and

$4,100 per community college student."[13] California's significant budget reductions in recent years have resulted in some creative negotiations with vendors. Some vendors have been proactive in suggesting special package arrangements to provide more resources for the same or a small additional amount of money. This has increased the amount of resources available to students with little additional cost. Other vendors only will offer pricing when they realize they are losing customers by not being more competitive. It would be helpful for vendors to offer an introductory price that would allow community colleges to purchase a product for a year to measure how useful the content is in the support of instruction. Vendors should also realize that as students become familiar with a resource at the community college level, they will seek out that same resource when they transfer to a four-year institution. Many alumni are now asking their institutions to provide access to databases which could expand the market for vendors to sell to a new, previously untapped, population.

Recognizing the needs of off-campus students, the larger vendors commonly include unlimited use of resources in their price. Some of the smaller vendors have been unable to provide the same type of pricing. With a database that would be used only by a select group of students, a helpful pricing model would base the cost on a smaller population keeping the costs in line with the target users of a resource. The differences in the community college population between those preparing for further academic study, those pursuing vocational careers, and members of the community seeking personal enrichment add up to pockets of users for which the library must provide adequate support with a materials budget far below a four-year institution. A general purpose aggregator database would serve a good portion of the academic sector and some needs of the other two. Community college libraries must also support the visual needs of programs such as interior design, photography, ceramics, and fashion design to name a few. The lack of good quality illustrations in most large aggregator databases means that libraries must continue to search for other resources to serve these types of programs. Online images are often withheld by the publisher or limited to individual subscribers. Instructors in these programs are stymied in their attempts to offer multimedia resources to their students both in face-to-face and distance learning courses because of the dearth of good-quality online images and the challenges of copyright compliance. Perhaps a partnership of librarians and vendors could persuade publishers and image copyright holders to open up their works to the academic market.

Courses in automobile repair, heating and air conditioning, hairdressing, and law enforcement have needs that go unmet in general databases. Therefore, as online resources to support these programs become available and community colleges are (or should be) target markets, it would be prudent for vendors to modify traditional FTE pricing models to allow community colleges to meet the information needs of these small and specialized programs. One possible model would be the consolidation of information resources for a particular vocation with marketing that could extend from the training programs (high schools, vocational schools, and community colleges) to the workplace. Using automobile repair as an example, a useful product would include online repair and body manuals, consolidated manufacturer and supplier information, certification requirements, how-to information on setting up and running a business, insurance information, and relevant laws and legislation. Much like the LexisNexis model, sizeable discounts could be offered to the institutions providing training, thus establishing product loyalty that will hopefully carry over to the business world.

There are vendors who offer favorable pricing to community colleges. The recently released ARTstor database of images for art history, design, history, and archaeology has tiered pricing based on the Carnegie Classification of Institutions of Higher Learning, with some modifications for FTES levels. Community colleges are classified separately from four-year and graduate institutions and the discount is significant.[14] Serials Solutions®, which facilitates access to journal and article-level materials in full-text databases, lowered their price for community colleges in 2004 in recognition of the budget challenges facing community colleges.

VENDOR RELATIONSHIPS

Positive vendor relationships, regardless of type of library, are the key to successful business transactions. The economic reality is that the time that a vendor spends with a library client is directly proportional to the size of the library's materials budget. Community colleges, on the low end of the equation, may have little direct contact with a vendor representative. For example, over the past year in California, some of the major database vendors broadened the territories of account representatives who worked primarily with community colleges to include campuses in the California State University System and/or the University of California campuses. Predictably, this business decision resulted in less attention paid to the needs of the community colleges. Proactive librarians can work within this model in several ways. Establish and maintain an e-mail and telephone relationship with vendors. Get a list of contacts that can troubleshoot or provide other forms of assistance. For a larger company, this can include not only information on the account representative, but also the inside contact at the vendor's headquarters, the customer service and technical support information. In some instances, the contact information for the product manager can be useful as well. Creative networking can also work to the advantage of the community college and the vendor. Organize a regional gathering of other community college librarians and invite one or more vendor representatives to meet with the group. Maintain a liaison with counterparts at the regional public libraries, colleges, and universities and set up demonstrations and discussions with appropriate vendors.

Community college librarians share several concerns regarding relationships with vendors. Most prefer communication via e-mail over telephone sales calls but occasionally, librarians feel their e-mails can fall into a black hole. 'Vendors not being responsive' is a very common complaint heard from librarians. While there may be good reasons that the vendor representative has not responded (such as a need to consult with their management), librarians would at least like to hear that the vendors are working on obtaining the answers. Vendors also appreciate timely communication with clients and prospective clients. Returning a vendor's e-mail or phone call can go a long way in promoting a successful business relationship. An enterprising vendor can gain insight into the community college market in several ways. Conversations with librarians are one approach but the Internet offers many more options. Perusing the college web site, including the catalog, will give insight into campus programs thus allowing for more focused marketing. As public institutions, most community college districts and systems have freely accessible web sites where budget and program transactions are posted. Several of the aggregator databases with current news content have alerting features whereby a vendor could be notified when an article appears that discusses colleges in their regions or territories. This kind of "insider" knowledge could give vendors a more competitive edge.

Many librarians are also unfamiliar with the mechanics of the database industry. The purchase of a small database or vendor by a larger conglomerate raises concerns of whether the quality/service of a product will continue. The reconfiguration of a database, whether by titles being removed from databases due to the loss of an agreement with a publisher, or to create a new database, is particularly vexing. Most community colleges do not have the funds to purchase many specialty databases and the loss of titles, particularly core titles, from a database is problematic. Overlap between databases is also a concern. Why buy databases with duplicate titles in a time when budgets are tight?

Unfortunately, some librarian/vendor relationships are adversarial with distrust of vendors an oft expressed sentiment.[15] The relationship between librarians and vendors should be symbiotic; libraries need the vendor's products and vendors need the revenue generated by library sales. Vendor's product pricing strategies are particularly frustrating for librarians. Electronic products never seem to have a set price and the first price given, much like a used car, is rarely the final price. As in any relationship, communication is the solution. Librarians should communicate their concerns about decisions that affect their libraries. Vendors need to present their products and pricing accurately without the hyperbole that often is used to tout features.

Vendors who market themselves as library partners seem to do better in the diverse library electronic market. Library partners solicit input from librarians as products are developed and changed. Community college librarian and student input would provide valuable insight into this often underserved market. In a recent display of commitment to the community college market, EBSCO formed a community college advisory board which will advise and advocate for community college-friendly products and pricing. ProQuest plans a similar partnership; Gale is considering the same.

CONCLUSION

In any library, the relationship between library staff/librarians and vendors is critical to the success of the library's services to students. This relationship must be based on mutual respect and an understanding of the needs and requirements of the other.

The 1,100 plus community colleges in the United States represent a sizeable market for those vendors who understand and address the unique needs and economic climate of the community college. Online products are needed to support allied health occupations, information technology programs, construction, repair, and service occupations without the expense of buying into aggregated products and packages where the majority of content is outside of the scope of community college program needs. Vendors should be encouraged to work with focus groups of community college students and librarians, and with the Community and Junior College Libraries Section of ACRL to help define needs of community college libraries.

Community college librarians need to take a more active roll in working collaboratively with vendors. Librarians can use conference exhibit visits and vendor sales calls as opportunities to express community college needs that should be addressed. Many vendors don't fully understand the unique requirements of community colleges, so it is up to the community college librarian to be proactive in educating vendors on academic and vocational needs, budget considerations and cycles, technical configurations and limitations, as well as student profiles and information-seeking behaviors.

NOTES

1. Board of Governors, California Community Colleges, *California Community Colleges 2005: A Strategic response for enabling community colleges to make a defining difference in the social and economic success of California in the 21st Century*, July 1998.

2. American Association of Community Colleges, "*Fast Facts*," http://www.aacc.nche.edu/Content/NavigationMenu/AboutCommunityColleges/Fast_Facts1/Fast_Facts.htm (accessed May 30, 2005).

3. Tidal Wave II is the term used for the children of the Baby Boom generation, i.e., those born between 1946 and 1964. Students in this demographic are beginning to swell the ranks of high schools and colleges.

4. Carol Tenopir, "Getting the User's Attention," *Library Journal*, 130, no. 8 (May 1, 2005): 32.

5. California Community Colleges Chancellor's office, http://www.cccco.edu/divisions/tris/mis/reports.htm (accessed November 10, 2004).

6. The California State University, http://www.calstate.edu/as/stat_reports/2002-2003/degree03.shtml, Table 20 (accessed December 16, 2004).

7. College Board, "*Pay for College*," http://www.collegeboard.com/article/0,3868,6-29-0-4494,00.html (accessed May 30, 2005).

8. Mary Ann Laun, "On-Ramps to Electronic Highways: Database Trends, Practices, and Expenditures in California's Community College Libraries," *Community & Junior College Libraries*, 9, no. 1 (January 1999):35-45.

9. California Community College, Council of Chief Librarians, http://cclccc.org/.

10. Community College League of California, http://www.ccleague.org/.

11. Daniel E. Hacker, "Occupational Employment Projections to 2012," *Monthly Labor Review* 127, no. 2 (February 2004):80-105, http://www.bls.gov/opub/mlr/2004/02/art5full.pdf (accessed January 9, 2005).

12. Carol Tenopir, "Vendor Communication," *Library Journal*, 130, no. 10 (June 1, 2005): 42.

13. Eleanor Yang, "Regents Skeptical About UC, CSU Enrollment Plan," *San Diego Union-Tribune*, January 16, 2004.

14. ARTstor, *"Higher Education: Participation Fees,"* http://www.artstor.org/info/participation_info/higher_education_fees.jsp (accessed June 5, 2005).

15. Paul Rux, "Predators or Partners?" *Book Report*, 15, no. 3 (Nov/Dec. 96): 28.

Electronic Discussion Lists

Bernie Sloan

SUMMARY. Electronic e-mail discussion lists have been used by librarians and vendors for twenty years. These lists have proliferated, especially in the last ten years, to the point where there are more than 250 library-related lists in use today. This paper describes the various types of lists, looks at the demographics of several library lists, and discusses how these lists can impact libraries and librarians. *[Article copies available for a fee from The Haworth Document Delivery Service: 1-800-HAWORTH. E-mail address: <docdelivery@haworthpress.com> Website: <http://www.HaworthPress.com> © 2006 by The Haworth Press, Inc. All rights reserved.]*

KEYWORDS. E-mail, electronic discussion lists, libraries, librarians, vendors, etiquette

A NOTE ON TERMINOLOGY

Electronic discussion lists are a form of communication that use e-mail to facilitate group discussions on a particular topic. There are a number of terms that people commonly use to refer to this form of communication including electronic discussion groups, e-mail discussion

---

Bernie Sloan is Senior Information Systems Consultant, Consortium of Academic and Research Libraries in Illinois (CARLI), a consortium providing various automated services to 181 academic and research libraries (E-mail: bernies@uillinois.edu). He also serves as a Listowner of the LIVEREFERENCE discussion list, and is on the Advisory Board for the Web4Lib list.

[Haworth co-indexing entry note]: "Electronic Discussion Lists." Sloan, Bernie. Co-published simultaneously in *Journal of Library Administration* (The Haworth Information Press, an imprint of The Haworth Press, Inc.) Vol. 44, No. 3/4, 2006, pp. 203-225; and: *Library/Vendor Relationships* (ed: Sam Brooks, and David H. Carlson) The Haworth Information Press, an imprint of The Haworth Press, Inc., 2006, pp. 203-225. Single or multiple copies of this article are available for a fee from The Haworth Document Delivery Service [1-800-HAWORTH, 9:00 a.m. - 5:00 p.m. (EST). E-mail address: docdelivery@haworthpress.com].

Available online at http://www.haworthpress.com/web/JLA
© 2006 by The Haworth Press, Inc. All rights reserved.
doi:10.1300/J111v44n03_16

groups, e-mail lists, etc. Perhaps the most commonly used term is "listserv." It is understandable that people might use the term "listserv" when referring to electronic discussion lists. The very first e-mail list management software was called "LISTSERV®" and debuted in 1986 (http://www.lsoft.com/products/listserv.asp). But "listserv" should not be used to generically describe electronic discussion lists as the term is a registered trademark licensed to L-Soft International, Inc. For the purpose of clarity, I will refer to the various types of e-mail management lists as simply "lists."

INTRODUCTION

I began working with vendors fifteen years ago with the Illinois Library Computer Systems Organization (ILCSO–http://office.ilcso.illinois.edu/). ILCSO's primary service was ILLINET Online, an automated system that serves each member library as an online catalog of its own collection, and which also provides the option to search the collections of all sixty-five ILCSO libraries at once. ILLINET Online supports local library operations (collection management and inventory control) for each member institution and provides a web interface for public access. ILCSO's open access and resource sharing policies allow its member library users to employ ILLINET Online to locate and request materials held at any of the ILCSO member libraries. ILCSO was founded in 1980 and celebrated its 25th anniversary at the American Library Association's annual conference in Chicago in June 2005. On July 1, 2005 ILCSO merged with the Illinois Cooperative Collection Management Program (ICCMP) and the Illinois Digital Academic Library (IDAL) to form the Consortium of Academic and Research Libraries in Illinois (CARLI–http://www.carli.illinois.edu/). With 181 academic and research libraries as members, CARLI will increase the efficiency and cost effectiveness of services, increase the effectiveness of consortial and member library staff efforts, and create opportunities to pursue new programs and services that the three constituent consortia would not have been able to provide on their own.

In 1990, ILCSO made a decision to broaden its programmatic activities beyond ILLINET Online and to investigate the consortial brokering of electronic resources. After discussions with several vendors, ILCSO decided to license the CARL Corporation's UnCover table of contents database. In the early days of ILCSO-brokered electronic resources, thirty-four libraries subscribed to a total of nine databases. By FY 2003,

ILCSO supported twenty-five databases used by forty-five libraries, with annual combined subscriptions in excess of one million dollars. For a year-by-year summary of ILCSO database subscriptions see: http://office.ilcso.illinois.edu/Reports/ERC/DB_subs_FY92-03.pdf. I have also participated, to a lesser degree, in the process of selecting integrated library systems from two vendors (Data Research Associates and Endeavor). Most recently I was the ILCSO staff liaison to a committee that selected three digital library products (OCLC's CONTENTdm digital object management system, the WebFeat federated search software, and ExLibris' SFX link resolver).

I began my list participation more than fifteen years ago on October 3, 1989, with my first posting to the PACS-L list. The topic was database pricing and access. I've continued to be an active participant in discussion lists over the years. In addition to being a frequent contributor to lists, I am also involved in lists from the management side. For nearly five years I have been an owner/moderator of the "livereference" list (http://groups.yahoo.com/group/livereference/), a group with nearly 1,000 subscribers that discusses live virtual reference services. For nearly five years I have also been a member of the Advisory Board for Web4Lib (http://lists.webjunction.org/web4lib/), a list with more than 3,000 subscribers that discusses libraries and the World Wide Web. The Advisory Board formulates and reviews list policies, advises the list owner on the enforcement of list policies, and provides input and advice on other issues relating to the management of the Web4Lib list.

A BRIEF HISTORY OF LISTS

In the mid-1980s academic institutions communicated via e-mail using BITNET ("because it's time" network), founded in 1981. In 1985 a student named Eric Thomas began working with the BITNET Network Information Center (NIC). The NIC had a rudimentary e-mail list function called LISTSERV that worked well enough as long as the volume of e-mail was relatively light. But as more and more people began using BITNET e-mail, and more and more lists were formed using the NIC software, the process became unwieldy. Thomas developed the LISTSERV software to make the process easier to manage. In the early 1990s Thomas founded L-Soft International to market and develop LISTSERV. For a more detailed overview of the history of the LISTSERV software see: http://www.lsoft.com/products/listserv-history. asp.

Along with the LISTSERV software, there were a number of competing projects in those early days, e.g., the Listproc software was developed for the Unix operating system in the 1980s, and the first Majordomo software debuted in 1992. Hosted lists came on the scene in the late 1990s and revolutionized the use of lists. Prior to the appearance of hosted lists one had to have access to a computer with mailing list software in order create a list. With hosted lists, anyone could start up a list, often free of charge. Hosted lists are maintained on the computers of companies or organizations that offer these services, obviating the need for a list owner to maintain his or her own hardware and software. One example of a company offering hosted lists was eGroups.com, developed in the late 1990s. eGroups became so successful that the company was purchased by Yahoo! in 2000, and renamed Yahoo! Groups in early 2001. Yahoo! Groups supports 16 general categories of lists, from "Business & Finance" to "Science." By itself, the "Business & Finance" category is comprised of more than 100,000 lists.

LIBRARIES AND LISTS

The library community was not far behind in making use of list software to communicate on a wide variety of topics. The Public-Access Computer Systems Forum (PACS-L–http://info.lib.uh.edu/pacsl.html) debuted in June 1989. PACS-L was established as a "list that deals with end-user computer systems in libraries. Utilizing PACS-L, subscribers discuss topics such as digital libraries, digital media, electronic books, electronic journals, electronic publishing, Internet information resources, and online catalogs" (http://info.lib.uh.edu/pacsl.html). While PACS-L was not the first library list, its precursors were focused on narrow topics, e.g., library vendor user groups. According to Walt Crawford, "PACS-L was *not* the first library list, but it was the first with broad appeal" (Crawford, Walt. *Talking About Public Access: PACS-L's First Decade.* http://home.att.net/~wcc.libmedx/pacsl.htm. Published April 2, 2000). PACS-L was dedicated to the discussion of publicly accessible library computer systems and at its peak had approximately 10,000 subscribers. PACS-L's prominence began to wane in the late 1990s as other more specifically topical library lists came into being. PACS-L's decline also coincided with the list's change from an unmoderated list to a moderated list. This switch from interactive, spontaneous discussion to a once-a-day distribution of messages was thought by some to take away one of the things that made PACS-L popular:

freewheeling debate. The list still exists, but the volume of postings is now down to a handful of e-mail notes per month. For an interesting and informative essay on the rise and fall of PACS-L and, by extension, the early history of library lists, see Crawford's *Talking About Public Access*.

There are hundreds of library lists available today, on a wide variety of topics. One source, *Library-Oriented Lists and Electronic Serials*, provides links to more than 250 library lists. The wide ranging topics include lists for acquisitions librarians, business librarians, health sciences librarians, library administrators, engineering librarians, and more. This list is available at: http://liblists.wrlc.org.

TYPES OF LISTS

While lists all serve the same basic function (allowing mass communication via e-mail) not all lists are the same. The "Mailing List Gurus" web site (http://lists.gurus.com) identifies the various types of lists as follows.

One distinction involves how the lists distribute information:

- An *announcement list* serves a function much like that of a newsletter. The communication is one way. Subscribers cannot post to the list. The list owner or moderator generally is the only person authorized to post items to the list. Subscribers play a passive role, simply receiving information.
- A *discussion list* is an interactive forum for communication. Subscribers may post an e-mail message to the list, with all subscribers receiving a copy of the message. Other subscribers may choose to respond to the initial message, with their e-mail reply also being distributed to all list subscribers. While discussion lists are an active form of communication, the volume of messages varies from list to list. Several library-related lists dealing with similar topics provide a good example. The DIG_REF and livereference groups both deal with the topic of virtual reference services. But the DIG_REF list is much more active than the livereference list. During November 2004 the DIG_REF list processed 278 e-mail messages, an average of nearly ten messages per day. In that same month, the livereference list handled twelve e-mail messages or an average of about one e-mail message every two days. Part of this discrepancy might be explained by the fact that DIG_REF has ap-

proximately twice as many subscribers as livereference, but that does not account for the entire discrepancy. Two other library lists dealing with similar topics demonstrate that more subscribers do not necessarily mean higher message traffic. These lists (Web4Lib and PACS-L) both deal generally with the use of technology in libraries. PACS-L has about 10,000 subscribers, three times the number of subscribers as Web4Lib, which has about 3,200 subscribers. But PACS-L processed only twenty-four messages in November 2004, compared with Web4Lib's volume of 315 e-mail messages during that same month.

The Mailing List Gurus site also differentiates between public and private lists:

- *Public lists* (also called open lists) place no restrictions on membership. Anyone interested in participating in the discussions may subscribe. The subscription process for public lists is often unmediated by the list owner (i.e., there is no person reviewing the subscription requests and they are processed automatically). But public lists sometimes require the list owner to review subscription requests. For example, I review subscription requests for the livereference list. The list began with a completely open subscription process, but subscription review requirements were put into place after spammers sent a series of notes to the list that many subscribers found offensive. Reviewing subscription requests put a stop to the spamming. The livereference list is still a public list, even with subscription request review, because no individual is turned away.
- *Private lists* (also called closed lists) are selective. The list owners review all requests for membership and may deny subscription requests if they fall outside of the target group. For example, a library automation vendor might make its customer list private and limit it to those individuals employed by client institutions. Conversely, a group of librarians might establish a private list to discuss vendors and their products, in order to promote open and frank discussion of various products. Or a committee might use a private list that is limited to committee members only.

Susan Tenby of techsoup.org (a web site dealing with technology for nonprofit organizations) identifies two additional distinctions:

- *Moderated lists* require a moderator to serve as an editor, making decisions on which e-mail messages get posted to the list. List subscribers post e-mail messages to the list, but the messages are not immediately routed to other subscribers. Incoming messages are stored until the moderator reviews them. The moderator determines whether each message conforms to the general purposes of the list. The moderator then either posts the message to the list, where it is delivered to the subscribers, or returns the message to the original sender, with an explanation as to why the note was not forwarded to the list. Generally, it is easy to tell when one subscribes to a moderated list because messages are received from the list in clusters. This is because the moderator typically checks for messages on a daily basis and processes them for distribution all at once. There are advantages and disadvantages to moderated lists. One obvious advantage is that moderated lists tend not to stray from their intended topic. But there are also disadvantages. A big disadvantage is that moderated lists are not very spontaneous. A message can be sent to the list, but it is not posted to the subscribers for a day, or sometimes even as much as a week, depending on the moderator's schedule. This can make it difficult to carry on a back-and-forth conversation. Some also feel that any editorial treatment of messages may pose a threat to free and unrestricted discussion. Another disadvantage is that a moderated list requires an extra commitment of time by the list managers, who need to regularly check and review incoming messages.
- *Unmoderated lists* distribute messages to subscribers without human editorial review. A subscriber sends an e-mail to the list address and the message is immediately posted to all subscribers. The major advantage of an unmoderated list is that the lack of moderation fosters interactive discussion. Subscribers can respond to a message immediately, which may result in further conversation by others. Unmoderated lists can exhibit a good deal of spontaneity, which helps promote the sharing of information and ideas. The obvious downside to an unmoderated list is the ease with which messages are sent to the list. It is easier to get off-topic. It is easier to post frivolous messages to the list, e.g., sending a message that simply says something like "I agree with the previous poster." It is also easier for misdirected messages to be distributed to subscribers. It is not uncommon to see people trying to sign off

of a list by sending "unsubscribe" messages to the distribution list, rather than sending them to the correct e-mail address for the list management software. And quite a few of us have had the unpleasant experience of inadvertently sending a personal note to the list. We might read a posting and make unflattering comments about the message or the sender, think we are sending it to a friend or colleague, not noticing that the e-mail address is for the list, and not for our friend or colleague. And finally, unmoderated lists can be less "genteel" than moderated lists. Because the messages are sent immediately, and because they are not reviewed by a moderator, tempers can flare and lead to extended arguments.

The following is a further distinction regarding lists:

- *Archived lists* automatically store every message processed by the list software. A good archive will allow you to search for past messages on a given topic, written by a specific person, etc. This comes in handy when looking for information on a specific product or solutions to a specific problem. A good archive can be a valuable information resource and can also cut down on the number of postings to a list when users search to see if a question has already been answered prior to asking that same question on the list. One very good example of a searchable list archive is the archive for the Web4Lib discussion list (http://sunsite.berkeley.edu/Web4Lib/archive.html). One can use a number of search parameters to refine the search, including limiting the search to "Subject & Body," "Subject Only," "Poster's Name," or "Poster's Email." The searcher can also specify date parameters including "All," "Today," "Yesterday," "This Week," "Last Week," "Last 90 Days," "This Month," or "Last Month," as well as a customized date range.
- *Unarchived lists* do not save copies of the messages posted to the list. Once you delete the message, it is gone. The only way you can get another copy of the message is by asking if other subscribers still have a copy. In my experience, unarchived lists are becoming less commonplace, but they are still out there. I subscribe to at least one. Determining whether or not a list has an archive is important. If a list is not archived, you will need to make a conscious effort to save any messages of interest.

LIST ETIQUETTE

Like any form of communication, a good list should have guidelines for acceptable and unacceptable use of the list. List guidelines can range from nonexistent to simple to elaborate. One example of a fairly comprehensive policy concerning the rules of posting and behavior guidelines comes from the Web4Lib list. The following is reproduced with the permission of Roy Tennant, Web4Lib list owner:

Posting Policy

The following policy governs all postings to the Web4Lib list. These policies will be enforced by the Web4Lib Advisory Board. Please note that repeated violations of these policies may result in the removal of offenders from the list.

1. All messages must relate, however slightly, to the general topic of World Wide Web systems and libraries or library staff. The list owner interprets this rather broadly, but messages that are clearly off-topic will not be tolerated.
2. Advertisements are not appropriate. This includes, but is not limited to, announcements of new products and free trials by those who stand to gain from such announcements. However, a simple statement that offers a way to follow-up for more information on a service or product is tolerated if it accompanies a substantive message discussing a subject appropriate to the list. Announcements of conferences, workshops, new publications, and position openings appropriate to the topic of the list are allowed.
3. Virus warnings (not bug reports) are strongly discouraged, and ONLY official CERT (http://www.cert.org/) or CIAC (http://ciac.llnl.gov/ciac/) advisories are acceptable. In addition, before forwarding any virus information, you may wish to check Internet Hoaxes (http://hoaxbusters.ciac.org/) and Virus Hoaxes (http://www.symantec.com/avcenter/hoax.html) for hoax information and how to spot hoaxes.
4. Personal attacks such as name calling and personal insults will not be tolerated. Comments that are intended only to enrage the recipient rather than contribute to thoughtful discussion are prohibited.
5. All postings must be free of copyright restrictions that limit distribution. For example, posting a significant amount of a copyrighted work verbatim requires the permission of the copyright

holder. To verify that such permission was obtained, all postings of this nature must include a statement that this is the case.

6. The preferred format for list messages is plain text. Subscribers whose mail clients default to other formats such as HTML should configure them to send plain text when posting to the list. Sending MIME file attachments of any kind is prohibited; to prevent the spread of viruses, etc., any attachments are automatically stripped from your message before posting.

The total size of any message should not exceed 10k.

Guidelines for Appropriate List Behavior

The following guidelines are offered as advice for how to best participate in this discussion in a manner that will both contribute to the experience of all readers and also reflect well on you.

- *Say something substantial.* Simply saying "I agree" (in so many words) or "I disagree" (in so many words) does not meet this guideline. Specific technical questions are, however, quite appropriate, as are brief answers to such questions.
- *Say something new.* Mere redundancy will not convince an opponent of their error. Explaining the same argument differently in an attempt to make them see the light has not been proven to be an effective strategy.
- *"Getting the last word" is for children.* We're all beyond the age when we should be concerned with being the one to end the argument. Just because you are the last to speak doesn't mean you won the argument.
- *Agree to disagree.* The likelihood of convincing someone to change a strongly held opinion is nil. State your case, but give up on the idea of converting the heathen.
- *Take "conversations" off the list.* When list interaction becomes two-sided (two individuals trading comments or arguments) it is a sign that you should take the discussion off the list and correspond with that person directly. If the discussion was of interest to the general membership you will see others posting on the topic as well.
- *Remember that you are being judged by the quality of your contributions.* No matter whether you are employed or not, or a certain age, or have a certain education, you can create a good professional reputation by how you contribute to a large electronic dis-

cussion like Web4Lib. On the other hand, you can ruin your reputation even faster and easier.

* *NEVER send e-mail in anger.* Go ahead and compose a message in anger, since that may help you work through what you're angry about, but don't send it. Sleep on it. You will nearly always decide to not send it or to recompose it. There's a reason for that.
* *Be civil.* Treat others how you wish to be treated. No matter how insulting someone is to you, you will always look better to the bystanders (of which there are many, I hasten to remind you) by responding politely.
* *Respect the rights of others.* An electronic discussion is a commons. Your right to post ends at the right of others to not be insulted, badgered, or to have their time needlessly wasted.

LIBRARY LIST DEMOGRAPHICS

Lists require an active population of subscribers in order to keep them going. Library lists can have hundreds or thousands of subscribers. What are the characteristics of list participants? Two methods that can be used to attempt to assess the demographics of a list are: breaking down list subscriptions by country, and studying frequency of posting by individual subscribers.

A commonly held view is that the vast majority of list subscribers play a passive role. The people in this silent majority are sometimes referred to as "lurkers" (i.e., they lurk on the list and observe, without participating in discussions). There is nothing inherently wrong with being a lurker. People can learn a lot and keep up with current topics by reading messages without becoming active participants in the discussion. And the lists would soon fall apart if every subscriber sent even one message per day. Handling hundreds or thousands of e-mail messages per day is simply not feasible for the average e-mail user. But the active posters are what make the list tick, and they provide the list with its personality, for better or for worse. I recently studied almost seven years of posting history (April 1995-January 2002) for the Web4Lib list to determine which people were the most active posters. Over that time frame, nearly 6,500 subscribers posted at least one message to the list (i.e., this does not include subscribers who have *never* posted to the list). One percent of these subscribers accounted for 25 percent of the messages posted to the list. The top twenty-five posters, representing only one half of one percent of the number of posters, accounted for 22 percent of the total messages sent. Nearly 90 percent of the subscribers who posted at least one message posted ten or fewer messages over the course of those seven years. Nearly 60 percent posted only one message during that time frame. The median number of postings was two, or about one every 3.5 years, and the mean was 6.36, or less than one per year. This data shows that a relatively small number of subscribers account for a significant amount of list traffic, and that the vast majority of subscribers post infrequently, if at all. What does this mean? In a sense it means that most list subscribers treat lists almost as if they were announcement lists. Most subscribers do not become involved in the discussions that take place on a list, even when that list is nominally a discussion list. Additionally, active participants may not be aware of the thousands of people that view their posts. Active participants may feel as if they are conversing with ten or twenty acquaintances, at the most, when the actual audience "viewing" their "performances" measures in the thousands. At the very least it should give pause to active list participants . . . remember that your casual conversations are viewed by large audiences.

Another interesting demographic aspect of library lists is the international flavor. Back in the days of BITNET and the BITNET NIC listserver, most list participants were from the U.S., or worked for research organizations in the U.S. While subscribers from the U.S. still account for the majority of subscribers to general library lists, there is also an international influence.

For example, the DIG_REF list fosters the discussion of virtual reference services. As of January 10, 2004, this list had 2,461 subscribers. While 78.4 percent of those subscribers were from the U.S., the total number of countries represented was forty nine. The country breakdown follows (in alphabetical order).

Country	Number of DIG_REF Subscribers
Argentina	3
Australia	90
Austria	5
Belgium	8
Brazil	4
Bulgaria	2
Canada	146
Chile	3
China	9
Colombia	2
Croatia/Hrvatska	3
Denmark	13

Egypt	1
Estonia	1
Finland	2
France	3
Germany	25
Great Britain	20
Greece	3
Hong Kong	7
Hungary	1
India	3
Indonesia	1
Ireland	1
Israel	14
Italy	30
Japan	11
Korea	9
Lebanon	1
Mexico	2
Micronesia, Federal States of	2
Netherlands	11
New Zealand	13
Norway	5
Peru	1
Portugal	7
Russian Federation	1
Saudi Arabia	1
Singapore	8
Slovakia	1
South Africa	9
Spain	12
Sweden	17
Switzerland	3
Taiwan	14
Thailand	4
Turkey	2
USA	1,929
United Arab Emirates	1

In another example, and an interesting parallel, the Web4Lib list, which discusses the management of library web services, also indicates that 79.3 percent of that list's subscribers were affiliated with the U.S. as of January 2003 (http://sunsite.berkeley.edu/Web4Lib/subscribers. html). Where the number of countries represented in the DIG_REF subscriber list was forty-nine, the country list for Web4Lib totaled fifty-three:

Country	Number of Web4Lib Subscribers
Armenia	3
Australia	128
Austria	1
Belgium	13
Brazil	5
Canada	193
Chile	2
China	1
Cuba	1
Czech Republic	3
Denmark	14
Dominican Republic 1	1
Egypt	1
Fiji	1
Finland	5
France	12
Germany	21
Greece	5
Hong Kong	3
Hungary	3
Iceland	1
India	3
Ireland	3
Israel	10
Italy	16
Japan	10
Korea	1
Lebanon	2
Lithuania	1
Luxembourg	1
Malaysia	2
Mexico	2
Namibia	3
Netherlands	22
New Zealand	30
Norway	12
Philippines	1
Poland	2
Russia	1
Singapore	3
Slovakia	1
South Africa	9
Spain	9

Sweden	13
Switzerland	5
Taiwan	10
Trinidad & Tobago	1
Turkey	2
United Arab Emirates	2
United Kingdom	69
United States	2,548
Uzbekistan	1
Venezuela	1

The PACS-L subscription list is slightly more international than the DIG_REF or Web4Lib lists. Where DIG_REF and Web4Lib show that 78.4 percent and 79.3 percent, respectively, of their subscribers are located in the U.S., PACS-L indicates that 71.1 percent of its subscribers are from the U.S. While DIG_REF boasts subscribers from forty-nine countries, and Web4Lib lists subscribers from fifty-three countries, PACS-L lists subscribers from seventy-one countries, as follows:

Country	Number of PACS-L Subscribers
Algeria	2
Argentina	8
Aruba	1
Australia	415
Austria	46
Bahrain	1
Belgium	19
Botswana	3
Brazil	44
Bulgaria	1
Canada	679
Chile	8
China	5
Cocos (Keeling) Islands	1
Colombia	1
Costa Rica	5
Croatia/Hrvatska	1
Cuba	8
Czech Republic	2
Denmark	21
Ecuador	4
Egypt	8
Estonia	4

Finland	25
France	53
Germany	53
Great Britain	260
Greece	12
Hong Kong	26
Hungary	32
Iceland	4
India	34
Iran	4
Ireland	20
Israel	111
Italy	66
Jamaica	4
Japan	63
Korea	21
Latvia	2
Lebanon	2
Lithuania	1
Macau	1
Malaysia	3
Mexico	67
Morocco	1
Netherlands	88
New Zealand	50
Norway	25
Peru	2
Poland	19
Portugal	7
Romania	4
Russian Federation	3
Saudi Arabia	5
Singapore	22
Slovenia	11
South Africa	49
Soviet Union	3
Spain	86
Sweden	30
Switzerland	19
Taiwan	212
Thailand	11
Turkey	61
USA	6,736

Ukraine	2
United Arab Emirates	7
Uruguay	1
Venezuela	4
Vietnam	1
Yugoslavia	4

A closer look of the data for each of these three lists indicates that there is some overlap in terms of country representation. The three lists show a total of 84 countries. Thirty-six countries (42.9 percent) are represented on all three lists. Eighteen countries (21.4 percent) are represented on two of the lists. Thirty countries (35.7 percent) are present on just one of the three lists.

LIBRARIES, LIBRARIANS, AND LISTS

The use of e-mail discussion lists benefits libraries and librarians in several ways, including information gathering/sharing, professional advancement, and organizational efficiency.

- *Information gathering/sharing*–Librarians who use lists can be divided into two general categories: those who recall the days before lists, and those who have always had lists available during their professional careers. The librarians in this latter group may take for granted the information gathering capabilities enabled by using lists. Those librarians in the former group can look back on the pre-list days and truly appreciate how much the information gathering process has improved since the widespread advent of lists. Tasks that are relatively simply undertaken via lists today would have been virtually impossible in the pre-list days. As an example, perhaps a library administrator has a question about how various peer institutions deal with using outsourcing for cataloging. In the past, the library administrator would have needed to conduct some research hoping that some of his or her peers had published information on how they had handled a particular issue. Today, that administrator simply needs to select a relevant list and post the question to the list. Within a brief amount of time, hundreds, if not thousands, of fellow administrators will have seen the question, and the administrator may receive dozens of useful responses before the day is over. This would not have been possible in the pre-list days. The same thing holds true with sharing information about how a library may have handled a particular issue. In the past, the administrator might have prepared an article for publication, and then hoped to find a publisher to accept it. Today, the administrator can describe the solution to an issue and have that information instantaneously distributed to hundreds or thousands of peers.

- *Professional advancement*–In the pre-list days, professional advancement could be a hit or miss process involving several different forms: publishing in journals, participating in professional committee activities, or presenting at conferences. Publishing in journals was a very competitive process, especially for a newcomer to the field. It could take several years of trial and error before landing one's first publication. Participating in committee activities might offer greater opportunities, but most likely this sort of professional advancement activity required travel to various conference venues or meeting sites to physically participate in meetings. Presenting at conferences was sort of a hybrid of the first two activities–it was a competitive process to have a paper accepted, and then one was required to travel to the conference venue to present the paper.

   The dynamics of this process have changed considerably in this age of discussion lists. One important aspect for success in these three forms of professional advancement is name recognition. The more widely known you are, the more likely it is that you might be invited to submit a publication or presentation, or participate in committee activities. Name recognition also helps when submitting a publication or a conference program proposal. While list participation does not replace publication, conference presentations, or committee activities as a form of professional advancement, it may increase the chances of success in these areas. It is important to insert a caveat here: while frequent list participation may increase name recognition, it may not necessarily translate into *positive* name recognition. Helpful or valuable contributions to list discussions can result in increased positive name recognition, but if postings are perceived in a negative light (due to content, or too frequent posting) by list subscribers they will have a damaging effect upon one's image.

- *Organizational effectiveness/efficiency*–Geographically dispersed organizations may benefit greatly from the use of discussion lists to promote enhanced communication. Many library consortia and professional organizations use discussion lists to conduct business in a way that is independent of time or place. For example, the Illinois Library Computer Systems Organization (ILCSO), with more than sixty member institutions spread across hundreds of miles within the state of Illinois, maintains discussion lists for each of its nearly thirty committees, task forces, and working groups. Much behind-the-scenes discussion and preparation of draft documents takes place via these e-mail lists. Conducting preliminary business in this manner results in more effective face-to-face-meetings, and can actually serve to reduce the number of face-to-face meetings required, resulting in significant savings in travel expenses. Professional associations, as well, can also benefit from conducting business virtually using e-mail lists. I can vouch for this from personal experience. I have been a member of two American Library Association ad hoc committees where much of the behind-the-scenes work was performed virtually, using e-mail lists. In each case, these committees were charged with producing or revising ALA guidelines in particular topical areas. Multiple versions of drafts of the guidelines were reviewed and revised using e-mail, significantly reducing the number of face-to-face meetings required to produce these documents. I co-chaired one of these ad hoc committees, and the background work via e-mail was so effective that I needed to attend only one face-to-face meeting of the group.

LIBRARIES, VENDORS, AND LISTS

In the early days of the Internet (mid-1980s until 1993) commercial activity was not permitted. The Internet was intended to be used for research and educational purposes. Library vendors could not use the Internet to conduct business with clients, and advertising or promotion of a product was especially frowned upon. Many early Internet users' views about proper use of the Internet, e-mail, and lists were formed during those formative years when commercial use of the Internet was perceived as a bad thing.

During the early days of the Clinton administration the National Science Foundation lifted the ban on commercial activity on the Internet as part of the President's plans to promote e-commerce. Lifting this ban resulted in a flurry of commercial activity on the Internet, some good, some not-so-good. Many of the Internet's early users are still around, and some are still influenced, consciously or subconsciously, by nearly ten years of experience on a non-commercial Internet. Many library list policies today reflect the early years' aversion towards advertising. For example, the Web4Lib posting policy (http://lists.webjunction.org/web4lib/) notes: "Advertisements are not appropriate. This includes, but is not limited to, announcements of new products and free trials by those who stand to gain from such announcements." Some lists (e.g., liblicense-l) are more lenient when it comes to product announcements, but the Web4Lib example shows how the past can have an influence on current list attitudes toward commercial activities.

Another issue dealing with vendors and lists is whether to allow vendors to subscribe to lists where librarians discuss vendors' products. List managers' attitudes vary on this issue much as they do on the "advertising" issue. Some lists, like Web4Lib and LIBLICENSE-L, are open to all subscribers, and the viewpoint seems to be that having vendor or publisher representatives on such lists can result in more productive discussion. Other lists, like the list for the International Coalition of Library Consortia (ICOLC) and the ERIL-L list, are closed to vendors, with the viewpoint being that list members need to have a certain degree of confidentiality when discussing vendor issues so that the discussion can be truly open. While the ERIL-L list is used mainly to discuss e-resource issues, the ICOLC list also serves as an organizing list to plan for that organization's annual meetings, and to get input from list members about official ICOLC documents that are being prepared for release to the general public. In this respect, the ICOLC list has a stronger rationale for limiting membership.

One of the major problems with closed lists is that invariably some postings get leaked to the "outside world." When a list has hundreds of subscribers (the ICOLC list has almost 400 subscribers, and ERIL-L has about 1,700 subscribers) there is plenty of opportunity for someone to forget that the list is closed, or for a subscriber to not understand that the list is closed. In most cases, the subscriber that distributes e-mail off-list is simply trying to be helpful. Perhaps they want to alert a vendor contact to a problem one of the vendor's customers is having, or they may want to share useful information with other colleagues. As an example of the latter, one closed list had to change the ID and password of a members-only web site after a "helpful" list member had forwarded this information to another list. Then someone on the other list forwarded the note to yet another list, and someone on that list forwarded the information to a third list! There is no telling how many unauthorized persons gained access to that confidential information.

Both the ICOLC list and ERIL-L have recently experienced situations in which notes posted to the lists were forwarded to non-subscribers. In each case, a list member made a comment about a service or product and in each case a vendor representative contacted the list member to discuss the perceived problem. The respective list members were understandably upset to find out that someone on these "confidential" lists had forwarded their complaint directly to the vendor. The list members who did this were most probably trying to be helpful, directing the complaints to someone who could address them. But the list members who posted the original complaints felt that their trust in the confidential nature of these lists had been betrayed. This sort of betrayal of trust, however inadvertent or well-intentioned, can do a great deal to stifle free-wheeling discussion on a closed membership list.

Various lists will deal with such breaches in different ways. In the case of the ICOLC list, reminders were distributed to the list urging subscribers to take care when distributing ICOLC information to non-subscribers. Ironically, in the case of ERIL-L, the breach prompted a discussion of whether the list should be closed or not. The list's moderators initiated the discussion. Interestingly, the bulk of those responding favored changing ERIL-L to an open subscription model. The argument was made by several subscribers that knowing that a product's vendor might be on the list might lead to people more carefully stating their case. And most respondents also indicated that discussions of a particular vendor's products might be enhanced if vendors were on the list and allowed to respond in kind. For example, a librarian might have a question that could be addressed easily if a vendor representative was on the list. There were several cautions against allowing advertising on the list, but most respondents seemed to think that vendors would abide by the rules. ERIL-L became an open subscription list in 2005.

CONCLUSION

To sum up, vendors can benefit from subscribing to lists, and librarians can benefit from vendor participation in lists. A few points to remember:

1. The Internet has a long standing history where commercial use of any kind was prohibited. Because of this, there sometimes may be an unconscious inherent bias against vendor participation in library lists. The strength of this bias, of course, will vary from individual to individual, and from list to list. If the individual's formative years of experience with the Internet occurred prior to 1993, that bias may be stronger. If the individual's experience with the Internet is relatively recent, there may be little or no bias. Some lists (e.g., Web4Lib) have written policy prohibiting advertisements and product announcements, while other lists (e.g., LIBLICENSE-L) appear to allow product announcements that relate to the list's theme.
2. Librarians and vendors should be aware of the rules of the road, and should be aware that the rules vary from one list to the next. What works on one list may be unacceptable on another.
3. Remember that active participation in lists can offer a great deal of visibility. While many library lists have thousands of subscribers, it is all too easy to forget this. Posting a note to a list requires the same level of effort as posting to an individual. Although the effort involved in posting may be minimal, the impact of posting to a list can be multiplied thousands of times. Posting to a list may bring you fame, or it may bring you notoriety. Active participation in a library list allows you to make an impression like nothing else can. Make sure it's a good impression.
4. By the same token, the visibility that active list participation brings to the individual can also carry over to the individual's institution or organization. Often the individual's e-mail address or e-mail signature block shows institutional affiliation. Positive and helpful participation can reflect nicely on the individual's organization, especially when the individual is associated with vendors or other commercial activities. An individual making a bad impression on list subscribers may also reflect poorly on his or her institution or organization. Commercial organizations, especially, might want to think about the implications of staff participation in discussion lists and consider policies or guidelines, if need be.

Electronic discussion lists offer librarians and vendors an opportunity to communicate more effectively. Lists also offer a means for sharing information quickly and broadly. To make the best use of this communication tool, all participants should remember one word to live by–responsibility:

- Responsibility on the part of librarians to consider the weight of what they post, bearing in mind that what they write will be read by hundreds or thousands of readers.
- Responsibility on the part of vendors to always represent themselves honestly and openly.

Index

Academic libraries, 58-60. *See also*
Libraries
Academic publishers
acquisitions and, 61-62
databases and, 63-64
focus groups and, 59-60
partnerships and, 62-63
peer review communities and, 67
serving needs of libraries and, 58-67
Acquisitions, academic publishers and,
61-62
ACS. *See* American Chemical Society
(ACS)
Advisory boards, 3
composition of, 90-91
in information industry, 88-90
librarians and, 9,91-92
overview of, 86-88
questions asked of publishers and
vendors for, 93
value of, 90-92
vendors and, 91
Aggregators, 7
Alford, Larry, 165
American Chemical Society (ACS), 13,19
American Institute of Physics (AIP),
13-14
American Psychological Association
(APA), 191-192
about, 26-27
books published by, 29
databases of, 29-33
development of new electronic
products and, 39-41
feedback and, 39-41
primary journals of, 27-29
training and support for products
by, 37-38

trends for products of, 38-39
vendors and, 33-37
benefits of working with, 33-34
communication issues, 36-37
complications in working with, 34
licensing and reporting issues
and, 34-35
matching products with
interface, 35-36
Anatolian University Libraries
Consortium (ANKOS), 70
background of, 70-71
experiences with vendors and,
74-76
growth of, 71-73
mode of operation of, 73-74
pricing negotiations and, 76-80
reflections on experiences of, 80-81
trialing of databases by, 74
Anderson, Rick, 183
Announcement lists, 207
APA. *See* American Psychological
Association (APA)
Application of integrated systems,
timeline for, 6-7
Archived lists, 210
Association of American Publishers
(AAP), 129
Association of Research Libraries
(ARL), 129
Atkinson, Hugh, 160
Authorized users, 13

Best practices, for vendor-library
software development,
150-152
BIS, 7

BOOK ORDER FORM!

Order a copy of this book with this form or online at:
http://www.HaworthPress.com/store/product.asp?sku= 5872

Library/Vendor Relationships

_____ in softbound at $24.95 ISBN-13: 978-0-7890-3352-9 / ISBN-10: 0-7890-3352-6.
_____ in hardbound at $39.95 ISBN-13: 978-0-7890-3351-2 / ISBN-10: 0-7890-3351-8.

COST OF BOOKS _____

POSTAGE & HANDLING _____
US: $4.00 for first book & $1.50
for each additional book
Outside US: $5.00 for first book
& $2.00 for each additional book.

SUBTOTAL _____

In Canada: add 6% GST. _____

STATE TAX _____
CA, IL, IN, MN, NJ, NY, OH, PA & SD residents
please add appropriate local sales tax.

FINAL TOTAL _____
If paying in Canadian funds, convert
using the current exchange rate,
UNESCO coupons welcome.

❏ BILL ME LATER:
Bill-me option is good on US/Canada/
Mexico orders only; not good to jobbers,
wholesalers, or subscription agencies.

❏ Signature _____

❏ Payment Enclosed: $_____

❏ PLEASE CHARGE TO MY CREDIT CARD:

❏ Visa ❏ MasterCard ❏ AmEx ❏ Discover
❏ Diner's Club ❏ Eurocard ❏ JCB

Account #_____

Exp Date_____

Signature_____
(Prices in US dollars and subject to change without notice.)

PLEASE PRINT ALL INFORMATION OR ATTACH YOUR BUSINESS CARD

Name

Address

City   State/Province   Zip/Postal Code

Country

Tel   Fax

E-Mail

May we use your e-mail address for confirmations and other types of information? ❏Yes ❏No We appreciate receiving
your e-mail address. Haworth would like to e-mail special discount offers to you, as a preferred customer.
We will never share, rent, or exchange your e-mail address. We regard such actions as an invasion of your privacy.

Order from your **local bookstore** or directly from
The Haworth Press, Inc. 10 Alice Street, Binghamton, New York 13904-1580 • USA
Call our toll-free number (1-800-429-6784) / Outside US/Canada: (607) 722-5857
Fax: 1-800-895-0582 / Outside US/Canada: (607) 771-0012
E-mail your order to us: orders@HaworthPress.com

For orders outside US and Canada, you may wish to order through your local
sales representative, distributor, or bookseller.
For information, see http://HaworthPress.com/distributors

(Discounts are available for individual orders in US and Canada only, not booksellers/distributors.)

Please photocopy this form for your personal use.
www.HaworthPress.com

 BOF06